THE GREAT BOOK OF MUSCLE CARS

BY THE AUTO EDITORS OF CONSUMER GUIDE®

Foulis

Haynes

A Foulis Motoring Book

This edition first published 1990.

Published by:
Haynes Publishing Group
Sparkford, Nr. Yeovil, Somerset BA227JJ
England

Manufactured in Yugoslavia.
8 7 6 5 4 3 2 1

ISBN 0-85429-886-X

CREDITS

Photography
The editors gratefully acknowledge the photographers who helped make this book possible:

Doug Mitchel—6, 7, 12—13, 14, 21, 30, 31, 35, 36, 37, 44, 50, 54, 55, 56, 57, 81, 82, 87, 98, 99, 100, 101, 106, 109, 110, 111, 115, 116, 117, 118, 119, 120, 130, 133, 134, 135, 141, 147, 148, 149, 152, 173, 174, 175, 183, 188, 197, 198, 199, 205, 222, 227, 228, 229, 230, 231, 233, 234, 235, 236, 244, 245, 246, 247, 249, 251; Mike Mueller—10, 11, 23, 24, 25, 28, 29, 32, 33, 38 46, 57, 58, 62, 63, 64, 65, 83, 84, 138, 139, 142, 143, 161, 170, 192, 193, 194, 201, 238, 252, 253; Sam Griffith—15, 16, 17, 29, 93, 94, 113, 114, 121, 122, 144, 145, 146, 172, 222, 223, 224, 225, 247, 249; Rithea Tep—18, 19, 22; Bud Juneau—20—21, 51, 52, 53, 60, 89, 92, 157, 167, 168, 181, 182, 216, 230, 231, 232; Mark Garcia—23; Jim Smart—24, 25, 39, 40, 41, 43, 45, 47, 48, 69, 102, 103, 123, 124, 129, 130, 132, 135, 176, 178, 180, 219, 226, 227, 228, 229, 237; Bob Garris—34; Jerry Heasley—39, 40, 70, 71, 80, 123, 124, 139, 169, 208, 242, 243, 251; Milton Gene Kieft—59, 177, 199, 204; Nicky Wright—61, 85, 104, 113, 114, 131, 132, 136, 137, 138, 140, 150, 151, 154, 155, 157, 158, 159, 162, 163, 164, 171, 172, 179, 180, 182, 184, 200, 206, 207, 209, 213, 214, 215; Bob Tenney—66, 68, 69; Gerald Sutphin—67, 187; Greg Barrow—67; Richard Spiegelman—72, 78, 79, 95, 96, 112; Thomas Glatch—86, 87, 91, 100, 101; David Patryas—96, 97; Studio Image—105; Ted Clow—107; Bob Trevarrow—125, 126; Ken Beebe/Kugler Studio—127,128; Alex Gabbard—135; Bower Corwin—156; Robert Sorgatz—165, 166; Dan Lyons—153; Jeff Medves—176; Vince Manocchi—185, 186; Photos by Morton—189; Joseph J. Bohovic—190, 191, 210, 211, 217, 218, 240, 241; Alan Hewko, DeChrisotpher's Studio—195, 196; David Temple—31; Frank Peiler—74; David Talbott—76, 77

Owners
Special thanks to the owners of the cars featured in this book for their enthusiastic cooperation. Listed by page number they are:

6-7, Jeffery L. Hill; 8, Jim Lojewski; 9, Bob Lojewski; 10, Dale Kumanchik; 11, Dale Kumanchik, Eugene Slocum; 12-13, 14, Rodney Brumbaugh; 15, 16, 17, Greg Mentzer; 18, 19, Brad & Barbara Hillick; 20-21, Greg Gyurina; 22, Bill Schroeder; 24, Carolina Classic Cars, Dennis M. Phipps; 25, Dennis M. Phipps; 28, Marion & Walter Gutowski; 29, Dennis Reboletti, Marion & Walter Gutowski; 30, Jerry & Pam Berger; 31, Jerry & Pam Berger, Jim Turner, Paul D. Pierce; 32, 33, Fernando F. Alvare; 34, Bob Masi; 35, Darryl McNabb; 36, Rusty Symmos; 37, Dan

Mamsen; 38, Jim Blaisdell; 39, Bill Kuntz; 40, 41, Doug Carter; 42, Dan Tessner; 43, Roger Brackett; 44, Ron Morz; 45, Maurice Bradley; 46, James E. Collins; 48, David Kissner; 51, Ramshead Auto Collection, Sacramento, CA.; 52, Steven Knutsen; 53, Charley Lillard; 54, Norman Andrews; 55, Norman Andrews, Jay Nolan; 56, Dan Parilli; 57, Kent Butterfield, Dan Parilli, Rick Cybul; 58, Paul McGuire; 59, Donald R. Crile; 60, Charley Lillard; 61, Stephen F. Collins; 62, 63, Phil Fair; 64, Phil Fair, Patti & J.R. Buxman; 65, Patti & J.R. Buxman; 66, Amos Minter; 67, Bob Burroughs, Bill Blair; 68, Amos Minter; 69, Paul Suloff, Amos Minter; 74, Frank Peiler; 75, 76, 77, Larry Barnett; 81, 82, Richard Hanley; 83, 84, Tony & Suzanne George; 89, Ramshead Auto Collection, Sacramento, CA.; 85, Bill Barnes; 86, Jeffery Baker; 87, Jeffery Baker, Nathan Studer; 91, Eric D. Rosynek; 92, Ramshead Auto Collection, Sacramento, CA.; 93, 94, Dennis Guest; 95, Glenn Cole; 96, Scott Rosenthal; 97, Scott Rosenthal; 98, 99, Andrew Peterson; 100, Thom Moerman, Andrew Peterson; 101, Andrew Peterson, Thom Moerman; 104, Larry Bell; 105, Joe Yanush; 107, Tom Amendola; 109, Bruce Rhoades; 110, John Wells; 111, Jeff Peterson; 112, Leon Pelissero; 113, Yoshio & Eric Nakayama; David Arent; 114, David Arent, Yoshio & Eric Nakayama; 115, 116, 117, Odus West; 118, Kenneth Jay Coleman; 119, Kenneth Jay Coleman, Alden Graber; 120, Terry Davis; 121, 122, Bill Jackson; 123, C.K. Spurlock; 124, Bobby Marburger; 127, 128, Frank Spittle; 130, Dennis Roxworthy; 131, Dean & Wanda Casey; 132, Jay F. Painter; 133, 134, 135, Ed Coughlin; 136, Richard A. Emry; 137, Jerry Buczkowski; 138, George N. Bowen, Jerry Buczkowski; 139, George N. Bowen; 140, Charles & Marie Cobb; 141, David L. Robb; 142, S. Pampanella Jr.; 143, Keith Hazley; 144, 145, 146, Edwin Putz; 147, Glen Moist; 148, 149, Ron Voxles; 150, 151, Thomas & Carol Podemski; 152, Jeff Knoll; 153, Robert Augustine; 154, 155, Greg & Rhonda Haynes; 157, Mark Johnstad; 157, Greg & Rhonda Haynes; 158, 159, Stephen Schonegg; 160, 161, Steve Ames; 162, Don Bergman; 163, 164, Dan & Karen Kerridge; 155, 166, Rare Performance Motors, Tempe, AZ.; 167, 168, Jack Karleskind; 170, Carl J. Beck; 171, Leo Bard; 172, Brian Kwiatkowski, Leo Bard; 173, Ron Voyles; 174, 175, John Cook; 176, William Petersen; 177, Dennis Urban; 179, James & Mary Engle; 180, Mike Furman, Ross Arterberry; 181, Michael Morocco; 182, Scott Campbell, Dave Cobble II, Trevor Badgley; 184, Terry Swisher; 185, 186, Bob Mosher; 187, Bob Burroughs; 188, Guy Mabee; 189, David B. Vedral; 190, 191, Walter Schenk; 194, Joe L. Saunders; 195, 196, Dave Bartholomew; 198, Jeff & Trish Holmes; 199, Jeff & Trish Holmes, The Beechy Family; 200, Robert Fraser; 201, Michael E. Hatch; 204, Robert Beechy; 206, 207, Rick Cain; 209, Doug Schliesser; 210, 211, Joseph "Whitey" Eberle; 212, Ronda Cunningham; 213, 214, 215, Jim Reginier; 216, Glen Stidger; 217, 218, Wayne Hartye; 220, Scott Sieveking; 222, Rich Antonacci, Allan & Louise Cartzman; 223, Allan & Louise Cartzman; 224, 225,

Richard Witek; 226, Walter Kuntz; Joe Kelly; 227, Walter Kuntz; Lynn Johnson; 228, 229, Reed Larson; 230, Chris Terry, Jeff Hare; 231, Chris Terry, Jeff Hare; 232, Don & Linda Davis; 233, Jeffery L. Hill; 234, Robert Lozins; 235, Felix Mozockie; 236, Mike Abbott; 238, Steve Maysonet; 240, 241, Ralph Milner; 246, Bruce Rhoades; 247, Russ Smith, Yoshio & Eric Nakayama; 249, Yoshio & Eric Nakayama, Ray Herman; 251, Kevin Cloubec; 252, 253, Gary Grillo

Very special thanks to:

Chrysler Historical Collection
Detroit, MI.

Helen J. Earley, Oldsmobile History Center
Lansing, MI

Jim Flammang

Larry Gustin, Buick Motor Public Relations
Flint, MI

Earl Hatfield, Mopar Muscle Club Int.
Washington, PA

Barbara Hillick, American Motoring
Atlanta, GA

Roy Murray

Charles Ordowski, Ford Photographic
Dept. Dearborn, MI

Pontiac Public Relations
Pontiac, MI

Technical Consultants:

AMC, Darryl Salisbury
American Motors Owners Association, Inc.
Portage, MI

BUICK, Rich Lasseter
Buick GS Club of America
Valdosta, GA

CHEVROLET, Ken Moorehead
Super Chevys Ltd.
Orlando, FL

DODGE/PLYMOUTH, Gary Rollins
RTS Warehouse
Detroit, MI

FORD/MERCURY, John R. Smith
Technical Services
Akron, OH

OLDSMOBILE, Dennis Casteele

PONTIAC, Mike Grippo

TABLE OF CONTENTS:

INTRODUCTION
ALL-AMERICAN
MUSCLE

Oldsmobile touched on the muscle-car concept way back in 1949 when it dropped the 135-horsepower Rocket V-8 from its Ninety-Eight series into the new, lightweight Futuramic Seventy-Six chassis. Presto! The Rocket 88. A legend in its time. That car set street-rodders' hearts aflutter and dominated NASCAR. In 1964, Pontiac took a page from the Rocket 88 book to create a legend of its own. Pontiac found a loophole in the General Motors corporate edict against intermediate cars with engines larger than 330 cubic inches. It was able to get its big-car 389-cubic-inch V-8 into its mid-size Tempest by making the engine part of an option package. Thus, the GTO, the first real muscle car.

In the strictest sense of the term, a muscle car is in fact a mid-size two-door model with a large-displacement V-8. A 1968 Hemi Road Runner or a '70 Chevelle SS 454 would define the breed. The intermediates were the smallest body style with an engine bay that could accommodate a big-block mill *and* the attendant exhaust system so vital to exploiting its power. These bodies were light, so they achieved a good power-to-weight ratio, but they also could transfer sufficient weight to the rear tires, which went begging for traction against a tornado's worth of torque. It took a quarter-mile time of 14 seconds or less and a trap speed of 100 mph or more to make the muscle major leagues. Big-block intermediates dominated the select group of cars that made the grade.

For *The Great Book of Muscle Cars* to take so narrow a view of the genre, however, would be to ignore the legion of other automobiles that breathed life into motoring's most exciting age.

For example, bona fide high-performance for the common man first reached the streets in full-size models. Blazing the trail were the 1962 Plymouths and Dodges with their dual-quad 413-cubic-inch wedge-head V-8s. These cars had a 116-inch wheelbase, which really was in the mid-size class, but they were considered their makers' full-size models. Later that same year, the genuinely full-sized Chevrolets became home to the 409 of song and celebration. Big-block power eventually embraced some of the smallest models. Pony cars like the Camaro SS 396 and Dodge Challenger R/T 440 Six Pack were threats to anything with wheels.

Meanwhile, muscle's family tree was branching out to include compacts such as the '68 Nova SS 350 and the '69 AMC-Hurst SC/Rambler. It cast a shadow over fast cars designed to handle the road, like the '69-70 Mustang Boss 302, and fast cars designed to coddle their occupants, such as the '69-70 Mercury Marauder X-100.

Some members of this extended family, such as the '64 Fairlane Thunderbolt, were full-out drag models too high strung really even to be driven to and from the strip. But there they were, available for street use to any buyer cagey enough to finagle one from the factory.

Other members of the brood blurred distinctions between muscle car and sports car; the '68-70 AMX and '65-66 Mustang Shelby GT-350 were equally at home on the quarter-mile at Pomona or the S-curve at Watkins Glen. There were branches with roots in NASCAR. Their vivid blossoms included the aerodynamic '69 Mercury Cyclone Spoiler II and the outrageous '70 Plymouth Superbird. Similarly, Trans Am racing spawned cars like the '70 Dodge Challenger T/A, which flowered for just one year, and the '67 Camaro Z-28, a classic with us still.

It might be said then that what really makes a muscle car is a certain quality born of a purpose and a time and a place. All these cars were fast, but more specifically, they were designed to accelerate in a straight line with lightning quickness. Even the road racers among them emphasized drag-strip rear-axle ratios and the like. While there were fast cars before and since, never was there such a focus on quarter-mile acceleration.

The other part of the formula has to do with America in the 1960s. Gas was cheap, the economy was strong, cars were not yet anti-social. Insurance companies, the safety lobby, and the environmentalists hadn't yet sedated Detroit's more brazen impulses. Youth and change were America's new buzzwords. Muscle cars were young people's cars and with each succeeding model year they expanded the frontiers of performance. Devil-may-care factory hot rods even reflected the '60s spirit of revolution.

If any auto flaunted authority, it was the roaring, rubber-burning, impractical muscle car. Buyers were asked to "Join the Dodge Rebellion." Pontiac played on contempt for the establishment, advertising that "The Judge can be bought."

All of this made for the grandest show. The muscle pageant reached a crescendo in 1970. But signs of a fall were there even then for those who chose to look. By 1972, the tenor of America itself had changed. Muscle cars had become a dalliance and Detroit drew the curtain on them with little ceremony.

There are, of course, those who remember. And there are those who are now just discovering an automotive universe unlike any other. This is the world of *The Great Book of Muscle Cars*.

The 1960s are memorable for a variety of reasons. To car buffs, the decade marked the fullest flowering of the muscle car, that peculiarly American hybrid of street-legal transportation and blistering straight-line acceleration. As typified by the 1967 Pontiac GTO seen above, muscle cars offered enough looks, style, and raw power to seduce even the most jaded driver.

1968-70
AMC
AMX 390

It was no surprise that an automaker synonymous with middle-of-the-road Rambler sedans would be out of its element in the fast-paced youth/performance market of the mid-1960s. Cash-strapped American Motors Corporation tried, but it just couldn't convincingly transform cars like the Marlin, Rebel, and Rogue from grocery getters into go-getters.

Then in 1968 AMC reached back for inspiration to the American Motors Experimental, its 1966 concept car, and unveiled a svelte fastback coupe called the Javelin. It had taken the Kenosha, Wisconsin, company more than three years to come up with a reply to the Mustang and Camaro, but at least the Javelin had the character to compete in the pony-car field. Javelin buyers could replace the standard six-cylinder engine with one of three optional V-8s and also could order such goodies as power front-disc brakes and a heavy-duty suspension. The car was a major step in AMC's plan to fashion for itself a new image as an aggressive, forward-thinking company. Then AMC went a step further.

Using the Javelin as a foundation, the company in February 1968 introduced the fastest, handsomest, best-handling car it ever built; an automobile that won a measure of respect from two diverse camps: the muscle-car guys and the sports-car people. The car was the AMX.

Engineers had sliced a foot from the Javelin's bodyshell to give the AMX a 97-inch wheelbase, one inch shorter than the Corvette's. The comparison is appropriate because AMC also yanked the Javelin's rear seats, allowing the AMX to join the Corvette as America's only other domestically produced two-seater. Tossing that rear bench sparked an immediate debate about whether the AMX was a sports car. Of course, some purists resisted the notion that even the Corvette was a true sports car, but AMC took comfort in the fact that it could at least sneak into such an argument, and at $1100 less than the least expensive 'Vette, to boot.

Its shortened platform gave the AMX a bobtail look compared to the Javelin, and its simpler, open grille gave it a cleaned-up nose of which any European design house would have been proud. The hood was cleaved by a pair of wedge-shaped extrusions, which served no performance function.

For your $3245 you got AMC's 290-cubic-inch small-block Typhoon V-8. With nearly square 3.75-inch bore and 3.28-inch stroke, it was a potential screamer; but with only 225 horses, it wasn't about to create a name for the AMX. AMC's 343-cubic-inch V-8 with 280 horsepower made for a fine upgrade.

Most buyers opted for the 315-horsepower 390-cubic-inch V-8. The AMX served to introduce this engine, which was the largest ever offered by AMC. It was derived from the 343 and used the same 10.2:1 compression ratio, but the 390 had a stronger block, forged instead of cast connecting rods and crankshaft, and larger bearings, among other improvements. All AMX engines used a single four-barrel carburetor.

Borg-Warner's T-10 four-speed manual transmission came standard with all engines in the AMX. Optionally available was B-W's three-speed automatic with floor-mounted shifter, dubbed Shift Command by AMC. Rear axle ratios ranged from 2.87:1

Not known for high-performance cars, American Motors scored a coup with the original AMX (both pages). It was a two-seater based on the Javelin, but was a foot shorter. A 315-bhp 390-cid V-8 was optional and with it, the AMX could turn mid-14s in the quarter-mile.

to 3.54:1, and dealer-installed 4.10:1 and 5.00:1 gears were available.

Car and Driver found the engine responsive up to its somewhat low rev limit of around 5200 rpm and said the automatic transmission's responsiveness was just shy of the quick, crisp shifts supplied by GM's Turbo Hydra-Matic. The four-speed manual was a major disappointment. "The shift linkage is an abomination," said *Car and Driver*. "It is a long, wobbly business with lots of play in every direction...." The magazine said the linkage was so bad that it negated any advantage of having a four-speed.

Underneath, the standard AMX boasted heavy-duty front coil springs and rear leaf springs, plus a large-diameter front sway bar and a pair of trailing arms (traction bars) to prevent rear-axle power hop. More precise steering could be had via an optional 19.3:1 ratio manual-steering gear or an 18.1:1 power-assisted unit.

Car and Driver said the 3245-pound AMX couldn't match the road manners of the contemporary independent-rear-suspension Corvette, which weighed 200 pounds less, "but it's infinitely superior to the old solid-axle jobs in both ride and road-holding....It's a suspension system that'll get you down the road and around the corners in admirable fashion, and get all the necessary going and stopping power properly spread around."

A popular AMX option was the "Go" package that consisted of either the 343 or 390 V-8, plus power front disc brakes, E70×14 Goodyear Polyglas Red Line tires, heavy-duty suspension with higher-rate springs, Twin-Grip differential, heavy-duty cooling, and twin racing stripes.

AMC portrayed the AMX as a limited-edition car and emphasized the point by attaching a production number to the dash of each one it built. The sales target for '68 was 10,000 AMXs and up to 20,000 annually after that. Just 6725 were produced during that first model year, however. Perhaps people weren't ready for a genuine performance machine from the Rambler people—especially one that could go fast in both a straight line and around turns. American-style power and European-style handling at family car prices? Pony car or sports car? Just what was this AMX?

1969

With only a half year under its belt, the AMX was treated to refinements rather than wholesale changes for 1969. A 140-mph speedometer was added, and you could order optional leather upholstery. More significantly, the shift linkage was replaced by a vastly superior one from Hurst.

AMC also made an all-out assault on quarter-mile performance with the Super Stock AMX. At $5994, some $1900 over a fully loaded regular '69 AMX, the SS/AMX ran with the 390 treated to twin Holley carburetors, 12.3:1 compression heads, a set of Doug's headers and exhaust system, plus a host of other modifications undertaken by Hurst. It was rated at 340 horsepower by AMC, but the National Hot Rod Association ultimately rated the SS/AMX at 420 horsepower and shuffled it among various classes: SS/G, SS/D, and SS/C. It could be ordered in all-white paint, or in the vertical red, white, and blue that banded the bodies of many AMC competition

A facelift for '70 (both pages) brought a hood scoop that could be fitted with optional Ram-Air hardware for 340 bhp. A 290-bhp 360-cid V-8 (top) replaced 290-cid V-8 as standard. AMX came with reclining buckets. It was a top road car, but this one (above) is set up for the strip.

cars of the day.

Since a production run of 50 units was required in order to compete in NHRA events, AMC/Hurst built that number, plus two for good measure. So highly strung was the SS/AMX that it came without a factory warranty. Its best recorded quarter-mile was 10.73 seconds at 128 mph.

AMX production was up for '69, but still came in at a disappointing 8293 units.

1970

A mild 1970 facelift of the Javelin also spilled over to AMX. The new grille ran the full width of the nose and was split horizontally by a rib.

AMC said that moving the parking light/turn signal lamps to the grille opened two holes in the front bumper that directed cooling air to the front brakes, though close inspection revealed that the ducts were too far from the brakes to do much good. Gone from the hood were the cleaves, replaced by a center scoop that could be fitted with optional vacuum-activated Ram-Air hardware. The taillights now ran the full width of the rear end.

The standard 225-horsepower 290-cubic-inch V-8 was replaced by a 360-cubic-inch V-8 rated at 290 horsepower. The optional 390 engine now made 325 horsepower, a gain of 10, and 340 horsepower with the Ram-Air option.

The front suspension was updated with upper and lower ball joints. The interior still had only two buckets, but these were now high-back models with integral head restraints.

AMX output for 1970 sank to a dismal 4116 units, incentive enough for AMC to discontinue the pert two-seater. As it turned out, the AMX befuddled most AMC dealers, didn't get its due respect on the street, and has been slow to garner wide-spread collector interest.

There are those, however, who celebrate it for the important and exciting automobile it is. Among them is the prestigious Milestone Car Society, which in 1985 recognized the AMX as a milestone car based on styling, engineering, performance, and innovation.

1968-70 AMC AMX

Facts At a Glance

Engine type:	V-8/AMC	V-8/AMC
Displacement (cid):	290	343
Horsepower @ rpm:	225 @ 4700	280 @ 4800
Torque (lbs/ft) @ rpm:	300 @ 3200	365 @ 3000
Compression ratio:	10.0:1	10.2:1
Bore (in.):	3.75	4.08
Stroke (in.):	3.28	3.28
Valve lifters:	Hydraulic	Hydraulic
Availability:	1968-69	1968-69

Engine type:	V-8/AMC	V-8/AMC
Displacement (cid):	360	390
Horsepower @ rpm:	290 @ 4800	315 @ 4600 (1968-69)
		325 @ 5000 (1970)[1]
Torque (lbs/ft) @ rpm:	395 @ 3200	425 @ 3200 (1968-69)
		420 @ 3000 (1970)
Compression ratio:	10.0:1	10.2:1 (1968-69)
		10.0:1 (1970)
Bore (in.):	4.08	4.17
Stroke (in.):	3.44	3.57
Valve lifters:	Hydraulic	Hydraulic
Availability:	1970	1968-70

[1]340 bhp with Ram-Air.

Magazine:	*Car and Driver* (March 1968)	*Motor Trend* (Dec. 1969)
Times:		
0-60 mph (sec):	6.6	6.56
0-100 mph (sec):	16.3	N/A
¼ mile (sec):	14.8 @ 95.0 mph	14.68 @ 92 mph
Top speed (mph):	122	N/A
Axle ratio:	3.15:1	3.54:1
Engine (cid/bhp):	390/315	390/325

1969½
AMC
HURST SC/RAMBLER

American Motors wasn't the first manufacturer to stuff its biggest engine into its mid-size model, but it was the first without enough money to really promote its potent new package. Too bad, because the junior muscle car that AMC made out of its 1969 Rambler Rogue was indeed potent.

How about a low, 14-second quarter-mile at 100 mph?

How about 390 cubic inches of rumbling V-8 fed at full throttle by a vacuum-operated hood scoop and hauled to a stop by front disc brakes?

How about a pedigree that comes from an association with hallowed Hurst Performance Research, Inc.?

AMC's marketing team tried to capitalize on the shock value of such credentials by simply heading one advertisement: "A Rambler that does the quarter mile in 14.3."

But they could afford only so many ads. So they made a billboard of the car itself.

Starting with a basic Rogue hardtop in plain appliance white they plastered the bodysides with brilliant red paint, bolted on bright mag wheels, blacked out the grille and tail panel, and hung racing mirrors on the doors. They placed in the middle of the hood a shirt-box-sized fiberglass scoop, the leading edge of which jutted skyward about 10 degrees like the nose of a hound who's caught the scent. Then they slapped the word "AIR" in red letters on either side of the scoop.

Really getting into the spirit now, they painted on the leading edge of the hood—as if being sucked up by that hound-snout scoop—a 12-inch-wide blue arrow inset with six-inch-high crimson-colored characters that read "390 CU.IN." The arrow continued over the roof and down the trunk lid as a big, blue racing stripe.

This was the 1969½ AMC SC/Rambler-Hurst. That was its official name; most just called it the Scrambler. And it got noticed.

Road Test said: "...the exterior trim of the SC/Rambler will turn more heads than a girl in a miniskirt tying her shoelaces." *Car and Driver* likened it to a "tri-colored nickelodeon...."

Once past the graphics, road testers seemed surprised to discover a genuinely good car.

"This is one of the best performing hot engines we have ever encountered," said *Road Test*, adding that the Hurst shift linkage also was among the smoothest in its experience. It concluded that the little Scrambler would "show the Hurst emblem on the back to a few GTOs, Cobra Jets, Road Runners, and Mach 1's."

Backing that claim was the 14.14-second quarter-mile at 100.44 mph turned by *Road Test. Car Life* gave the SC/Rambler a go in May 1969 and saw 0-60 mph in 6.3 seconds, 0-100 in 14.1, and the quarter-mile in 14.2 seconds at 100.8 mph.

It's important to note that the Scrambler wasn't the first time AMC had attempted to inject the Rogue with some muscle. In '67, the two-door hardtop was available with a 343-cubic-inch V-8 producing 280 horsepower at 4800 rpm. The 343 Rogue covered the quarter-mile in 15.8 seconds at 88 miles per hour, considerably faster than the "Flash-O-Matic"-equipped six-cylinder Ramblers America had known for years, but not in the Scrambler's league.

Just 500 SC/Ramblers were slated for production, and at a price few could pass up—$2998 delivered complete, ready for the road or strip. The only option was a $61 dealer-installed AM radio.

Road Test magazine got the message, calling the SC/Rambler a "drag strip eliminator at a penny pinching price," a car that "follows the econo-racer concept of austere sedan body with super-car drivetrain and running gear established by the Plymouth Road Runner."

That drivetrain and running gear included the 315-

AMC teamed with Hurst Performance to create the cartoonish but quick Scrambler. Shirt-box hood-scoop fed a 390-cid V-8. About 1000 of the 1512 Scramblers built had these full "Yankee Doodle" graphics.

horsepower, four-barrel 390 V-8 lifted directly out of the AMX. It had a heavy-duty cooling system and a power-flex fan that flattened out at higher speeds to conserve power. Backing this up was the tough Borg-Warner four-speed manual gearbox with a T-handle Hurst floor shifter, 3.54:1 rear-axle gearing, and Twin-Grip limited-slip differential. Topping it all off was a straight-through dual exhaust system with chrome extensions.

The suspension, with front coils and rear leaf springs, boasted heavy-duty shocks, anti-sway bar, and twin torque links at the rear to fight axle hop. Rolling stock consisted of six-inch-wide mag-style wheels and E70×14 Goodyear Polyglas Red Line bias-belted tires. The AMX's optional heavy-duty braking system was a Scrambler standard and consisted of 11.2-inch Bendix front discs augmenting rear drums.

The first 500 SC/Ramblers received the "Yankee Doodle" graphics. After they sold out, an additional 1000 or so were run off, about half with the original graphics and half with narrower red and blue stripes. A total of 1512 Scramblers were built.

The interiors featured reclining bucket seats in charcoal gray vinyl and a wood-rimmed steering wheel. Instrumentation was standard Rogue, but with a Sun 8000-rpm tachometer strapped hot-rodder style to the steering column. The wild exterior graphics were carried over via red, white, and blue headrests.

Road Test magazine complained that the steering wheel was too close to the driver and that the tach blocked some gauges, but overall was pleased to find that the 3160-pound curb weight in combination with the taut suspension and wide tires made the Scrambler an impressive handler under hard driving.

"Although the SC/Rambler doesn't create the world's best visual impression," said the magazine's editors, "when it comes down to the business of go and stop, this little machine comes on with the best." Sharp of them to notice.

1969½ AMC-Hurst SC/Rambler

Facts At a Glance

Engine type:	V-8/AMC
Displacement (cid):	390
Horsepower @ rpm:	315 @ 4600
Torque (lbs/ft)	
@ rpm:	425 @ 3200
Compression ratio:	10.2:1
Bore (in.):	4.17
Stroke (in.):	3.75
Valve lifters:	Hydraulic
Availability:	1969

Magazine:	Car and Driver (May 1969)	Car Life (May 1969)
Times:		
0-60 mph (sec):	6.3	6.3
0-100 mph (sec):	15.8	14.1
¼ mile (sec):	14.7 @ 96.3 mph	14.2 @ 100.8 mph
Top speed (mph):	114 (est)	108
Axle ratio:	3.54:1	N/A

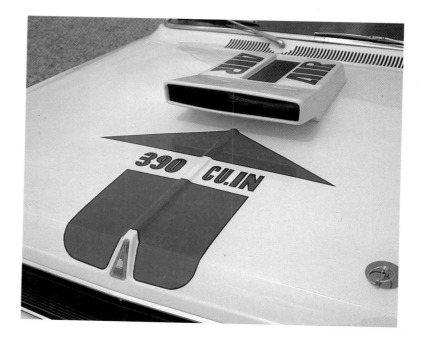

Above left is one of about 500 Scramblers with the more conservative paint treatment. Ram-air hardware (above) helped generate 315 bhp. Rogue-based Scrambler was offered for 1969 only; it cost $2998.

1970
AMC
REBEL MACHINE

Even two years after the debut of the AMX, "American
Motors" and "performance" didn't seem to belong in the
same sentence. AMC had begun sponsoring professional drag-
racing and road-racing teams. It had attempted to make all
the noise it could with its quick and colorful Hurst-SC/Rambler.
But its image car, the AMX, wasn't selling well and the
Rogue upon which the Scrambler was based had been dropped
for 1970.

For respect on the street and strip, AMC turned to its mid-
size Rebel, then took more than a passing glance back at the
strategy that got the Scrambler noticed. With its odd hood
scoop and "Laugh-In" graphics, the SC/Rambler was a kind of
cartoon muscle car. Its Rebel follow-up was slightly less
garish; more of a muscle-car caricature. But AMC carried
through on the tongue-in-cheek spirit in naming the car, calling
its new model the Machine.

A performance takeoff on the fastback Rebel SST
intermediate hardtop, the Machine retained the Scrambler's
flag-waving paint scheme, but toned it down, relegating it
primarily to a highly reflective red side stripe linked across the
trunk lid by red, white, and blue bands. The motif was carried
over into the upholstery of the front seat armrest and onto the
lower lip of the grille. After the first 1000 or so Machines
were produced, AMC made this performance package available
in any regular Rebel color and even offered a vinyl roof. All
shared a hood air scoop with vacuum-activated ducts that fed
directly to the air cleaner. Built into the driver's side of the
hood scoop was an 8000-rpm tachometer.

With a wheelbase of 114 inches, an overall body length of

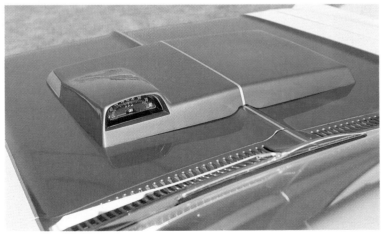

*AMC's tongue-in-cheek follow-up to the garish Scrambler was the Rebel
Machine. Patriotic paint scheme was mandatory on the first 1000. Rain and
glare from the sun cut legibility of the hood-mounted tachometer.*

1970 AMC Rebel Machine

Facts At a Glance

Engine type:	V-8/AMC
Displacement (cid):	390
Horsepower @ rpm:	340 @ 5100
Torque (lbs/ft) @ rpm:	430 @ 3600
Compression ratio:	10.0:1
Bore (in.):	4.17
Stroke (in.):	3.57
Valve lifters:	Hydraulic
Availability:	1970

Magazine:	Road Test (May 1970)	Motor Trend (Nov. 1969)
Times:		
0-60 mph (sec):	7.0 (est)	6.4
0-100 mph (sec):	17.0 (est)	N/A
¼ mile (sec):	14.57 @ 92.77 mph	14.4 @ 99.0 mph
Top speed (mph):	120 (est)	N/A
Axle ratio:	3.91:1	N/A

Station-wagon rear springs gave the Machine a raked stance that hurt traction off the line. Overall handling was above average, however. The Machine had AMC's most powerful standard engine ever, a 340-bhp 390-cid with ram air. Four-speed with Hurst shifter was standard.

16

199 inches, and a curb weight of 3650 pounds, the Machine was considerably bulkier than the Scrambler, which had a 106-inch wheelbase and a 3160-pound curb weight. AMC tried to offset this heft by building the Machine around the most powerful engine it ever offered: its 390-cubic-inch V-8, here rated at 340 horsepower at 5100 rpm and 430 pounds/feet of torque at 3600.

Helping out were a heavy-duty cooling package with flexible fan for efficiency, dual exhausts, and 15×7-inch mag-styled steel wheels that held fat E60×15 glass-belted tires. The Warner T-10 four-speed gearbox carried a Hurst shifter and the Twin-Grip differential came with a standard 3.54:1 axle; gearing up to 5.00:1 was available through the dealer.

Road Test magazine tried a Machine with the optional 3.91:1 gears and saw a quarter-mile best of 14.57 seconds at 92.77 mph. Severe wheel hop and weight—the test car tipped the scales at 3800 pounds—were blamed for the fair-to-middling performance. In everyday use, though, *Road Test* said the powertrain got the Machine moving "with surprising verve" and returned 11 miles per gallon, which it deemed acceptable for a muscle car.

And testers liked the way it handled. The Machine got an upgraded suspension that included front and rear anti-sway bars and heavy-duty rear springs from the Rebel station wagon. These springs helped raise the rear end, which AMC advertising said gave the Machine "a raked, just mowed the lawn look." *Road Test*, however, blamed the raised tail for contributing to that nasty wheel hop off the line; it said that keeping the rear-end pasted to the pavement might cut the quarter-mile time to 14 seconds flat and get the speed to 100 mph.

The optional power steering was deemed grossly overassisted, but all in all, *Road Test* was impressed with the handling. "The whole effect [of the heavy-duty suspension] is to tie the Machine down with close to Ben Hur chariot springing," the editors wrote. "While you can feel anything thicker than a cigarette paper under your wheels, you also get around corners with sports car aplomb...."

They praised the brakes—11.19-inch Bendix discs at the front, 10-inch drums in the rear—but derided the instrumentation, which consisted primarily of the Rebel's horizontal speedometer and little else. The hood-mounted tachometer came in for special criticism: Its face was rendered invisible by the sun's glare or rain.

Overall, the Machine was a handsome intermediate designed for a combination of street/strip driving at a tempting starting price of just $3475. And unlike the SC/Rambler, the Machine could be ordered with a selection of extra-cost options.

AMC maintained a refreshing sense of forthrightness in promoting the Machine. "Incidentally," said its introductory advertisement, "if you have delusions of entering the Daytona 500 with the Machine, or challenging people at random, the Machine is not that fast. You should know that.

"For instance," continued the ad, "it is not as fast on the getaway as a 427 Corvette, or a Hemi, but it is faster on the getaway than a Volkswagen, a slow freight train, and your old man's Cadillac."

Alas, of the 49,725 Rebels built in 1970, only 2326 were Machines. That was bad for AMC then, but it's good for collectors now.

1971
AMC
HORNET SC/360

By the early 1970s the sun was beginning to set on the full-bore muscle car. All-out performance machines had become quite expensive to insure and selling thinly disguised racers for the street was not the kind of image Detroit wanted to cultivate in the eyes of an increasingly safety- and regulatory-minded Washington, D.C.

So the automakers turned to something slightly less conspicuous. Offerings like the popular Plymouth Duster 340 showed that a compact with a relatively conservative V-8 could provide bundles of performance without the drawbacks associated with big-block muscle.

American Motors for 1970 had replaced its Rambler American with a new compact, the Hornet, which initially was offered with only six-cylinder power. For '71, AMC made a 304-cubic-inch V-8 optional in the Hornet, but it was the hot, underrated Hornet SC/360 that got it into the boy-racer ranks.

AMC made it clear from the start that its new offering was tailored to this new performance niche. "Introducing a sensible alternative to the money-squeezing, insurance-strangling muscle cars of America. The Hornet SC/360," said an early ad.

The "SC" designation was familiar enough, recalled by enthusiasts from the 390-cubic-inch/315-horse AMC-Hurst SC/Rambler offered only in 1969. For the Hornet, AMC took a base two-door version of its new compact with the standard three-place split-bench front seat, then added some well-thought-

out performance touches. These included a sport steering wheel, a heavy-duty suspension with a front anti-sway bar, slotted-steel wheels, and modest SC/360 rally striping graphics that followed the upper front fenders rearward to eventually curve over the rear window in a horseshoe effect.

Initial plans had called for both an SC/360 and SC/401, but when AMC discovered that a 401-cubic-inch Hornet probably wouldn't provide enough of an insurance advantage, the peppy 360 V-8 alone was borrowed from the Javelin AMX.

In standard form, the 360 developed 245 horsepower using an Autolite 2100 series two-barrel carburetor. But many buyers demanded more, so a large chunk of Hornet SC/360 production was ordered with the "Go" package, which was also available on the Javelin. This $199 option added the four-barrel 360 V-8 with Ram-Air that cranked out a more satisfying 285 horses. Other options included dual exhausts, a tachometer, white-letter tires, and a handling package.

Behind the two 360 V-8s stood a standard three-speed manual or an optional Hurst-shifted four-speed. A column-mounted Torque Command automatic also was optional. Twin-Grip differential was a popular upgrade, especially by those who chose the more powerful four-barrel 360.

All in all, the SC/360 was a tempting choice for those seeking both a "sleeper" and reasonable insurance rates. And with a base price of $2663, it ranked as one of the most affordable muscle cars ever offered.

As for straight-line performance, the SC/360 couldn't stay with the monster-engine road burners, but it did all right. *Muscle Car Review* lists a 14.9-second quarter-mile time at 95.3 mph. This respectable go power combined with a taut suspension, big tires, and modest size to give the SC/360 a dimension most all-out muscle cars didn't have: reasonable all-around road manners. *Motor Trend*'s testers wrung it out around the Trans Am road course at Michigan International Speedway and found the super Hornet "just a plain gas to drive...it handles like a dream."

Even so, SC/360 output amounted to only 667 units out of nearly 75,000 '71 Hornets. AMC offered V-8s in subsequent Hornets, but never again offered a package that duplicated the appeal of the 1971 SC/360. It was one of the rarest of performance machines of its time and remains a well-kept secret even today.

1971 AMC Hornet SC/360

Facts At a Glance

Engine type:	V-8/AMC	V-8/AMC
Displacement (cid):	360 (2v)	360 (4v)[1]
Horsepower @ rpm:	245 @ 4400	285 @ 4800
Torque (lbs/ft) @ rpm:	365 @ 2600	390 @ 3200
Compression ratio:	8.5:1	8.5:1
Bore (in.):	4.08	4.08
Stroke (in.):	3.44	3.44
Valve lifters:	Hydraulic	Hydraulic
Availability:	1971	1971

[1]With Ram-Air induction

Magazine:	Muscle Car Review (1987 Annual)	Motor Trend (January 1971)
Times:		
0-60 mph (sec):	6.5 (est)	6.7
0-100 mph (sec):	15.5 (est)	N/A
¼-mile (sec):	14.91 @ 95.33 mph	15.0 @ 94.0 mph
Top speed (mph):	N/A	109 (est)
Axle ratio:	3.54:1	3.54:1
Engine type:	360 (4v)	360 (4v)

1971-74
AMC
JAVELIN AMX 401

By 1971, the ponycar had taken a turn for the bigger, if not better, and AMC was going with the flow. The revamped '71 Javelin was longer, lower, wider, and heavier than its predecessor. Gone was the gentle, tucked-in look of the original. This second-generation Javelin was characterized by severe fender arches that were awkwardly sculpted attempts to mimic the Corvette.

Gone also was the AMX as a distinct model. The original AMX was based on a Javelin shortened from a wheelbase of 109 inches to 97. It was a svelte two-seater with a legitimate claim as a genuine sports car. For '71, the Javelin AMX was essentially a decor option group added to the same 110-inch wheelbase and four-passenger body used by all the other Javelins. Any Javelin, in fact, could be ordered with the Javelin AMX's power and performance options. Javelin offerings included a base model and the more luxurious SST, but the Javelin AMX was AMC's performance flagship.

At $3432, the Javelin AMX was about $300 more expensive than an SST V-8. Part of the difference was that the SST came standard with a 210-horsepower 304-cubic-inch V-8 while the Javelin AMX's standard powerplant was a 360-cubic-inch V-8 that developed 245 horses with a two-barrel carburetor. For an extra $49, a four-barrel carb brought 285 horsepower, down five from 1970's four-barrel power rating. As before, the buyer could choose between a three- or four-speed manual transmission or Shift Command automatic transmission with a column- or floor-mounted lever. Twin-Grip limited-slip differential remained a desirable option, especially with the four-speed.

The big news for '71 was the introduction of a 401-cubic-inch V-8, a bored-and-stroked version of the earlier 290- to 390-cubic-inch AMC V-8s. For only $137, the 401 helped the Javelin AMX come alive with 330 advertised horsepower at 5000 rpm. With the extra cubes, however, came a less-than-super 9.5:1 compression ratio for compatibility with low lead, low octane gas.

Externally, the Javelin AMX boasted its own grille, a flush-mounted wire mesh affair that was simply mounted ahead of the standard Javelin grille. Optional on all Javelins, but standard on the Javelin AMX were front and rear spoilers. A reverse-flow cowl vent package that used the high-pressure area at the base of the windshield for a carburetor-induction effect was an extra-cost item.

The optional "Go" package included a T stripe decal on the hood, Rally Pac instruments, a handling package, heavy-duty cooling, Twin-Grip limited-slip differential, power front disc brakes, Goodyear E60×15 Polyglas white-letter tires, and the same slot-styled steel wheels used on the '70 AMC Rebel Machine.

Despite its larger size and an extra 100 or so pounds of curb weight compared to the '70 AMX, the 3244-pound '71 Javelin AMX with a 401 was able to run the quarter-mile in the credible mid 14s at around 93 mph.

The new Javelin AMX's spoilers and cowl-induction hood were supposedly inspired by Mark Donohue's experience racing Javelins in Sports Car Club of America Trans Am competition. AMC wrung as much publicity mileage as it could out of the Trans Am championships that Donohue and others won with the Javelin. Unfortunately, this didn't leave much of an impression on potential Javelin AMX buyers. Some 2054 Javelin AMXs were built in '71—just seven percent of Javelin production—and only 745 are believed to have been equipped with the 401 V-8.

1972

Slightly redesigned taillamps distinguished the '72 Javelin AMX externally, but there were more important changes under

the hood. As were its Motown rivals, AMC was scaling back performance under pressure from increasingly stringent exhaust-emission standards and oppressive insurance rates.

So the AMC 304-cubic-inch V-8 became the standard Javelin AMX engine for '72; the 360 was now an option along with the 401. Underscoring this retreat, the manufacturers began to list net horsepower ratings—the engine with all its accessories as installed in the car—rather than gross horsepower—essentially the engine free of encumbrances.

The 304 was listed at 210 horsepower in '71, but only 150 under the new rating system in '72. Estimates of the 304's gross horsepower ran around 200, but regardless, the 304 proved a disappointment to buyers pursuing more horsepower for their Javelin AMX. Most opted for the larger 360, a $188 extra. This engine was down to 175 horsepower with the two barrel, 195 with a four barrel and single exhaust, and 220 for the four barrel with dual exhaust. Compression was down to 8.5:1 for more efficient use with the unleaded fuels that were now required. Included with the 360 were E70×14 Goodyear Polyglas tires and other features.

The 401-cubic-inch V-8 remained an option and was now

Second-generation AMX was no longer a two-seater or a distinct model and was instead an option package for the new bigger and heavier Javelin. It had its own mesh grille mounted ahead of the stock unit.

1971-74 AMC Javelin AMX

Facts At a Glance

Engine type:	V-8/AMC	V-8/AMC
Displacement (cid):	360	401
Horsepower @ rpm:	285 @ 4800 (245 @ 4800 2v)	330 @ 5000
Torque (lbs/ft) @ rpm:	390 @ 3200 (365 @ 3200 2v)	430 @ 3400
Compression ratio:	8.5:1	9.5:1
Bore (in.):	4.08	4.17
Stroke (in.):	3.44	3.68
Valve lifters:	Hydraulic	Hydraulic
Availability:	1971	1971

Engine type:	V-8/AMC	V-8/AMC
Displacement (cid):	304	401
Horsepower @ rpm:	150 @ 4200	255 @ 4600
Torque (lbs/ft) @ rpm:	245 @ 2500	345 @ 3300
Compression ratio:	8.4:1	8.5:1
Bore (in.):	3.75	4.17
Stroke (in.):	3.44	3.68
Valve lifters:	Hydraulic	Hydraulic
Availability:	1972-74	1972-74

Engine type:	V-8/AMC
Displacement (cid):	360
Horsepower @ rpm:	220 @ 4400[1] (175 @ 4000 2V)
Torque (lbs/ft) @ rpm:	315 @ 3100[2] (285 @ 2400 2V)
Compression ratio:	8.4:1
Bore (in.):	4.08
Stroke (in.):	3.44
Valve lifters:	Hydraulic
Availability:	1972-74

[1]195 @ 4400 single exhaust
[2]295 @ 2900 single exhaust

Magazine:	Muscle Car Review (1987 Annual)	Motor Trend (July 1973)
Times:		
0-60 mph:	N/A	7.7
0-100 mph:	N/A	N/A
¼ mile (sec):	14.65 @ 92.97 mph	15.5 @ 90 mph
Top speed:	N/A	115.53
Axle ratio:	N/A	3.54:1
Engine (cid/bhp):	401/330	401/255
Model year:	1971	1973

rated at 255 horsepower at 4600 rpm.

As in 1968-71, the optional "Go" package was a tempting tick on the Javelin options sheet. It contained Cowl-Air induction, heavy-duty suspension, E60×15 Goodyear Polyglas tires, racing stripes, Rally Pac instrumentation, hood T-stripe decal, and related appearance/performance features.

1973

The 1973 Javelin AMX was mostly a carryover, with the exception of new taillights and backup lights. The 401 kept its 255-horsepower rating and nearly identical choice of powertrains—a standard four-speed or optional Torque Command automatic transmission.

Straight-line performance took a beating. *Motor Trend* saw a mediocre 15.5 at 90 mph in the quarter with a 401.

But for evidence of how manufacturers were de-emphasizing all-out go, you had to look no further than an AMC advertisement for the '73 Javelin AMX. It touted the car's continued Trans Am success, but absent was the excited rundown of horsepower, transmissions, and drag-strip-axle ratios that had spiced up earlier ads. Instead, the copy talked about the room in the back seat, "the nice balance of performance and comfort," and AMC's warranty plan. There even was a tag line that read "Buckle up for safety."

Evidently this kind of appeal worked, for Javelin AMX sales jumped a dramatic 73 percent in 1973, to an all-time high of 4737. That was nearly 18 percent of Javelin production.

1974

The ponycar war was grinding to a conclusion. Ford had given up the ship in 1973 with the "last" of its high-performance V-8 Mustangs and Cougars. Both Chevrolet and Pontiac were scaling back their performance Camaros and Firebirds. Chrysler was preparing to axe the Barracuda and Challenger. AMC soldiered on with the Javelin AMX in this, the last year for an AMC ponycar.

Under the hood, the 304 remained the standard V-8, with the optional 360 and 401 still in the arsenal. The last big one continued to crank out its rated 255 net horsepower, with the assistance of a Motorcraft 4300 four-barrel carburetor and dual exhausts. A standard three-speed and optional four-speed continued as the manual-transmission choices; Torque Command automatic and Twin-Grip remained other choices.

The '74 AMX didn't do well in the marketplace compared to Camaro, Firebird, and the downsized Mustang II, all of which saw increased sales. Javelin production, meanwhile, reached a second-generation high of 27,696 units. Of that number, 4980, or about 15 percent, were Javelin AMX models. AMC would resurrect the AMX tag, attaching it to the Hornet, Concord, and Spirit in subsequent years. But none had the muscle-car mystique that the Javelin AMX strived for, and certainly none could hold a candle to the classic, original 1968-70 AMX.

Javelin AMX styling changed little through '74, though optional spoilers, vinyl roof, and stripes—inside and out—could alter its appearance. Hottest available engine was the four-barrel 401, which declined from 330 bhp in '71 to 255 by '74. AMX badge had tarnished.

1965-67
BUICK
GRAN SPORT

Buick put its 325-bhp 401-cid "Wildcat 455" (bottom) into the '65 Skylark (opposite) to create the Gran Sport. It had less horsepower but more torque than GTO; quarter-miles times were in the mid-15s. Blackened grille, fake hood and fender vents marked '66 GS (below and opposite page bottom).

The name Buick conjures visions of sedate drives in the country with Grandma and Granddad in maybe a big, soft '55 Special sedan. But there was another breed of Buick and they were tire-smoking, road-ripping rivals to the baddest muscle cars in the land. Their story begins in 1965.

In 1964, performance at Buick and the other GM divisions was constrained by a corporate edict that permitted nothing larger than a 330-cubic-inch engine in an intermediate body. That left Buick with a 300-cubic-inch V-8 as its largest offering for the mid-size, 115-inch-wheelbase Special/Skylark. An enlarged version of the famed 215-cubic-inch aluminum V-8, the 300-incher also had an aluminum block and was good for 210 or 250 horsepower and up to 335 pounds/feet of torque. Buick might have been content with the 300 V-8. But Pontiac had gotten around the GM ruling with its 389-cubic-inch Tempest GTO and Buick was itching to join the big-bore fray.

In '65, GM raised the cubic-inch limit to 400 and Buick seized the chance to revitalize its Skylark. Buick looked to the 401 "Nail-Head" V-8 (so-called for its small, vertical valves), which was standard in most big Buicks. At 401 cubic inches, however, this engine just exceeded GM's 400-cube limit. Undeterred, Buick simply renamed the 401 the "400" and slipped it into the Skylark.

Introduced at midyear, the new Skylark option was labeled Gran Sport, or "GS" for short, and it joined a beefed-up Wildcat and the Riviera Gran Sport in the Buick performance stable.

Advertised as "A howitzer with windshield wipers," the GS packed the "Wildcat 445" engine, which made 325 horses at 4400 rpm. That was slightly under the horsepower of the GTO and Oldsmobile 4-4-2, but the Gran Sport had more torque; a tarmac-tearing 445 pounds/feet at 2800 rpm. The Nail-Head was mated with a three-speed full-synchro stick as standard, but a close-ratio four-speed manual and a two-speed Super Turbine automatic also were available. Standard with the manual transmissions was a 3.36:1 axle ratio; the automatic came with a 3.08:1. Ratios up to 3.73:1 were optionally available with either type of gearbox. Like all Buicks, the GS had a luxury slant, so very few ended up with the four-speed.

Bucket seats, a center console (optional with the manual transmission only), and GS badges were the main visual cues to the '65 Gran Sport. Standard firepower in addition to the 401 included dual exhausts, a reinforced frame from the Skylark convertible, heavy-duty springs and shocks, and a stabilizer bar that was roughly twice as stiff as the normal Skylark's. Heavy-duty upper control-arm bushings helped snub axle wind-up and 7.75×14 tires on six-inch rims (chromed steel wheels were optional) got the power down. Instrumentation was modest, with the same horizontal-sweep speedometer found in the base Special models, though a tachometer was available at extra cost.

The '65 Buick Gran Sport came in three body styles: hardtop, thin-pillar Sport Coupe, and convertible. At $3149 for the Sport Coupe and $3299 for the ragtop, the GS was about $460 more expensive than the regular Skylarks.

1966

Skylark got fresh new lines for 1966 highlighted by sloping sail panels that extended the roofline beyond the recessed back window. The Gran Sport was distinguished by its blacked-out grille, new Gran Sport nameplate, dual simulated rear-facing hood scoops, and a fake fender vent just aft of the front wheels.

The GS option again included the 325-horse 401 along with a choice of three- and four-speed manuals or the Super Turbine automatic transmission. For a few bucks extra, a 340-horse version of the 401 was available.

Buick had an honest performance vehicle in the Skylark Gran Sport. Its 0-60-mph clocking of 7.6 seconds and quarter-mile time of 15.47 at 90.54 mph, as recorded by *Motor Trend*, were nearly identical to the performance posted by the magazine's GTO test car. Buick also had a better reputation for assembly quality than Chevrolet, Pontiac, or even Oldsmobile. So at $2956 for the thin-pillar coupe, $3019 for the Sport Coupe, and $3167 for the convertible, the GS represented a remarkable performance value.

Unfortunately, it also was an underappreciated performance value. Sales were soft, with 13,816 '66 GS models built; 1835 were pillared coupes and 2047 were ragtops.

1967

While 1967 was largely a carryover year for the hottest Skylark, the Gran Sport name was dropped and the car was rechristened the GS-400 in honor of its new engine. On the outside was a new red-banded grille, blacked-out headlamp bezels, and fresh taillamps. The hood scoops now faced forward and the simulated air extractors just behind the front wheels were of a slightly different design. Inside, the horizontal-sweep speedometer remained.

The new engine was a new-generation Buick 400-cubic-inch V-8. Though displacement was nearly the same as the discontinued 401 Nail-Head, the new 400 was very different from its predecessor. With its 4.04-inch bore and 3.90-inch stroke, the 400 GS V-8 developed 340 horsepower and the ability to pull more revs through the gears.

Driveline choices included a standard three-speed stick, a Muncie four-speed, or the Super Turbine automatic. Positive Traction limited-slip differential was a desirable option.

With prices unchanged for '67, GS output again hovered around 13,800. Seeking to broaden the model's appeal, Buick offered a GS-340 for '67. It had a 260-horsepower 340-cubic-inch V-8 and sold for $2845, but just 3692 GS-340s were built.

The 1965-67 Buick Gran Sport was Buick's interpretation of mid-size muscle and so it was blessed with Buick quality, but also burdened with Buick's staid image. It never had the flamboyance or the following of the GTO, the Chevelle SS models, or even the 4-4-2. But it was Buick's first step down a road that would eventually lead it to build some of the most potent muscle cars ever.

1965-67 Buick Gran Sport

Facts At a Glance

Engine type/maker:	V-8/Buick Nail-Head	V-8/Buick
Displacement (cid):	401	400
Horsepower @ rpm:	325 @ 4400	340 @ 5000
	340 @ 4600 (1966)	
Torque (lbs/ft) @ rpm:	445 @ 2800	440 @ 3200
		445 @ 3200 (1966)
Compression ratio:	10.25:1	10.25:1
Bore (in.):	4.18	4.04
Stroke (in.):	3.64	3.90
Valve lifters:	Hydraulic	Hydraulic
Availability:	1965-66	1967

Magazine:	*Car and Driver* (1966)	*Motor Trend* (May 1965)
Times:		
0-60 mph (sec):	6.8	7.8
0-100 mph (sec):	17.0	N/A
¼ mile (sec):	14.92 @ 95.13 mph	16.6 @ 86 mph
Top speed (mph):	120	116
Axle ratio:	3.36:1	3.36:1
Engine type:	401/4V	401/4V

Magazine:	*Motor Trend* (Dec. 1967)	*Motor Trend* (April 1967)
Times:		
0-60 mph (sec):	7.6	6.6
0-100 mph (sec):	N/A	N/A
¼ mile (sec):	15.5 @ 90.5 mph	15.2 @ 95 mph
Top speed (mph):	N/A	N/A
Axle ratio:	N/A	3.36:1
Engine (cid/bhp):	401/325	401/340

Recessed backlight and fresh body contours help separate '66 GS from '65 (opposite, bottom). In '67, Buick renamed it the GS-400 (opposite, top) in honor of its new 400-cid V-8.

1968-72
BUICK
SKYLARK GS

General Motors' mid-size lineup got new bodies on a shorter, 112-inch wheelbase for 1968 and that meant big styling changes for the Chevrolet Chevelle, Oldsmobile 4-4-2, Pontiac GTO, and Buick's Skylark.

The new GS 400 was able to trade its sedan-like proportions for the long-hood/short-deck lines that spelled performance in the public eye. It got a new chrome-wrapped grille set between quad headlamps. The roof took on semi-fastback form and a strong character line swept from just aft of the headlamps to the bottom leading edge of the rear wheelwell. This made the rear portion of the car look quite massive, especially in hardtop form, where the rear flanks ran virtually uninterrupted into the sail panels. Indeed, despite a three-inch shorter wheelbase and a four-inch shorter overall length, the new Skylarks weighed slightly more than the old.

Most GSs were either hardtops or convertibles for '68, though some Buick dealers stocked a pillared coupe known as the California GS.

Inside, enthusiasts of European-inspired instrumentation would have to look to the GTO and its round gauges; the GS 400 kept its traditional horizontal-sweep speedometer and relegated a host of monitoring functions to idiot lights.

GS 400 powertrain choices remained the same as in 1967, with the standard 400 cubic-inch Buick V-8 producing 340 horsepower at 5000 rpm and 440 pounds/feet of torque at 3200 rpm. Carburetion was via a single Rochester Quadrajet four barrel. Mid-range torque was this engine's forte. It delivered strong seat-of-the-pants performance without the peakiness and fussiness of most high-performance engines. Transmission choices continued from the year before, as did the Posi-Traction option.

Prices were up barely $100 over 1967 and the new styling helped make the '68 GS a best seller. Production nearly doubled over 1967, with a record 21,514 built: 10,743 were GS 400 hardtops, 2454 were GS 400 convertibles and 8317 were "little brother" GS 350s with 280-horsepower 350-cubic-inch V-8s. The California coupes used the 350 engine.

1969

The big news was introduction of the Stage I and Stage II engine options. These packages added to the standard 400-cubic-inch V-8 a high-lift cam, special Quadrajet four-barrel carburetor, and larger low-restriction dual exhausts. A 3.64:1 rear axle was part of the group when a four-speed manual transmission was ordered; specifying the automatic brought a 3.42:1 gear. Buick also threw in a Positive Traction limited-slip differential.

The Stage II used an even higher lift cam and assorted other performance-enhancers. Coupled with Cool-Air induction, the Stage engines did their best breathing at highway speeds. But how much power they actually made is open to debate. The standard mill was rated at 340 horsepower at 5000 rpm. Various sources list the Stage I output at either 345 or 350 horsepower at 5800 rpm, while the Stage II is thought to have produced as much as 360 horsepower.

A heavy-duty Rallye suspension and front disc brakes were optional on all GS 400s.

Styling changed little, with a new rear bumper and exterior graphics complementing a slightly altered grille that was unique to the GS 400 this year. Subtle twin hood scoops on all GS 400s fed cold air to the carburetor through dual snorkels.

Despite a slight price hike, GS production climbed by nearly 6000 units in 1969: 10,743 GS 400 coupes; 8317 GS 350 coupes; 4831 California GS coupes; and 2454 GS 400 convertibles.

1970

For 1970, the new "Light your fire Buicks" turned mean with a new engine that won the GS a place in the muscle-car hall of fame. They also got fresh styling. Wheelbase was unchanged, but Skylark's body grew by two inches thanks to handsome new sheetmetal. Sharper definition in the rear flanks corrected the car's previous problems with proportion and suddenly the GS looked even more macho. Inside, the sporting driver finally got circular gauges to go along with a new sport steering wheel, comfortable bucket seats, and console.

GS nomenclature also was changed. The new base model was simply called the GS and it came standard with a 315-horsepower 350-cubic-inch four-barrel V-8. Benched was the GS 400 name along with the 400-cubic-inch V-8. Stepping up to the plate in its place was the GS 455, so named for its new 455-cubic-inch V-8. Not only did the new 455 offer advantages of displacement over the 400, it had bigger valves, better heads, and a hotter camshaft. Horsepower was 350 at 4600 rpm, torque a prodigious 510 pounds/feet at 2800 rpm. The only production passenger car engine to make more torque was the 500-cubic-inch V-8 in the Cadillac Eldorado, at 550 pounds/feet.

To those for whom too much was never enough, Buick offered the GS 455 Stage I performance package. Torque was unchanged, but there was a higher-lift cam, slightly larger valves, and a compression of 10.25:1 compared to 10.0:1. Horsepower climbed to 360.

This is the engine that made the GS an all-star. *Motor Trend* rode one to 13.38 second quarter-mile at 105.5 mph. The magazine's editors crowned the GS 455 Stage 1 "the quickest American production car we had ever tested."

The standard 455 was available with either a three- or a four-speed manual transmission with a 3.42:1 rear axle ratio or an automatic trans with a 2.93:1 gear. For the $199 extra cost of the Stage 1 option, Buick threw in a Posi-Traction rear axle that had the same 3.64:1 rear-axle ratio with either manual or automatic transmission.

Halfway through the '70 model year, Buick introduced a variation of the GS called the GSX. Basically a GS 455 Sport Coupe usually outfitted in Stage I gear, the '70 GSX's special graphics and aero add ons made it one of the hottest looking muscle cars of the era.

Available in two colors, Apollo White and Saturn Yellow, its unique graphics consisted of narrow side stripes that gradually widened as they spread to the rear fender and over the decklid spoiler. The interior featured buckets, Rallye clock, 15-inch steering wheel, and GSX ornamentation; a tachometer was mounted on the hood in front of the driver. The $1195 GSX package also brought lucky buyers stiffer springs, tighter shock dampening, and heavy-duty suspension components. G60×15 Goodyear Polyglas GTs with chromed Magnum-style steel wheels rounded out the GSX chassis group. Just 678 1970 GSXs were built.

Overall GS sales slipped to 20,096 units, including 9948 small-block GS models, 8732 GS 455 hardtops, and 1416 GS 455 convertibles.

1971

As with most muscle cars that survived to see 1971, the Buick GS seemed defused. Stricter exhaust-emissions standards were strangling engine output.

1968-72 Buick Gran Sport

Facts At a Glance

Engine type:	V-8/Buick	V-8/Buick
Displacement (cid):	400	455
Horsepower @ rpm:	340 @ 5000	350 @ 4600
	350 @ 4800 (1969)[1]	360 @ 4600[1]

Torque (lbs/ft)		
@ rpm:	440 @ 3200	510 @ 2800
Compression ratio:	10.25:1	10.5:1/10.0:1
Bore (in.):	4.04	4.31
Stroke (in.):	3.90	3.90
Valve lifters:	Hydraulic	Hydraulic
Availability:	1968-69	1970

[1]Stage 1

Engine type:	V-8/Buick	V-8/Buick
Displacement (cid):	455	455
Horsepower @ rpm:	315 @ 4400	225 @ 4400
	345 @ 4000[1]	275 @ 4400[1]
Torque (lbs/ft)		
@ rpm:	450 @ 2800	360 @ 2600
	460 @ 3000[1]	395 @ 2600[1]
Compression ratio:	8.5:1	8.5:1
Bore (in.):	4.31	4.31
Stroke (in.):	3.90	3.90
Valve lifters:	Hydraulic	Hydraulic
Availability:	1971	1972

[1]Stage 1

Magazine:	*Motor Trend* *(January 1969)*	*Motor Trend* *(January 1970)*
Times:		
0-60 mph (sec):	7.7	5.5
0-100 mph (sec):	N/A	12.0 (est)
¼-mile (sec):	15.9 @ 89.0 mph	13.38 @ 105.5 mph
Top speed (mph):	N/A	N/A
Axle ratio:	2.93:1	3.64:1
Engine type:	400	455 Stage 1
Model year:	1969	1970

Magazine:	*Hi-Performance* *Cars (Oct. 1970)*
Times:	
0-60 mph (sec):	6.2
0-100 mph (sec):	N/A
¼-mile (sec):	14.0 @ 103 mph
Top speed (mph):	115
Axle ratio:	3.64:1
Engine type:	455 Stage 1
Model year:	GSX Stage 1

Magazine:	*Motor Trend* *(June 1972)*
Times:	
0-60 mph (sec):	5.8
0-100 mph (sec):	N/A
¼-mile (sec):	14.10 @ 97.0 mph
Top speed (mph):	N/A
Axle ratio:	4.30:1
Engine type:	455 Stage 1
Model year:	1972

The 350-cube V-8 in the base GS 350 fell to 260 horsepower, the GS 455's engine slipped to 315 horsepower, while the 455 Stage 1 dropped to 345 at 5000 rpm. Compression ratios scaled back to 8.5:1 for use with low lead, low octane fuels. Although not quite the engine it had been in 1970, the Stage 1 still managed to get the job done with 460 pounds/feet of torque. Cool-Air induction remained a vital part of the package.

The GSX kept its high-profile exterior graphics, but items previously exclusive to it were now available as individual options on any GS.

As before, the GS boasted a heavy-duty suspension—with heavier Rallye Firm Ride and Handling options available—and G60×15 bias-belted tires.

Transmission choices for the 350 engine were a standard three-on-the-tree, or optional four-speed or THM 350 Turbo Hydra-Matic. GS 455 buyers got either the four-speed gearbox or THM 400 Turbo Hydra-Matic. Axle ratios also were toned down; the 3.64:1 was dropped and the 3.42:1 took over as the top performance gear.

The bloom was off the muscle-car rose. GS sales plunged more than 50 percent, to 8268 hardtops and 902 ragtops. Of those, only 801 coupes and 81 convertibles received the Stage 1 package.

1972

The '72 Gran Sport was virtually a carryover from 1971, aside from minor grille and graphics changes. Gone was the limited-production GSX option, although the 455 and 455 Stage 1 V-8s hung on as attitude enhancers for a dying breed. Adding insult to injury, manufacturers began listing net horsepower— the engine with accessories attached—instead of gross horsepower.

Thus, the standard 350 V-8 was rated at 195 horsepower. The 455 four-barrel V-8 with Cool-Air induction remained the performance mainstay, but its horsepower rating dropped to 225. Back for another round was the 455 Stage 1, listed at 270 horses.

The '72 Gran Sport received a shot in the arm toward the end of the model year, when Stage 2 cylinder heads were made available over the counter. But it wasn't enough to halt the march away from mid-size Buick performance.

Prices were reduced $60 to $70, so the GS Sport Coupe ran $3225 and the convertible $3406. But only 8575 Skylark GSs were built, including just 852 ragtops. Production of 1972 Stage 1 models came to a modest 809 units, making them as rare as the 1970 and '71 GSX models.

Handsome '70 restyle made a worthy platform for the hot GSX (opposite page and top), most of which had the mighty 455 Stage I with 360 bhp good for sub-14-second ETs. Hood-mounted tach was standard; exclusive black graphics contrasted with Saturn Yellow paint. Ragtop on this page is among only 902 '71 GS 455 convertibles; the swan-song '72 is pictured above.

1973-74
BUICK
GRAN SPORT 455

Muscle car buffs can be excused for not equating a 1973 or '74 Buick Gran Sport with a high-performance engine. Fact is, the '73 Buick Gran Sport could be fitted with a 455 Stage 1 V-8—but Buick built just 728 of them for the '73 model year.

Motor Trend, in fact, noted that the "sedate Buick has a cousin no one talks about on the TV commercials." Unlike its intermediate Skylark-based predecessors, this overlooked Gran Sport was based on the slippery lines of the all-new Century Colonnade coupe. The base Century Colonnade coupe retailed at $3057, rode a 112-inch wheelbase, and stretched 208 inches overall. The Gran Sport option cost $173.

Unlike the last few years of the Skylark incarnation, in which only the letters "GS" were used, the Century-based cars used the full "Gran Sport" name. Exterior cues included a black-out grille and headlight bezels, special rear-deck trim, and "gran sport" lettering on the rear flanks. To aid both handling and aesthetics, Buick endowed the Gran Sport with 14×7-inch sport wheels that wore bias-belted, wide-profile tires.

Most '73 Gran Sports used the standard 350-cubic-inch V-8, which was rated at 150 horsepower with a two barrel carburetor and single exhaust or 190 with a four-barrel and dual exhausts. While the 455 Stage 1 Gran Sports are quite rare, regular 225-horsepower 455 Gran Sports aren't far behind, not with a total of only 979 units built. Buick threw in a dual exhaust setup with this engine on GS models.

A 225-horsepower 455-cubic-inch V-8 could be ordered with any Century Colonnade coupe, but only Gran Sports were eligible for the Stage 1 option. The '73 Buick GS with Stage 1

Buick transferred the Gran Sport name to the new mid-size Century for '73. Standard was a mild 350-cid V-8, but this '73 Gran Sport (both pages) has the optional 455 Stage I. Rated at 270 bhp net, the four-barrel big-block propelled the 3800-lb Colonnade coupe to low-15-second ETs.

option, which cost $546 extra, provided a 270-horsepower 455 fortified with Stage 1-grade camshaft and heads, Rochester Quadra-Jet carb, factory dual exhausts, and a dual-snorkel air cleaner. Of the 728 Stage 1s produced, 721 left the factory with the heavy-duty Turbo Hydra-Matic 400 transmission. Having this gearbox on board guaranteed that every flexing of the 455 Stage 1's 390 pounds/feet of torque would be channeled to the standard Posi-Traction 3.42:1 rear end.

1974

The Gran Sport option remained on the books for 1974, as did the Stage 1 engine, which now was rated at only 255 horsepower. Three other choices were available: a 175-horsepower 350-cube V-8 with two-barrel carburetor; a 190-horse two-barrel 455; or a four-barrel, 230-horsepower 455.

While horsepower was succumbing to clean-air regulations, curb weights were rising to accommodate five-mile-per-hour bumpers and other safety-related equipment. In Buick's case, that translated into about 250 pounds of extra heft for 1973. The '73 Century tipped the scales at a burly 3700 pounds without options; it gained another 130 pounds for '74. Perhaps that's why Buick billed its 1973 models as the cars with "the solid feeling." Still, *Motor Trend* clocked a '73 Stage 1 at 15.3 and 90 mph in the quarter-mile. Apart from the Corvette, little else out of Detroit was much faster.

After 1974, Buick dropped the Stage 1 engine and the Gran Sport option.

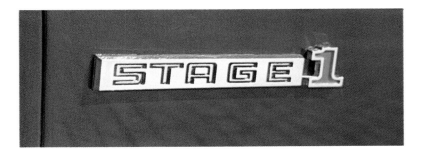

Century Gran Sport was little changed in '74, its second and final season (this page). This also marked the end of the 455-cid engine and the Stage I option. It went out fighting with 90-mph quarter-miles.

1973-74 Buick Gran Sport 455

Facts At a Glance

Engine type:	V-8/Buick	V-8/Buick
Displacement (cid):	455	455 (Stage 1)
Horsepower @ rpm:	225 @ 4000 (1973)	270 @ 4400 (1973)
	190 @ 3600 (1974)	255 @ 4400 (1974)
		230 @ 3800 (1974)
Torque (lbs/ft)	375 @ 2800 (1973)	390 @ 3000 (1973)
@ rpm:	370 @ 2000 (1974)	370 @ 2800 (1974)
		355 @ 2200 (1974)
Compression ratio:	8.5:1	8.5:1
Bore (in.):	4.31	4.31
Stroke (in.):	3.90	3.90
Valve lifters:	Hydraulic	Hydraulic
Availability:	1973-74	1973-74

Magazine:	**Motor Trend (July 1973)**
Times:	
0-60 mph (sec):	7.4
0-100 mph (sec):	N/A
¼-mile (sec):	15.3 @ 90 mph
Top speed:	115.97
Axle ratio:	3.42:1
Engine type:	455 Stage 1 (1973)

1961-65 CHEVROLET 409

The Beach Boys sang about it, competitors cried it about it, and Chevy fans loved their 409. The 360-bhp V-8's debut coincided with that of the Impala's Super Sport option package. When ordered together, as on the '62 pictured here, few cars on the road could match the big bowtie's combination of class and sass. Motor Trend ran one with a 4.56:1 gear to a 14.02-second ET at 98.12 mph.

I t was derived from a truck engine. It did not lend itself well to serious high-performance modifications. It hadn't been out a full model year before it was eclipsed in popularity by a smaller engine. Rival big-blocks ran roughshod over it on the glamorous NASCAR superspeedways. And at no time in its brief four-and-and-a-half-year life was it installed in more than one percent of the cars that could be ordered with it. Why then was Chevrolet's 409-cubic-inch V-8 of 1961-65 the most renowned engine of its era?

Probably because it was the first motor of the muscle age to have charisma. Sure, it wasn't a dazzling skunk-works wonder like Chrysler's original 426 Hemi. But the 409 was celebrated on the street precisely because it wasn't some unattainable high-tech contrivance. And granted, it wasn't a NASCAR champ. But muscle fanatics always were suspicious about stock-car-racing's relevance, anyway. No, when it came down to run-what-ya-brung at the drive-in or drag strip, a 409 was royalty. And when the Beach Boys eulogized it in the 1962 hit, "409"—one of the first car anthems of the '60s—it won something no other engine had. It got an identity.

Chevy introduced the 409 in mid-1961 after deciding it could no longer stand pat with its 348-cubic-inch V-8, even if it did make 350 horsepower with its available three two-barrel carburetors. The 348 had been developed in the late 1950s for double duty in cars and trucks. In concept, the 409 was supposed to be merely a bored-out 348, but it ended up with only a few parts that were interchangeable. Still, the two engines shared block, heads, and wedge-shaped combustion chambers. That was important because the wedge was formed not in the heads, but by cutting off the top of the block at a 74-degree angle from the plane of the cylinder walls. The design precluded high-compression heads and made it difficult to "hot rod" the 348 and 409, a trait largely responsible for the short life span of both engines.

Upgrading the 348 to the 409 also added such components

The serious street/strip crowd preferred their 409s in Bel Airs like the '62 models pictured on both pages. It was less expensive and 100 pounds lighter than the Impala and retained the sporty "slantback" roof. For '62, the 409 was rated at 380 bhp in single four-barrel guise (opposite, top left). The Bel Air Sport Coupe pictured above has the optional dual-quad version of the 409, which upped the ante to the magical one horsepower per cubic inch.

as forged-aluminum pistons, stronger valve springs, and thicker pushrods. Compression was bumped to 11.25:1 and a wilder camshaft specified. It used solid lifters, a big four-barrel Carter AFB carb on an aluminum manifold, and a dual-snorkel air cleaner. No multiple-carb setups were offered with the 409, which breathed well enough to be rated at 360 horsepower.

Helping raise the profile of the new 409 was the concurrent introduction of the Super Sport option, which was available on any Impala model. It cost $53.80 and included Super Sport exterior trim, power steering, power brakes with sintered Morraine metallic linings, and full wheel covers with tri-blade spinner. Inside was a Corvette-type grab bar in front of the passenger, more special trim, and a console for the floor shift. A column-mounted 7000-rpm tachometer was included, but Chevy put it behind the steering-wheel spoke, where it was hard to see unless the wheel was turned. Bucket seats were unavailable on the '61 SSs. Power for the SS was limited to the 348 or the 409. A four-speed manual transmission was mandatory with all but the least powerful SS engine, the 305-horsepower 348, which could be fitted with Powerglide. The 409 had to use the four-speed and was listed only with a 3.36:1 rear-axle ratio, though extra-cost 4.10:1 and 4.56:1 gears were popular over-the-counter replacements.

Chevy built 705,000 Impalas in '61, but just 453 had the SS package. Installation of the 409 was even rarer, with only 142 delivered. Most of these engines went for media testing, to favored drag racers, and to others who had pull with the factory. But the 409's reputation outdistanced its numbers from the very start.

1962

The 409 became more readily available in 1962, and 15,019 were ordered. The engine option added $428 to the cost of any full-size Chevy and, with revised cams and heads, was rated at 380 horsepower and 420 pounds/feet of torque. For another $60, dual Carter AFBs raised the ante to 409 horsepower at 6000 rpm. Manual transmission was again mandatory, but a three-speed was now also available.

Chevy also built a very limited run of late-'62 lightweight 409 specials with aluminum front end parts that shaved 130 pounds from the nose. It even sold aluminum replacement body panels over the counter. Also, about 57 cars were built in 1963 with the 409 stretched to 427 cubic inches. This also was the year that the newly enlarged 327-cubic-inch small-block bowed.

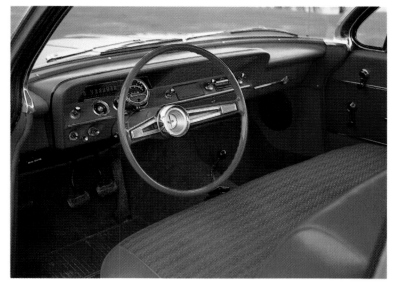

A replacement for the 348, it was available in 250- and 300-horsepower tune. More flexible than the 409 at low speed, the 327 also had tremendous mid-range poke, good off-the-line dig, more refined highway behavior, and better fuel economy. Not surprisingly, it handily outsold the 409.

1963

This would be the peak year for 409 production, with 16,902 ordered. Nonetheless, that was only one percent of the 1.4 million full-size Chevys built for '63. The upturn was fueled by the introduction of a more streetable, slightly detuned 409. It was rated at 340 horsepower and had hydraulic lifters, 10.0:1 compression, and a cast-iron induction manifold. It was the only 409 available with Powerglide. A step up the performance ladder brought 400 horsepower from another four-barrel 409, but with 11.0:1 compression and solid lifters. On the top rung stood the 425-horsepower dual-quad 409, also with solid lifters and 11.0:1 compression. For all-out drag duty, Chevy built the limited-production Z-11, a 427-cubic-inch version of the 409 rated at 430 horsepower and offered only to factory-approved buyers. It was usually teamed with the aluminum-front-end cars, which this year used aluminum bumpers to save a total of 180 pounds.

As for that "mild" 409, it was no milquetoast, not with 420 pounds/feet of torque at 3200. That was just shy of the 425 pounds/feet at 3600 churned out by its mechanical-lifter brothers. *Car Life* drove one to 60 mph in 6.6 seconds and saw 124 mph with Powerglide and the 3.36:1 rear axle. *Motor Trend* ran another automatic to a 15.9-second quarter at 88 mph. All 409 engines this year were garnished with brightwork, including chrome air cleaner, valve covers, automatic-choke tube, dipstick, oil-filler cap, fuel-filter top, and fuel line.

1964-65

Having targeted the youth market with their new mid-size Chevelle, stylists gave the regular Chevys a larger, more formal look for 1964. Impala's Super Sport was upgraded to a series that consisted of coupe and convertible.

The 409s were back in 340-, 400-, and 425-horsepower form, but the competition—principally Ford's 427 and MoPar's 426 wedge and Hemi—was tougher than ever. Chevy fought back with revised rear-axle ratios for the four-speeds. The M20 box got numerically lower ratios in gears one through three while the M21 close-ratio box qualified for a 4.11:1 or 4.56:1 with Positraction. The Z-11 did not return. Most of the 185,325 SS Impalas ordered for '64 were loaded with luxury equipment, and those fitted with air conditioning couldn't have the 400- or 425-horsepower 409. Moreover, the market as a whole was about to turn quickly away from thinking of big cars as performance cars, for 1964 saw the debut of the Ford Mustang and the Pontiac GTO. Production of the 409 dropped by 48 percent, to 8864 engines.

Chevy's full-size cars got a radical redesign for 1965, trading their squared-off shape for rounded contours and a graceful fastback roof. The 409 returned, but its days were numbered. The 340-horse version carried over unchanged, but the hottest setup for '65 was the 400-horsepower 409 with its aluminum intake manifold 11.:1 compression and solid lifters. It lasted only until mid-year, however, and died when Chevy introduced its glittering new big-block: the 396 Mark IV. Including the 2828 built for '65, Chevrolet equipped just 43,775 cars with the 409. That the engine's legend is far out of proportion to its production numbers speaks volumes about its impact on the early muscle years.

Chevy offered the 409 in any full-size model, but the rarest application may be this '63 four-door. The engine could be had in 340- and 400-bhp tune for '63, but this sedan has the all-out 425-bhp version with twin Carter AFB carbs. The engine added $376 to the $2768 base price. The four-speed gearbox was a madatory $236 option and with such extra-cost items as a 4.11:1 positraction axle and sintered metallic brakes, brought this car's total to $3225.

1961-65 Chevrolet 409

Facts At a Glance

Engine type:	V-8/W-series
Displacement (cid):	409
Horsepower @ rpm:	360 @ 5800 (1961)
	380 @ 5800 (1962)
	409 @ 6000 (1962)
	430 @ 6000 (1963)[1]
	340 @ 5000 (1963-65)[2]
	400 @ 5800 (1963-65)
	425 @ 6000 (1963-64)
Torque (lbs/ft) @ rpm:	409 @ 3600 (1961)
	420 @ 3200 (1962)
	420 @ 4000 (1962)
	425 @ 4200 (1963)[1]
	420 @ 3200 (1963-65)[2]
	425 @ 3600 (1963-65)
	425 @ 4200 (1963-64)
Compression ratio:	11.25:1 (1961)
	11.0:1 (1962-65)
	10.0:1 (1963-65)[2]
Bore (in.):	4.31
Stroke (in.):	3.50
Valve lifters:	Mechanical
Availability:	All 1961-65 full-size Chevrolets

[1]Z-11 option (427 cubic-inches).
[2]340-bhp engine had 10.0:1 compression and hydraulic lifters.

Magazine:	*Car Life* (Dec. 1964)	*Car and Driver* (March 1962)
Times:		
0-60 mph (sec):	8.0	7.3
0-100 mph (sec):	20.0	N/A
¼-mile (sec):	16.4 @ 91 mph	14.9 @ 94
Top speed (mph):	132	N/A
Axle ratio:	3.31:1	3.70:1
Engine type:	409/340	409/380
Model year:	1965	1962

1964-67
CHEVROLET
CHEVELLE SS

To those in the market for a sensible intermediate in 1964, Chevrolet's all-new Chevelle looked great. It was bigger than the compact Chevy II, but had nearly the interior room of the Impala without the big car's acres of sheetmetal. The whole range of two- and four-door body styles were available, as well as a cute two-door wagon and a cool open-bed El Camino. Six-cylinder and V-8 power was offered across the board. Of course, enthusiasts seldom take the purely "sensible" view, and they were quick to notice that the Chevelle's 115-inch wheelbase was the same as that of the 1955-57 Chevy.

The best expression of this revival came in a Chevelle equipped with the $162 Super Sport package. Available on the upscale Malibu two-door hardtop and convertible models, the option added special exterior brightwork with SS emblems and the 14-inch full-disc wheel covers from the Impala SS. Inside was a vinyl bucket-seat interior that featured a floor console for models equipped with the optional Muncie aluminum four-speed-manual or Powerglide two-speed automatic instead of the standard three-speed manual. Super Sport Malibu also got a four-gauge cluster in place of engine warning lights, and a dash-mounted tachometer was optional. Kinship to those Chevys of yore was sealed by the availability of a 283-cubic-inch four-barrel dual-exhaust V-8 engine rated at 220-horsepower, the exact same rating as the celebrated 1957 Power-Pak 283.

But while the 1964 Malibu SS may have recalled past glories, the future was available over at Pontiac. There, Chevelle's Tempest corporate cousin had been stuffed with a 389-cubic-inch V-8 to create the 325-horsepower GTO. Oldsmobile followed quickly with a 310-horse 330-cube 4-4-2. That was all it took for Chevy to break GM's 326-cubic-inch ceiling for intermediate-car engines. Starting in mid-1964, the Chevelle could be ordered with the division's fine 327-cubic-inch V-8, in either 250 or 300 horsepower. Both used a four-barrel carb

The '62 Chevelle SS (above) revived the power/size balance of the classic '55-57 Chevys. It bowed with an available 283-cid V-8, but a 300-bhp 327 quickly joined the options list. Chevy stylists effectively updated the '65 Chevelle (top). Very serious performance was now on tap with a 350-bhp 327 or, as this car has, the limited-edition Z-16, a 375-bhp 396.

and 10.5:1 compression, and could hold their own against 289 Fairlanes and 273 Barracudas. But muscle fans would demand more, and get it. Still, for those "sensible" buyers, the Chevelle was obviously appealing and Chevy built 294,160 this first year, including 76,860 SS models.

1965

Chevy honed Chevelle's appearance for 1965 with some carefully considered detail changes inside and out, but the car's character was unaltered. Distinguishing the Super Sports this year was a black-out grille treatment, but there was big news behind the grille, as well. For well-rounded street and strip performance, the 327 was an excellent choice, especially now that a 350-horse version had joined the 250- and 300-horsepower carryovers. Listed as the L79 engine and available at mid-year in regular and SS Malibus, the 350-horse 327 bulked up on some internals from the Corvette's 365-horse 327, though it used hydraulic lifters to the 'Vette's solid lifters. It wasn't available with Powerglide, but with a four-speed, Positraction, and the standard 3.31:1 rear axle, quarter-mile times in the high 14s were within easy reach. This was among the hottest street setups of '65, but both the GTO and the 4-4-2 had already upped the ante to 400 cubic inches.

Chevy counterpunched at mid-year with the Z-16, a 375-horsepower 396 cubic-inch V-8. This was a limited-edition offering installed in just 200 Malibu SS hardtops and one convertible for '65. Records are sketchy, but it appears the

majority of these Turbo-Jet 396s were essentially hydraulic-lifter versions of the 375-horse 396 available in the Corvette.

More than just an engine, however, the $1500 Z-16 package that created an SS 396 Chevelle also brought a fortified convertible-type frame, a strengthened front suspension, front and rear anti-roll bars, bigger brakes, and faster power-assisted steering. A Muncie four-speed manual was mandatory and came with a 3.31:1 gear, though ratios as high as 4.56:1 were available. Inside, the Z-16 group included a 160-mph speedometer, a tach redlined at 6000 rpm, and an AM-FM stereo radio. Nearly 58 percent of the SS 396 Chevelle's weight was on its front wheels, so even the beefed-up suspension couldn't do much to keep it from plowing through most changes of direction. But of course, its mission was to go straight real fast and mid-14-second quarters at around 100 mph were just a hint of what was to come.

Super Sport production peaked this year, accounting for 101,577 of the 326,977 Chevelles built.

1966

Chevelle shelved its boxy look in 1966 for a graceful new skin. Built again on the 115-inch wheelbase, the new Chevelle appeared larger than its predecessor, though its dimensions were virtually identical. Momentum had been building behind the Malibu Super Sport and Chevy rolled with it this year by making the 396 V-8 standard. This was the first SS based on an engine rather than simply being a trim option and no other Chevelle—save the El Camino Custom—could have a 396. In

The squared lines of the '65 Chevelle (opposite, top left) gave way to the rounded forms of '66 (other photos). All '66 SS Chevelles came with the 396-cid V-8. A 325-bhp version was standard; the 360-bhp L34 was the most common optional upgrade (opposite right).

base form, the 396 Turbo-Jet made 325 horsepower at 4800 rpm, using a mild camshaft with hydraulic lifters and Holley carburetion. This engine was big on torque, cranking out 410 pounds/feet at 3200 rpm. With a taller camshaft, a larger four-barrel and a stronger four-bolt main block, the optional L34 396 generated 360 horsepower at 5200 rpm, with an extra 10 pounds/feet of torque. Both had a 10.25:1 compression ratio. A three-speed manual was standard and a four-speed manual optional with both engines; an improved Powerglide with liquid cooling was now also available with either one.

There also was a third SS 396, the limited-production 375-horsepower L78. It was installed in only about 100 Malibu Super Sports for '66 and was essentially an updated Z-16. Closely related to the Corvette's mighty 425-horsepower 396, the L78 had a heavy-duty block with four-bolt mains, 11.0:1 compression, solid lifters, and an 800cfm Holly four-barrel on an aluminum intake manifold.

The 3375-pound Malibu SS hardtop listed for $2776 and the 3470-pound convertible cost $2984. The gap between SS and lesser Malibus had widened for '66, and it was clear most of the extra cost was for the engine and associated heavy-duty hardware. Bucket seats and full wheel covers, for instance, were now SS options. Still, a base SS 396 with its red-line 7.75×14 nylon tires, body-colored steel wheels, and tiny hub cabs had a pleasing, no-nonsense air about it.

Because the 396 turned the '66 Chevelle SS into such a smashing success, a word on its origins is in order. It roots were in NASCAR competition as a pure-race 427. That engine, about which Chevrolet was quite secretive, used a canted-valve design that produced a prickly pattern of rocker arm studs, a pattern that gave it its "porcupine-head" nickname. The design was carried over to the production 396 and allowed for better airflow through large, round ports.

Though this engine was exclusive to the Super Sport in the Chevelle line for '66, Chevy small-block loyalists could order the L79 350-horse 327 in a Malibu, which may have hurt some SS sales. Sure enough, Malibu SS production slipped to 72,300 out of 380,100 Chevelles for '66.

1967

Chevelle was mildly facelifted for 1967 and the SS received a new grille and taillamps, and got bright metal wheelhouse moldings. The non-functional hood blisters that appeared in '66 returned and the cabin got only minor trim and upholstery changes.

Mechanical changes also were minimal. The 325-horsepower 396 was again standard, but the L34 option lost 10 horsepower and now was rated at 350. The 375-horse L78 396 was no longer listed, though a handful are likely to have made it into a select group of SS Malibus. Chevy's three-speed Turbo Hydra-Matic joined the two-speed Powerglide as an optional automatic transmission choice.

At $2825 for the coupe and $3033 for the ragtop, the Super Sports cost about $285 more than comparable Malibu models.

1964-67 Chevrolet Chevelle SS

Facts At a Glance

Engine type:	V-8/small block	V-8/small block
Displacement (cid):	283	327
Horsepower @ rpm:	195 @ 4800	250 @ 4400
	220 @ 4800[1]	300 @ 5000
		350 @ 5800 (1965)
Torque (lbs/ft)		
@ rpm:	285 @ 2400	350 @ 2800
	295 @ 3200[1]	360 @ 3200
		360 @ 3600 (1965)
Compression ratio:	9.25:1	10.5:1/11.0:1[2]
Bore (in.):	3.87	4.00
Stroke (in.):	3.00	3.25
Valve lifters:	Hydraulic	Hydraulic
Availability:	1964-65	1964-65

[1]Four-barrel
[2]350-bhp engine

Engine type:	V-8/big block/Mark IV
Displacement (cid):	396
Horsepower @ rpm:	325 @ 4800 (1966-67)
	360 @ 5200 (1966)
	350 @ 5200 (1967)
	375 @ 5600[1]
Torque (lbs/ft)	
@ rpm:	410 @ 3200 (1966-67)
	420 @ 3600 (1966)
	415 @ 3200 (1967)
	420 @ 3600 (1965)[1]
	415 @ 3600 (1966-67)[1]
Compression ratio:	10.25:1/11.0:1[1]
Bore (in.):	4.09
Stroke (in.):	3.76
Valve lifters:	Hydraulic/Mechanical[1]
Availability:	1965-67

[1]Z-16 (1965); L78 (1966-67).

Magazine:	Car and Driver (Nov. 1963)	Car and Driver (March 1966)
Times:		
0-60 mph (sec):	8.5	6.0 (est)
0-100 mph (sec):	27.8	15.0 (est)
¼-mile (sec):	16.6[1]	14.66 @ 99.88
Top speed (mph):	N/A	115 (est)
Axle ratio:	3.08:1	3.65:1
Engine (cid/bhp):	283/220	396/360
Model year:	1964 SS	1966 SS 396

[1]Trap speed not indicated.

Chevelle SS 396 was little changed for '67, though the L34 option (above right) was rated at 350 bhp, a loss of 10 bhp from '66. Power front disc brakes were a new option. Ordering them brought Rally-style 14-inch slotted wheels with bright trim rings (top). Red strip tires were standard. Strato bucket seats and center console with tachometer were boss options (above left).

1965-69 CHEVROLET 396/427

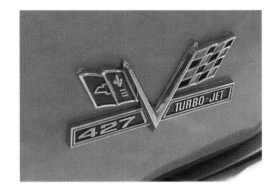

High-performance headlines moved quickly from full-size cars to intermediates in 1964 with the blockbuster debut of the Pontiac Tempest GTO. But even as the automakers scrambled to create mid-size factory hot rods, they couldn't ignore the market for big muscle.

At Chevrolet, the 1965 Impala, Bel Air, and Biscayne had shed their crate-like lines for curvy new bodywork. Though the previous 119-inch wheelbase was retained, these new full-size Chevys were three-inches longer and 2.6-inches wider than the '64s.

As the '65 model year opened, those serious about muscle in any of the big Chevys sought out the warhorse 409 and its 400 horsepower. But rumors were growing that the bowtie brigade would replace this engine with a version of the 427-cubic-inch Mark II 1963 "mystery motor"—the mill that had blown the doors off Ford and Chrysler in NASCAR, then vanished as Chevy withdrew from racing. Its most sensational feature was its "porcupine heads," so named for the bristly arrangement of the rocker studs. By February 1965, the motor was a mystery no more.

The Mark IV big-block appeared mid-year as the Turbo-Jet 396 and sure enough, there was the porcupine head design. Its arrival sent the 409 to its grave and finally gave Chevy a big engine that could be readily bored and stroked—all the way to 500 cubic inches if need be. Its original 396-cubic-inch displacement apparently reflected Chevy's desire to meet NASCAR's anticipated ban on engines over 400 cubic inches, and, since the mill also was destined for the Chevelle, to stay within GM's 400-cube ceiling on intermediate-car powerplants.

Two versions of the 396 were released. In base form it made 325 horsepower with hydraulic lifters and a 10.25:1 compression. This variant was the recipient of Rochester's new Quadri-Jet

Holding fast against mid-size muscle in the mid-'60s were full-size big-block stormers like this '66 Chevy Biscayne with the optional 427-cid V-8. This sedate-looking sedan conceals the "special performance" solid-lifter 425-bhp 427. Styling was littled altered from the '65 models, which had been revamped inside and out.

four-barrel with huge, venturiless secondaries. A second 396 used solid lifters, a wilder cam, and an 11.0:1 compression to produce an astonishing 425 horsepower—1.073 horsepower per cubic inch. Both had remarkably good breathing, high reliability, and lots of torque. The 325-horsepower 396 could be ordered only in the Impala, Impala SS, and Caprice. The 425-horsepower version could be ordered in the Corvette, as well as in any full-size model, making for some very potent two-door Biscayne sleepers. Behind the 396, a buyer could have a three- or four-speed manual or GM's new Turbo Hydra-Matic. A 12-bolt Positraction differential was optional.

Chevy built a record 2.6 million cars in 1965, with much of the demand fueled by the new full-size models, of which 1.6 million were produced. Even though it was a mid-year offering, almost 60,000 396 Mark IVs were ordered—a number not even imagined with the 409.

1966

Chevy retrenched this year, improving the Impala frame, hyping the Caprice, but altering the appearance of its big cars only with a new grille and by the substitution of horizontal taillamps for the previous round ones. The 396 returned unchanged in 325-horsepower guise only for the big cars, but in mid-year, Chevy bored and stroked the 396 to unleash the 427-cubic-inch version of the Mark IV block. For street use there was a 427 with 390 horsepower. A "special performance" version had solid lifters, special performance camshaft, a four-bolt main block, and 425 horsepower. This replaced the 425-horsepower 396 screamer as the top big block. The 427's 425 horsepower peaked 800 rpm sooner than that 396's, and its added displacement brought more torque at lower revs.

Standard with the 396 and 427 was a three-speed heavy-duty manual gearbox. A four-speed was optional with either, though the 427 got exclusive rights to the M21 close-ratio box and to the new M22 "rock crusher" four speed, so named for

its super-tough but noisy gears. The 396 could be ordered with either the Powerglide two-speed automatic or Turbo-Hydra-matic three-speed. The 425-horsepower 427 wasn't available with automatic, though the 390-horsepower version could be ordered with Turbo-Hydra-matic. Despite impressive credentials, the big-block full-size Chevys had only sporadic racing success. One notable exception was the 427 drag-racing Biscayne that won Junior Stock Eliminator at the '66 NHRA Winternationals. Impala SS sales fell by more than half as luxury buyers went for the Caprice and sporty types for the Chevelle SS 396.

1967

Chevy's big cars got a minor restyle for 1967. The hood now dipped over the grille in a handsome brow, the coupe's roof mated with the rear deck in a graceful semi-fastback line, and the taillamps were inset in a cleaner-looking tail. Any big Chevy could still be ordered with the 396, back again at 325 horsepower, or with the 427, this year offered only in a 385-horsepower version. Once again, either big block could be ordered with a three- or four-speed manual, while the 396 could use Powerglide or Turbo-Hydra-matic and the 427 could use only the Turbo-Hydra-matic.

The Impala in SS guise was de-emphasized for '67. Its exterior trim was brought closer to that of the regular Impala, and bucket seats, console, and full instrumentation relegated to the options list. SS Impalas could be ordered with six-cylinder or V-8 power, but Chevy this year took a page from the Chevelle SS 396 book—in which a model was created around an engine—to create the SS 427 Impala.

"For the man who'd buy a sports car if it had this much room," was how Chevy advertised the SS 427, and indeed, it was about as sporty as a 212-inch-long coupe or convertible on a 119-inch wheelbase could be. The 385-horsepower 427 Mark IV was standard; the usual 427 transmission choices were offered, with the four-speed's 3.73:1 rear-axle ratio the most aggressive

Chevy created the SS 427 Impala in '67, but the 385-bhp big block could still be ordered in plainer Impalas like the clean base hardtop (left). In '68, the SS 427 (above) was demoted to an Impala subseries. It also traded the previous year's domed hood with its brushed aluminum ducts for a trio of simulated bodyside vents.

1965-69 Chevrolet 396/427

Facts At a Glance

Engine type:	V-8/Big block/Mark IV	V-8/Big block/Mark IV
Displacement (cid):	396	427
Horsepower @ rpm:	325 @ 4800 (1965-68)	390 @ 5200 (1966)
	425 @ 6400 (1965)	425 @ 5600 (1966)
		385 @ 5200 (1967-68)
		390 @ 5400 (1969)
Torque (lbs/ft) @ rpm:	410 @ 3200 (1965-68)	460 @ 3600 (1966)
	415 @ 4000 (1965)	460 @ 4000 (1966)
		460 @ 3400 (1967-68)
		460 @ 3600 (1969)
Compression ratio:	10.25:1/11.0:1[1]	10.25:1/11.0:1[2]
Bore (in.):	4.09	4.25
Stroke (in.):	3.76	3.76
Valve lifters:	Hydraulic/Mechanical[1]	Hydraulic/Mechanical[2]
Availability:	All full-size models	All full-size models

[1]396/425-bhp.
[2]427/425-bhp.

Magazine:	*Car Life* (May 1967)
Times:	
0-60 mph (sec):	8.4
0-100 mph (sec):	N/A
¼-mile (sec):	15.75 @ 86.5 mph
Top speed (mph):	125
Axle ratio:	N/A
Engine type:	427/385
Model year:	1967

gear. Stiffer springs, shocks, and front stabilizer bar were fitted and 8.24×14 red-stripe tires were mounted on six-inch rims.

1968

Aside from changes in the grille and taillamps and a turn to hidden windshield wipers, the 1968 Chevrolet was pretty much a carryover. The focus was on safety, with front shoulder belts, revised door handles, and ignition-key reminder buzzer, among other new features. On the performance front, the 396 and 427 returned unchanged and still available in any full-size Chevy.

But Biscaynes, Bel Airs, and Impalas with 427 power were increasingly scarce; it didn't help that air conditioning wasn't offered with this engine. A sure sign of the move away from sporty big cars was the demotion of the Impala SS to a subseries of the Impala line for the first time since 1963. The $179.05 SS option package was available on three '68 Impalas: the semi-fastback hardtop, the convertible, and the new formal-roof Custom hardtop coupe. An investment of $358.10 bought the SS 427 package, which added to the base SS a domed hood with four vents near the windshield, three tall vertical louvers behind the front wheels, and of course, the 385-horsepower 427.

1969

The 1969 Chevy was reskinned in a more formal mode with puffed-out lines designed to make its body's stretch to 216 inches look even longer. Gone was the sporty semi-fastback roofline, replaced by the notchback Sport Coupe. The 396 and 427 were back in any full-size model, and revised pistons and cylinder heads upped the 427's horsepower by five, to 390 at 5400 rpm.

This was the last year for the Impala SS, and Chevrolet sent it out in style, making the 427 standard. The SS 427 was available in coupe or convertible for a $422.35 premium. It was identified by its black-accented grille and SS badges. A buyer could choose among a three-speed and two four-speed manuals, or Turbo Hydra-Matic, along with the extra-cost Positraction differential. Also listed were an upgraded suspension and red-line tires as in '68. This closed the curtain on full-size Chevy muscle. Neither the 396 nor the 427 would return and while the '70 models could be equipped with a 390-horsepower 454-cubic-inch V-8, they had abandoned any high-performance pretense.

Chevy sent the SS Impala out in style for '69 by making the 427-cid V-8 standard. The Mark IV big block gained 5 bhp, to 390, and was available in the notch-back Sport Coupe or the convertible (above). An upgraded suspension and red-line tires were options. The '69 SS Impala closed the curtain on an era of full-size Chevy muscle.

1965-72 CHEVROLET NOVA SS

Perhaps the toughest little overachiever ever to harass the traditional muscle intermediates was Chevy's Nova Super Sport. Never a style leader, this was the compact for the serious enthusiast, the individualist whose goal was not to wow the easily impressed, but to go fast on guile and light weight.

Nova originally was the name of the top-of-the-line Chevy II, a compact that debuted in 1962 as GM's answer to the Ford Falcon. A boxy design on a 110-inch wheelbase, it was available with four- and six-cylinder engines.

The Chevy II had been designed from the outset for a V-8 and indeed, some hot rodders had delighted in dropping in a hot 327 Corvette engine. But not until the '64 model year was a V-8 officially offered as a Chevy II option, and then it was the 195-horsepower, two-barrel 283. The good news was that the Chevy II's 283 could be teamed with the M20 four-speed manual gearbox. The bad news for '64 was that Chevy had dropped the spry Chevy II convertible and the Nova SS. The ragtop never would return, but the SS was back by mid-year, and it was about come into its own as something more than a tame little sporty compact.

In 1965, Chevrolet made the Chevy II available with its

tough 327-cubic-inch V-8 and things really began to heat up. In L74 guise, the 327 four-barrel cranked out 300 horsepower. Though the SS model was its most logical home, the L74 made for a very effective Q-Ship when ordered in a dressed-down Chevy II two-door sedan. A 250-horsepower version of the 327 also was offered, as was a four-barrel, dual exhaust 220-horsepower 283. Three-speed manuals were standard with these V-8s and Powerglide was optional. But the most fun was the Muncie four-speed gearbox and Positraction differential. Worthwhile options included upgraded suspension components, sintered metallic brake linings, and a tachometer.

Available only in hardtop form, the 1964-65 Nova SS was dashing enough, but it was upstaged by the Chevelle Malibu SS 396, a bigger car that cost only about $100 more.

1966

Chevy II got its first reskin in 1966 and the look was more masculine than the decidedly unthreatening original. The SS package was a $159 option and included Strato-bucket front seats with a console when the optional four-speed manual or

Nova had been part of the Chevy II lineup since '62, but not until '65, when it became available with the 327-cid V-8, did it grow real fangs. The '65 Nova Super Sport (above) was available only as a hardtop. Its top engine was the 300-bhp 327 four-barrel.

Powerglide was ordered.

SS models could be had with six-cylinder engines of 120- or 140-horsepower, though the 220-horsepower four-barrel 283 was more in keeping with the car's character. A new 275-horsepower version of the 327 with a new four-barrel carb and a revised spark advance curve replaced the previous 250- and 300-horse variants. It was capable of ETs in the low-16s. To hard-core muscle fans, however, the real news was Chevy's decision to offer the Chevy II with the 350-horsepower 327. This was the 11.0:1-compression L79 engine, first found in '65 Chevelles. It would shoot the 3000-pound Chevy II through the quarter in the high 14s.

"The 350-hp 327 in approximately Corvette tune, dropped into a Chevy II, didn't have the juke-box magic of a 409 or a 427. Still, that combination made for one of the sneakiest muscle cars ever built," remembers Patrick Bedard, writing of his top-10 all-time muscle cars in the January 1990 issue of *Car and Driver*.

1967-68

The handsome '67 Nova SS sported some exterior trim changes and '65 Impala SS hubcaps, but otherwise returned pretty much unchanged with its bucket seats and sporty appointments.

Enthusiasts were crestfallen at the passing of the L79 350-horsepower 327 from the regular options list, though apparently a handful were installed in Chevy IIs through special orders. That left the 275-horsepower 327 as the top power option. Transmission choices were 1966 carryovers, although the axle ratio options were shuffled a bit.

Chevy II sales fell considerably for 1967, perhaps partly as a result of the Camaro's introduction that year. Just 106,000 Chevy IIs were built and only 10,100 were Nova SS models, both six and V-8.

The Chevy II car line underwent its most extensive styling change for 1968. At the same time, the Chevy II Nova SS was granted a new high-performance personality. A 350-cubic-inch four barrel was made the base engine for the '68 Nova SS. Proven in the '67 Camaro RS/SS, it cranked out 295 horsepower. Late in the model run Chevrolet added to the SS options list two 396s, the 350-horsepower L34 and the 375-horsepower L78. With the $500.30 solid-lifter L78 option, the giant-killer Nova SS 396 could hit 100 mph in 14 seconds.

As a reasonably priced $211 option package, the basic '68 Nova SS offered go for the dough, but without many frills. There was no hardtop, for example, just a frumpy two-door pillared sedan with a low-key SS appearance group and fake hood air intakes. Even the E70×14 Tiger Paw tires surrounded humdrum Chevy II hubcaps. Bucket seats, console, and full instrumentation were options.

Sales went soft that year, with just 5571 Nova SS models built, including 234 L34s and 667 L78s.

1969-72

The Chevy II designation was phased out after 1968, but few changes were made to the one-year-old Nova design. Powertrains remained the same, though the 350-cube V-8 boasted a strengthened block and a five-horsepower-boost to an even 300. Power front disc brakes were SS standards, as were a heavy-duty suspension and three-speed manual. Turbo Hydra-Matic also joined the options list this year. The SS 350 came at a $280 premium over the regular Nova for '69, while the SS 396s were a bit more costly: $464 and $596 over the base coupe. This was the first full year for Nova SS 396 production and Chevy built 1947 of the 350-horsepower units and 5262 375-horsepower cars. Nova SS output totaled 17,654.

The Nova SS sailed into the '70s with a revised grille and taillights and three hash marks on the front fenders. Engine offerings went unchanged, but variable-ratio power steering became available. SS output hit 19,558 units for 1970, but how many were 396s isn't known. Worth noting is that this year's Turbo-Jet 396 wasn't a 396 at all, but displaced 402 cubic inches.

With the muscle era on the wane, Chevy dropped the 396 from the Nova in '71. The surviving 350 two-barrel had 245 horses while the four-barrel offered 270. An 8.5:1 compression ratio allowed these engines to burn regular gas. Gone along with the front-fender hash marks were many of the SS's mechanical and chassis upgrade options. Nova SS output skidded to 7015 units. Late in the '71 model year, Chevy brought out the Rally Nova, essentially a tarted-up SS.

Nova's final performance season was 1972. This was the year Detroit turned to net horsepower ratings, that is, engine power with all the accessories attached and running. Thus, the Nova SS with the 350 four-barrel had 200 *net* horsepower. That translated to 260 *gross* horsepower on the dynamometer. The SS was again little changed, although the three-speed manual shift was dropped, forcing the buyer to pay extra for a four-speed manual or Turbo Hydra-Matic. The '72 Nova SS was still a good performer for its day. *Hot Rod* clocked a four-barrel 350 at 15.42 at 88.40 mph in the quarter. Nova SS production spiked to 12,309 for 1972, as the death of muscle cars from other makers sent enthusiasts to Chevy showrooms.

The Nova SS returned for 1973 with new sheet metal, a hatchback option, and two available 350 V-8s, but the thrill was gone. The SS could be found clear through 1976, though performance options were rare. No, it was the frisky, tough, no-nonsense '65-72 Chevy IIs and Nova SSs with their all-star power-to-weight ratios that earned this compact its place in the Chevy muscle hall of fame.

1965-72 Chevrolet Nova SS V-8

Facts At a Glance

Engine type:	V-8/Small block	V-8/Small block
Displacement (cid):	283	327
Horsepower @ rpm:	195 @ 4800	250 @ 4400 (1965)
	220 @ 4800	300 @ 5000 (1965)
	275 @ 4800 (66-67)	350 @ 5800 (1966)[1]
Torque (lbs/ft) @ rpm:	285 @ 2400	350 @ 2800 (1965)
	295 @ 3200	360 @ 3200 (1965)
	355 @ 3200 (66-67)	360 @ 3600 (1966)[1]
Compression ratio:	9.25:1	10.0:1/10.25:1
Bore (in.):	3.87	4.00
Stroke (in.):	3.00	3.25
Valve lifters:	Hydraulic	Hydraulic
Availability:	1965-67	1965-67

[1]L79 option with 11.0:1 compression.

Engine type:	V-8/Small block	V-8/Big block/ Mark IV
Displacement (cid):	350	396[1]
Horsepower @ rpm:	295 @ 4800	350 @ 5200
		375 @ 5600[2]
Torque (lbs/ft) @ rpm:	380 @ 3200	415 @ 3400
		415 @ 3600[2]
Compression ratio:	10.25:1	10.25:1/11.0:1[2]
Bore (in.):	4.00	4.09
Stroke (in.):	3.48	3.76
Valve lifters:	Hydraulic	Hydraulic/ Mechanical
Availability:	1968	1968-70

[1]1970 Turbo-Jet 396 actually displaced 402 cubic inches.
[2]375-hp version had 11.0:1 compression.

Engine type:	V-8/Small block
Displacement (cid):	350

Horsepower @ rpm:	255 @ 4800 (1969)
	250 @ 4800 (1970)
	300 @ 4800 (1969-70)
	245 @ 4800 (1971)
	270 @ 4800 (1971)
	200 @ 4400 (1972)
Torque (lbs/ft) @ rpm:	
	365 @ 3200 (1969)
	345 @ 2800 (1970)
	380 @ 3200 (1969-70)
	350 @ 2800 (1971)
	360 @ 3200 (1971)
	300 @ 2800 (1972)
Compression ratio:	10.25:1/9.0:1[1]/8.5:1[2]
Bore (in.):	4.00
Stroke (in.):	3.48
Valve lifters:	Hydraulic
Availability:	1969-72

[1]All 1969-70 with two-barrel carburetor.
[2]All 1971-72.

Magazine:	*Car Life* (1966)	*Car and Driver* (August 1968)
Times:		
0-60 mph (sec):	7.2	5.9
0-100 mph (sec):	18.2	14.3
¼-mile (sec):	15.1 @ 93 mph	14.5 @ 101.1 mph
Top speed (mph):	N/A	121 (est)
Axle ratio:	3.31:1	3.55:1
Engine (cid/bhp):	327/350	396/375
Model year:	1966	1968

Magazine:	*Hot Rod* (July 1969)	*Car and Driver* (August 1968)
Times:		
0-60 mph (sec):	5.8 (est)	5.9
0-100 mph (sec):	12.8 (est)	14.3
¼-mile (sec):	13.87 @ 105.14 mph	14.5 @ 101.1 mph
Top speed (mph):	115 (est)	121 (est)
Axle ratio:	3.55:1	3.55:1
Engine type:	396/375	396/375
Model year:	1969	1968

1967-70 CHEVROLET CAMARO SS

Chevrolet's Corvair may have been a more sophisticated car than Ford's Mustang, but its rear-mounted air-cooled engine was too unorthodox a design to score with the masses. General Motors had to fight back with a genuine pony car, so in August 1964, it started a crash program to create a Mustang fighter. On September 29, 1966—more than two years and 1.3-million Mustangs later—the Chevrolet Camaro was unveiled.

Camaro bowed as a '67 coupe and convertible on a 108-inch wheelbase. It had pony-car proportions, an array of engine choices, bucket seats, and a long options list, but it wasn't quite a Mustang copycat. Its styling was curvier, even cleaner. And while the Camaro could be outfitted as a $2500 six-cylinder sporty pretender, it also could be optioned into a genuine high-performance threat.

Right from the start Camaro featured a Super Sport edition that was an authoritative counterpunch to both the Mustang GT and Plymouth Barracuda Formula S. It added $210 to the $2572 Sport Coupe or $2809 convertible and featured the new 295-horsepower 350-cubic-inch dual-exhaust V-8. Then, just a few months into the model year, Chevy really took the gloves off and introduced the big-block 396 V-8. It was available only with the SS package and came in two levels of tune, a 325-horsepower version that tacked on $263 to the SS group, and a 375-horse variant that added $500.

A three-speed, fully-synchronized manual gearbox was standard; the Muncie four-speed manual, available in close- and wide-ratio gearing, was a popular $184.35 extra on SS models, as was the $194.35 two-speed Powerglide automatic. SS 396s came only with the four-speed or the $226.45 three-speed Turbo Hydra-Matic. A Positraction limited-slip differential ($42.15) was available in a wide variety of axle ratios.

Camaro SS models were distinguished by a domed hood with dual simulated vents and SS emblems. An accent stripe banded its nose (the stripe would become optional on any Camaro later in the year). SS models had a stouter suspension with high-rate springs and stiffer shocks and Wide Oval red-stripe D70×14 bias-belted tires on six-inch Rally wheels.

A companion option package was the $105 Rally Sport group, which included a blacked-out grille and concealed headlamps. It could be combined with the SS package.

These first Camaros suffered severe rear-wheel hop under hard braking or all-out acceleration. Blame went to the inadequate single-leaf rear springs and a near-vertical mounting of the rear shock absorbers. A last-minute change to larger tires ate up suspension travel, so the '67s also tended to bottom out too easily. Overall though, the market accepted Camaro as a solid response to Mustang. Moreover, it was instantly a better high-performance car than the Ford. Camaro's eager 396s decimated the 320-horsepower 390 Mustang while its new 350 was more than a match for Mustang's 271-horsepower 289. *Car Life* ran a 325-horsepower 396 to a 15.1-second quarter-mile at 91.8 mph. Camaro sales in this first year trailed Mustang by a wide margin, though production was a very respectable 220,906, including 25,141 convertibles. More than 34,000 had the SS package, nearly 65,000 the RS group.

1968

Refinement was the byword for 1968. Camaro got side marker lights and its vent wing windows disappeared in favor of the new Astro-Ventilation system that circulated fresh air through the interior. SS models with Turbo Hydra-Matic got a stirrup-shaped shifter and Chevy combined the optional

Camaro came in Super Sport form right from its debut as a '67 model (opposite). V-8s of 350- and 396-cid were offered. The '68 SS 396 (below) was available in 325-, 350-, and 375-bhp form and got a unique hood with dual banks of non-functional ports (bottom).

tachometer and clock into one gauge, which it dubbed the Tick-Tock Tach.

The SS again started with a standard 295-horse 350, but a 350-horsepower version of the 396 joined the 325- and 375-horse carryovers. About 270 396s received special-order aluminum cylinder heads, though these parts didn't change the 375-horsepower rating. The SS 396, meanwhile, got its own hood, which featured dual banks of four non-functional ports. The axle tromp was diminished with the addition of staggered rear shocks to all Camaros, plus SS models got five-leaf rear springs. This was also the first full year for the Z-28 model, which is covered elsewhere in this book. Of the 235,147 Camaros built for '68, 27,844 had the SS package.

1969

All new sheetmetal made for a strikingly different Camaro in 1969. The new models retained the previous wheelbase and running gear, but were more angular for a look unlike any Camaro before or since. With the standard 210-horsepower 327, the base Sport Coupe V-8 cost $2727, while the base V-8 convertible was $2940. The Rally Sport again had hidden headlamps and could be combined with the $295.95 SS option. A rear lip spoiler was a new option. Inside, square instrument binnacles replaced round ones.

SS engine choices were unchanged and included the 375-horse 396, a $316 option, and for $711, the 396 with aluminum heads. SS Camaros were identified by their dual-bulge hood, all of which got the simulated port design previously used only by the SS 396. Wide Oval white-letter bias-belted F70×14 tires, Rally wheels, heavy-duty suspension, power front disc brakes, close-ratio three-speed transmission, and chromed engine appointments were SS standards. The optional Muncie four-speed got Hurst linkage for '69 in place of the bulky-shifting Chevy unit. Powerglide was the automatic option, though Turbo Hydra-Matic was available with the 396. Optional on SS and Z-28 models was the Super Scoop, a force-air induction hood that drew on the high-pressure area at the base of the windshield.

The most desirable limited-edition '67-69 Camaros were the hyper-performance 427s. These were of two principal varieties and were usually referred to as COPO (Corporate Office Production Order) cars. The first batch was a run of 69 1969 aluminum-block 430-horsepower 427s bearing the factory ZL-1 code. These were $7300-drag-racing specials sold through selected Chevy dealers. The second category was the Yenko Camaro, named for Don Yenko, a performance-oriented Chevrolet dealer in Cannonsburg, Pennsylvania. Yenko had been adding 427s to SS 396 Camaros and badging them all with his own graphics and SYC insignia. For '69, Yenko got Chevrolet

to factory-equip special-order Camaros with the iron-block L72 427. Chevy rated these cars at 425 horsepower, though Yenko listed them at 450. Some 201 of these SYC Camaros were produced, all with Z-28 suspension, close-ratio Muncie four-speed gearbox, and a 140-mph speedometer. Other dealers were able to place similar orders, but how many 427 factory-built Camaros were produced is uncertain.

A labor strike against GM extended the 1969 model year by about five months, so the 243,085 '69 Camaros sold—a record that stood until 1978—comes with an asterisk. It should also be noted that in September 1969, Chevy's 396 actually grew to displace 402 cubic inches, a change that was phased into '69 Camaro production.

1970

The redesigned 1970 Camaro was an undisputed classic. So right were its lines that the car stayed in production with very few changes until 1982. Curvaceous and sexy, it had European-exotic looks at American-pony-car prices. Dynamically, there was no better-handling mainstream American car. Its redesigned suspension had a lower roll rate, its steering was revised, and it could be fitted with state-of-the art 60-series Wide Oval tires.

Labor troubles and engineering and tooling problems had delayed introduction of this second-generation Camaro until February 1970. Designed jointly by Chevy and Pontiac, which would get a Firerbird version, the new car retained the 108-inch wheelbase, but was longer, lower, and wider than its predecessor, yet was smaller on the inside. It was available only as a coupe.

Under the hood, Chevy carried on with its 1969 engine lineup. The SS package added $289 to the $2839 base price of the V-8 Sport Coupe and included the 300-horse 350-cubic-inch four-barrel. Optional was the 350- or 375-horsepower 396, the latter not available with air conditioning. All SS models got the Muncie four-speed as standard and, except for the 375-horsepower 396, could be ordered with the optional Turbo Hydra-Matic. Positraction, at $44.25, was recommended. The F41 special-performance suspension—an option on all Camaros— was standard on the SS 396. Except for their badging, the SS models had no special trim. Rally Sport Camaros, however, eschewed the full-width front bumper and steel nose for two bumperettes, a urethane cap on the snout, and turn-signal lamps inboard of the headlights. Inside, all Camaros had front bucket seats; a bench wasn't offered.

Chevrolet would go on to build nearly two million of these second-generation pony cars over the next 12 years, but the best high-performance offerings of the lot arguably were the 1970 SS and Z-28.

1967-70 Chevrolet Camaro SS

Facts At a Glance

Engine type:	V-8/Small block	V-8/Big block/ Mark IV
Displacement (cid):	350	396[1]
Horsepower @ rpm:	295 @ 4800 (1967-68) 300 @ 4800 (1969-70)	325 @ 4800 (67-69) 350 @ 5200 (68-70) 375 @ 5600
Torque (lbs/ft) @ rpm:	380 @ 3200 (1967-68) 380 @ 3200 (1969-70)	415 @ 3200 (67-69) 415 @ 3400 (68-70) 415 @ 3600
Compression ratio:	10.25:1	10.25:1/11.0:1[2]
Bore (in.):	4.00	4.09
Stroke (in.):	3.48	3.76
Valve lifters:	Hydraulic	Hydraulic/ Mechanical[2]
Availability:	1967-70	1967-70

[1]402-cid in 1970.
[2]375-bhp version.

Engine type:	V-8/Big block/Mark IV (aluminum)
Displacement:	427 (COPO ZL-1)
Horsepower @ rpm:	425 @ 5600 (3x2v)
Torque (lbs/ft) @ rpm:	460 @ 4400
Compression ratio:	11.0:1
Bore (in.):	4.25
Stroke (in.):	3.76
Valve lifters:	Mechanical
Availability:	1969 (Corporate Office Production Order)

Camaro paced the Indy 500 in '67 and '69. Only in '69 did Chevy offer a pace-car replica to the public. Of the 3675 built, most had the 350-cid V-8, but about 100 had the 396. All were painted white with "hugger" orange racing stripes and black/orange seat inserts, as is this SS 396 coupe (opposite). SS 396 ragtop (top) was quick and cool in '69. Above: SS Camaro's 300-bhp 350 was a small-block star.

Magazine:	Muscle Car Review (1987)	Car and Driver (November 1966)
Times:		
0-60 mph (sec):	5.2 (est)	7.8
0-100 mph (sec):	10.5 (est)	23.0
¼-mile (sec):	12.76 @ 107 mph	16.1 @ 86.5 mph
Top speed:	N/A	N/A
Axle ratio:	N/A	3.31:1
Engine:	427/425 ZL-1	350/295
Model year:	1969	1967

1968-72 CHEVROLET CHEVELLE SS

The 1968-70 Chevelle SS was as close to an Everymans' muscle car as Detroit would ever get. With standard 396-cubic-inch power, these shapely Super Sports bestowed upon big-block intermediates the Chevrolet hallo of reliability and respectability. They sold in larger numbers than any other true high-performance car of their time and included among their numbers one of the most potent automobiles ever unleashed on the streets.

General Motors' mid-size cars got fresh sheet metal and a redesigned chassis for '68. Chevelle hardtops got graceful fastback lines and, along with the convertibles, were sized right on a 112-inch wheelbase—down three inches from '67. Their stance was more bossy and broad-shouldered, too, thanks to a one-inch wider track, a rounded new beltline, and standard F70×14 Firestone Wide Oval tires.

In '68 Super Sport Chevelle coupes and convertibles were redesignated as a distinct series called the SS 396. The 325-horsepower 396-cubic-inch Turbo-Jet V-8 was standard. Two versions of the 396 were optional. The L-34 was rated at 350 horsepower and was the most common upgrade. Then came the mighty solid-lifter L-78 396 with its 375 horsepower, 11.0:1 compression, and Holley four-barrel on a low-rise aluminum manifold. Just 4751 '68 models got one, but these L-78 SS 396s could scale muscle's twin peaks: 14 seconds and 100 mph in the quarter mile.

Standard with all engines was the three-speed manual transmission; optional were the Muncie four-speed manual and Powerglide or Turbo Hydra-Matic automatics. Axle ratios began with 2.73:1 highway gearing and ended with 4.56:1 drag strip cogs. All were encased in a sturdy GM 12-bolt housing.

SS 396 Chevelles had their grille and rear panel blacked out and light-colored cars got a blackened lower body treatment. The double-dome hood was carried from the previous generation and all SS 396's got Chevy's Hide-A-Way hidden windshield wipers. The new cabin featured a revised dash, though a tachometer, bucket seats, and a console were optional. For the first time, Chevy's pickup truck-like El Camino also could be ordered as an SS 396.

Chevy built 62,785 SS 396 Chevelles for '68, about the same as in 1967; only 2286 were ragtops.

1969

For 1969, Chevy made the SS 396 an option package (RPO Z-25) rather than a separate model or series. It was available on the Chevelle Sport Coupe and on the Malibu Sport Coupe and convertible. Plus, for the first time, a pillared coupe could get the SS 396 treatment on the Chevelle 300 Deluxe model. In addition to the 396 engine, the SS option added a redesigned black-out horizontal grille, revised taillamps, bright wheel-opening moldings, and five-spoke chrome Sport Wheels. Ordering the optional bucket seats triggered the addition of a console. Manual-transmission cars used a floor shift with or without bucket seats; automatics were column mounted unless buckets were specified.

Buyers still chose among 396s of 325, 350, and 375 horsepower. About 500 Chevelles were fitted with the Corvette L-72 engine, an aluminum-head 427 rated at 425 horses. These were COPO (Central Office Production Order) units and were parceled out only to those who had some pull with the factory or dealer body.

Making the SS 396 an option package turned out to be a smart move, with a record 86,307 ordered in the Chevelle/Malibu line.

1970

The age of muscle peaked in 1970 and Chevelle was there to herald its ascent. The year owes its distinction in no small measure to a GM decision that allowed engines of more than 400 cubic inches in its intermediates. The Pontiac GTO, Oldsmobile 4-4-2, and Buick Gran Sport all responded with 455-cube mills that made 370 horsepower in their most pumped-up tune. Chevy's retort was a stroked 427 option that created the Chevelle SS 454. This engine *started* at 360 horsepower and ended with the LS-6 at a drop-dead 450 horses. This was

The '68-72 SS Chevelles enjoyed the best-selling four-year run of any muscle car ever, and with good reason. They were fast, affordable, and good looking. Downsized and restyled, the '68 (opposite) launched the new look and with the solid-lifter 375-bhp L-78 396 (below) launched itself to hyper-quick ETs. The '69 model (bottom two photos) set an all-time Chevelle SS sales record.

muscle's summit.

In LS-6 tune, the 454 had solid-lifters, 11.0:1 compression, four-bolt mains, and an 800cfm Holley four-barrel. Its ultra high-performance internals included a forged steel crank, forged steel connecting rods, and forged aluminum TRW pistons. Peak horsepower was achieved at 5400 rpm. A rubber-roasting 500 pounds/feet of torque was on tap at 3600. Appropriately enough, Muncie's celebrated M22 "Rockcrusher" four-speed was the only manual tough enough for the LS-6, while heavy-duty M40 Turbo Hydra-matic was the only automatic to make the grade. Rear-axles ranged from 3.31:1 to 4.10:1. The LS-6 cost a hefty $767 and would easily push the price of an SS 454 into the $5000 range. Only 4475 were produced, but this was a car that left an indelible mark on all who drove it.

The solid-lifter 454 could be a temperamental beast, however, so most SS 454s had the hydraulic-lifter LS-5. This one had a Quadrajet and a more practical 10.25:1 compression ratio. It was rated at 360 horses, but still delivered 500 pounds/feet of torque at 3200 rpm. It cost an extra $504. The entry-level Chevelle SS engine was still the 396, but was now the 350-horsepower L-34. It was included in the $445 SS package. In January 1970, Chevy replaced the 396 with a 402-cubic-inch V-8, but continued to use the well-established 396 label and 350-horse rating. *Road Test* magazine ran a 396/350 with Turbo Hydra-Matic and reported a quarter-mile time of 15.27 seconds at 92 mph. Little publicized but still available was the 375-horsepower L-78 version of the 396. It cost $656 and an additional $184 got it aluminum heads. Only 18 L-78s were built for '70.

Chevy packaged all this new hardware in a restyled Chevelle body. Its lines were squarer than the '68-69 models and when dressed in SS garb, made the car look even more like a street tough. The Super Sport option was offered only on the Chevelle coupe and convertible and the El Camino for '70. It now included a domed hood with chrome tie-down pins. Inside was a revised dashboard borrowed from the new Monte Carlo.

The muscle market was saturated in '70, and despite new levels of style and power, production of the SS 396 fell to 53,559; 8773 SS 454s were built.

1971-72

Insurance adjusters, safety lobbyists, and environmentalists had all been pressuring Detroit to scale back on fast, youth-oriented, high-octane-gulping cars and by autumn 1970, it was clear that the market for muscle was shrinking. Compression ratios fell for the '71 model year and GM was poised to switch to the more benign-sounding net horsepower ratings.

In the SS Chevelle range, the hallowed 396 label was dropped, though the 402-cube V-8 was carried over under the Turbo-Jet 400 badge. Compression declined from 10.25:1 to 8.5:1 and horsepower dropped to 300. Also available on Super Sport models was the Turbo-Fire 350-cubic-inch V-8 with 245 or 270 horsepower. The LS-6 was gone, but the basic LS-5 454 survived. Despite a compression drop to 8.5:1, it was rated at 365 horsepower, up five from '70, thanks to a freshened head design and a revised camshaft. Transmission choices for the 454 and 402 were unchanged, though axle-ratio options were fewer.

Chevelle switched to single headlamps set within a new fascia for '71, but little of significance was altered inside or out. The $357 SS package continued on coupe and ragtop models and upped its standard tire size to F60×15. The domed hood and power front disc brakes remained standard, and cowl induction was again an option.

Following Detroit's drift toward muscle pretenders was the Heavy Chevy of '71-72. This was a budget SS with a cutesy

1968-72 Chevelle SS

Facts At a Glance

Engine type:	V-8/Big block/ Mark IV	V-8/Big block/ Mark IV
Displacement (cid):	396	402
Horsepower @ rpm:	325 @ 4800 350 @ 5200 375 @ 5600[1]	350 @ 5200 375 @ 5600[1] 300 @ 4800 (1971) 240 @ 4400 (1972)
Torque (lbs/ft) @ rpm:	410 @ 3200 415 @ 3400 415 @ 3600[1]	415 @ 3400 415 @ 3600[1] 400 @ 3200 (1971) 345 @ 3200 (1972)
Compression ratio:	10.25:1/11.0:1	10.25:1/8.5:1
Bore (in.):	4.09	4.12
Stroke (in.):	3.76	3.76
Valve lifters:	Hydraulic/Mechanical[1]	Hydraulic
Availability:	1968-69	1970-72

[1]L-78 (1969-70)

Engine type:		V-8/Big block/ Mark V
Displacement (cid):		454
Horsepower @ rpm:		360 @ 4400 (1970) 365 @ 4800 (1971) 450 @ 5600 (1970)[1]
Torque (lbs/ft) @ rpm:		500 @ 3200 (1970) 465 @ 3200 (1971) 500 @ 3600 (1970)[1]
Compression ratio:		10.25:1/11.25:1[1]/ 8.5:1
Bore (in.):		4.25
Stroke (in.):		4.00
Valve lifters:		Hydraulic/ Mechanical[1]
Availability:		1970-72

[1]LS-6

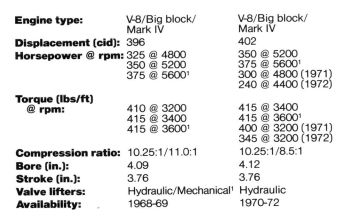

Magazine:	Car and Driver (Jan 1969)	Muscle Car Review
Times:		
0-60 mph (sec):	5.8	6.0 (est)
0-100 mph (sec):	15.2	14.20 (est)
1/4-mile (sec):	14.41 @ 97.35 mph	14.20 @ 100 mph
Top speed (mph):	116 (est)	120 (est)
Axle ratio:	3.55:1	3.31:1
Engine:	396/325	454/360 LS-5
Model year:	1969	1970

Magazine:	Muscle Car Review
Times:	
0-60 mph (sec):	5.5 (est)
0-100 mph (sec):	14.0 (est)
1/4-mile (sec):	13.75 @ 98.46 mph
Top speed (mph):	N/A
Axle ratio:	N/A
Engine:	454/450 LS-6
Model year:	1970

name, its own exterior graphics, and 14-inch tires. Heavy Chevy V-8 choices ranged from the 307 V-8 to the Turbo-Fire 400-cube small block. Production totals for the 402- and 350-cube SS Chevelles are sketchy, but some sources put the number around 60,000. Chevy researchers say 9402 SS 454 Chevelles were built for '71.

For '72, the net horsepower ratings kicked in and engines were rated with all their power-robbing accessories attached. The LS-5 454's rating under this system was 270 horsepower. The Turbo-Jet 400 came in at 240 net horsepower. Few of these big blocks were ordered, though, as SS Chevelle buyers opted for an expanded range of more docile V-8s. There was the 350 in 165-and 175-horse trim, and this year even the 130-horsepower 307 was available in an SS. The Super Sport package itself changed little and still made the Chevelle look brawny, no matter the engine. All LS-5s were mated to the Rockcrusher four-speed, while the other V-8s got either the three- or four-speed manual, depending on horsepower. And since power had fallen to ranges that wouldn't damage the Powerglide two-speed automatic, it now joined the Hydra-matic on the options list. A 3.31:1 gear was now the strongest performance ratio available.

Chevelle SS production fell to 24,946. The LS-5 found only 5333 takers, including a handful who ordered SS 454 convertibles, the last of the Super Sport Chevelle ragtops.

In 1973, the proud Super Sport name withered and died on a redesigned Chevelle that was bigger and heavier than any before it. The SS package went on the Chevelle "Colonnade" coupe and also could be ordered on the Chevelle station wagon! A handful were equipped with the 245-horsepower LS-4 454, but most had a 307 or a 350. Chevy built nearly 296,000 SS 396 and SS 454 Chevelles from 1968-72. No muscle car ever had a higher-volume four-year run. The Super Sport Chevelle: quantity and quality.

Styling of the '70 Chevelle (left and above) was squared. Opposite: Breathing of standard 350-bhp 396 V-8 could be aided via cowl induction. New SS dashboard was shared with the Monte Carlo and was not used with any other Chevelle. The "396" was dropped from the SS badge in '71. By the '72 model (bottom) V-8 engine choices ranged from 307- to 454-cid.

1967-70 CHEVROLET CAMARO Z-28

Chevrolet was acutely aware of Mustang's success in Sports Car Club of America competition, particularly in the tough Trans American sedan series. Trans Am was the premier racing showcase for pony cars as the 1967 Camaro was launched and Chevy knew the new car would have to score here if it was to chip away at the entrenched Mustang.

Trans Am rules specified a production-based car with an engine no larger than 305 cubic inches. Ford had run its 289-cubic-inch V-8s to great success and would soon aim its new tunnel port 302 at the winner's circle. Camaro's smallest V-8 was the 327, so Chevy engineers did some off-the-shelf engineering. They worked the steel-forged crankshaft from their 283-cubic-inch V-8 into the 327 to achieve a 302-cubic-inch displacement. Then they continued the part swap with big-port heads from the Corvette L-69 engine, added solid lifters, a hot cam, a baffled oil pan, and hooked up a high-pressure oil pump. A Holley four-barrel on a tuned aluminum manifold was specified and the package was finished off with chrome on the air cleaner, valve covers, and oil-filler tube and cap. Compression was 11.1:1, horsepower was rated at 290 at 5800 rpm. True horsepower was likely close to 400.

Corporate policy prevented Chevrolet's direct involvement in racing, so the division turned to Roger Penske and Mark Donohue to develop and campaign the new Camaro. The car didn't unseat the Mustangs that first year—and, in fact, its competition history would turn out to be but a footnote to its story.

Manufacturers at that time had to produce at least 1000 streetable examples of their Trans Am racers before the car could compete. Chevy went about meeting that requirement by making the 302 engine the heart of a Camaro Regular Production Option Code. It did this in a very low-key fashion. It didn't advertise the car, didn't even mention it in sales literature. To acquire one, the knowledgeable buyer had to order a base Camaro ($2466), then scan the order sheet for what turned out to be the most famous RPO in history: Z-28. That $400.25 package brought the new 302 engine, as well as the F-41 handling suspension, 7.35×15 Goodyear tires on Corvette six-inch Rally wheels, and quick-ratio manual steering. Mandatory with RPO Z-28 were a Muncie four-speed manual transmission and power front disc brakes, which pushed the list price to around $3150.

Trans Am competition spawned the Z-28 Camaro, a barely tamed racer for the street. It bowed in '67 (opposite) with racing stripes, but no special badging. Fender emblems were added for '68 (below). The Z-28 pictured has the hidden-headlamp RS package.

The Z-28 Camaro was available on the coupe only and could not be ordered with automatic transmission or air conditioning. It could, however, be combined with the Rally Sport option group, the most noticeable feature of which was the hidden-headlamp grille. The Z-28 came with a cast-iron exhaust manifold and a single exhaust, but Chevy offered optional headers and a variety of carburetion setups, including dual quads. These were shipped from the factory in the trunk, to be installed by the dealer or owner. There were no Z-28 emblems on the car its first year, but the Z-28 package did include a pair of broad racing stripes on the hood and trunk. The regular Camaro rear lip spoiler also was a popular option.

The '67 Z-28 was a rough-riding, rip-snorting racer barely tamed for the street. Its 302 was a peaky devil, hard to launch and even lethargic under 3000 rpm or so. Above that, it was a hurricane, propelling the 3200-pound coupe to mid-14-second quarter-miles at 100 mph. Find enough road, and it would top out at more than 130 mph. Just 602 were ordered that first year.

1968

Chevy added Z-28 badges—or on some cars, 302 insignia—to the front fenders of its hot new Camaro for 1968. And while it still wasn't in sales literature, the Z-28 was advertised in the enthusiast press under the banner, "Closest thing to a Corvette yet."

The Z-28 package itself was largely unaltered, though it now was available with a heavy-duty four-speed or with the tougher still four-speed used with the L-88 350-cube V-8 (L-88 denoted a dealer-installed factory-option dual-quad kit). A 3.73:1 rear axle was standard, but ratios up to 4.88:1 were available when Positraction was ordered. Like all high-performance Camaros for '68, the Z-28 got multi-leaf rear springs and staggered rear shocks, a change that helped minimize the severe axle tramp that had plagued the hot '67 models.

In Trans Am, Chevy finally accomplished what it had set out to do with the Z-28. Mark Donohue's No. 6 Sunoco Camaro won 10 of the 11 races in the series to capture the championship.

Not only were the '68 Z-28 Camaros successful in competition, they performed well at the showroom. Production totaled 7198 for the model year.

1969

Camaro for 1969 got a fresh skin that featured sharper lines and horizontal brows over the wheels.

The Z-28 group was again available only on the coupe and added $458.15 to the $2726 base price (the package price rose to $506.60 after May 1). Returning was the solid-lifter, dual-exhaust four-barrel 302, though four-bolt main bearing caps were added this year for improved durability. Horsepower was again underrated at 290. In place of the standard 3.73:1 rear axle, buyers could order ratios ranging from 3.07:1 to 4.10:1. Among

other Z-28 changes for '69 was the availability of a rear-facing hood scoop to enhance engine breathing. Tire size was upped to E70×15 and they now were raised-letter Firestone SC-200s. Corvette-type four-wheel disc brakes were a new option, but cost $500 and most of the roughly 200 ordered were for race use. Fast 17.9:1-ratio power-assisted steering could be ordered in place of the already quickened 21.4:1 ratio.

Ford countered Chevy in '69 with the Boss 302, a Trans Am-homologated Mustang just as raucous as the Z-28. But now it was the Chevy that had the head start, and production of the Z-28 reached 19,014, to just 1934 for the Boss 302. It was Chevy again on the racetrack, too, as Donohue's 170-mph Z-28 Camaro won a second Trans Am championship.

1970

Camaro kept its 108-inch wheelbase for 1970, but otherwise underwent wholesale change. Its new coupe body was an instant classic and was the foundation for what most bowtie fans regard as the baddest Z-28 of all.

Trans Am rules now allowed destroked engines, so Chevy shelved the 302 and made a 350 the new standard Z-28 street powerplant. This was the LT-1 Corvette 350. It had solid lifters, a hot cam, big valves, extruded aluminum pistons, 11.0:1 compression, and a Holley 780cfm four-barrel. It made 370 horsepower in the 'Vette and was rated at 360 in the Z-28. Handling was better in all '70 Camaros due to an improved suspension. The Z-28 again had the stiffer F-41 underpinnings and improved even more with state-of-the-art F60×15 fiberglass-belted tires. A Muncie four-speed box with Hurst linkage remained standard, but Turbo Hydra-Matic was now an option. Listing for $3412, the Z-28 could again be ordered in tandem with the RS package. Which added $168. That gave it the unique RS nose treatment that featured an soft Endura grille surround and two bumperettes instead of a full-width bumper. A rear spoiler was made standard for '70.

"It's not for everybody," said Chevy in this year's Z-28 advertising, and indeed it wasn't. Unfortunately, among those were Penske and Donohue, who left Chevy to campaign factory-backed AMC Javelins in the 1970 Trans Am season. Ford's Boss 302 won the championship. The racing Z-28 team, headed by Jim Hall of Chaparral fame, finished off the pace. On the street, however, the Z-28 was at its pinnacle. No Z-28 ever was faster, quicker, or handled better. The following year compression would drop to 9.0:1 and horsepower would fall to 330. That would begin a steady decline in specification until the Z-28 actually was dropped between 1975 and February 1977. It was supplanted by the Camaro IROC-Z in 1988-89, but returned for 1990. It's significant that the Z-28 name far outlived Chevy's proud Super Sport tag. That's a testament to the high-performance pedigree originated in those untamed 1967-70 Z-28s.

Z-28 was restyled for '69 (opposite), but retained the solid-lifter 302-cid V-8. All-new Z-28 for '70 (below) handled better and had enduring looks. Its 350-cid (bottom) made 360 bhp. This was the bloodthirstiest Z-28 of all.

1967-70 Chevrolet Camaro

Z-28

Facts At a Glance

Engine type:	V-8/Small block	V-8/Small block
Displacement (cid):	302	350
Horsepower @ rpm:	290 @ 5800	360 @ 6000
Torque (lbs/ft) @ rpm:	290 @ 4200	380 @ 4500
Compression ratio:	11.0:1	11.0:1
Bore (in.):	4.00	4.00
Stroke (in.):	3.00	3.48
Valve lifters:	Mechanical	Mechanical
Availability:	1967-69	1970

Magazine:	Car and Driver (March 1967)	Hi Performance Cars (1968)
Times:		
0-60 mph (sec):	6.7	5.5 (est)
0-100 mph (sec):	16.2	12.50 (est)
¼-mile (sec):	14.9 @ 97 mph	13.75 @ 107 mph
Top speed (mph):	124	115
Axle ratio:	3.70:1	4.10:1
Engine:	302	302 (2x4v)[1]
Model year:	1967	1968

[1]With dealer installed stock modifications.

Magazine:	Car and Driver (May 1970)
Times:	
0-60 mph (sec):	5.8
0-100 mph (sec):	14.2
¼-mile (sec):	14.2 @ 100.3 mph
Top speed (mph):	118
Axle ratio:	4.10:1
Engine:	350
Model year:	1970

1962
DODGE
DART 413

One of the watershed years of the early muscle era was 1962. Chevrolet's fine 409 was made available to the public in wide numbers for the first time and was terrorizing street and strip with one horsepower per cubic inch in dual-quad form. Over at Ford, that magic threshold had been broached with the brand new 405 horsepower tri-carb 406. Chrysler, meanwhile, had introduced a 413-cubic-inch V-8 way back in 1959, but it wasn't until '61 that it found its way out of the big Chryslers and into the smaller Dodges and Plymouths. Its peak output of 375 horsepower with dual quads was very respectable, but not up to the standards that Chevy and Ford had in store for '62.

So MoPar engineers went back to their drawing boards and emerged with the Max Wedge 413. All 413s had wedge-shaped combustion chambers, but at 410 horsepower, only this one was strong enough to wear the "maximum wedge" title. Both Dodge and Plymouth got this engine. Dodge dubbed it the Ram-Charger 413, Plymouth the Super Stock 413. Perhaps Plymouth's name was the more accurate, for Chrysler specified that the engine was to be used for sanctioned acceleration trials, and not as a street mill, though of course, some did show up to do battle on the boulevards and back roads.

Dodge made it a special option in its Dart. The Dart tag would subsequently become synonymous with the company's compact models, but in '62, it was billed as a standard-size Dodge. Its wheelbase had been shortened from 118 inches to 116 for '62, which was just a half-inch shorter than Ford's new-for-1962 intermediate Fairlane. Thus, the '62 Dodge might best be thought of as a mid-size. Its maker described it as "The new lean breed of Dodge!" Styling was another matter. In one sense, it was typical of Chrysler chief designer Virgil Exner's later days with the firm—that is to say, flamboyant, oddball, and out of step with GM and Ford. On the other hand, it might also be described as daring and even appealing. The '62 Dart featured beltline fins and heavy bodyside sculpting coupled with such jet-age appointments as "turbine" taillamps.

The Dart's ace in the hole was its light weight. At 3260 pounds, even the top-of-the-line Dart 440 two-door hardtop was 200 pounds lighter than a Chevy Bel Air and 300 pounds lighter than a Ford Galaxie. Dodge simply pointed out that there's "more live action because there's less dead weight."

But it was the 413 that made Dart one of the few early high-performance cars worthy of super-car status. Costing only $374.40 more than a 230-horsepower Dart, the Ram-Charger 413 package, said *Motor Trend* at the time, "gives more performance per dollar than any other factory-assembled car in America."

As installed in the Dart, this solid-lifter 413 pumped out 410 or 415 horses, both outputs with dual four-barrel 650cfm Carter

Dodge downsized its standard models for '62. When equipped with the solid-lifer dual-quad 413-cid Ram-Charger V-8, like this Dart, they had a supercar power-to-weight ratio. Conservative cabin (bottom) featured dash-mounted transmission-control buttons to the left of the steering wheel. Exterior styling was flamboyant, but Motor Trend called the 413's upswept exhaust manifolds the "most efficient and beautiful ever put on an American car."

Dart pillared coupe (opposite top) was the sleeper of the Ram-Charger-equipped models, while the dressier Polara hardtop (other photos) added some show to the 413's go. Compare this interior with its bucket seats, snazzier steering wheel, and floor shift, to the Dart's cabin on page 63. "Max Wedge" was a nickname bestowed on the engine by the street/strip crowd; MoPar never officially used it.

1962 Dodge Dart 413

Facts At a Glance

Engine type:	V-8/RB-block/Wedge
Displacement (cid):	413
Horsepower @ rpm:	410/415 @ 5600
Torque (lbs/ft) @ rpm:	470 @ 3600
Compression ratio:	11.0:1/12.0:1
Bore (in.):	4.19
Stroke (in.):	3.75
Valve lifters:	Mechanical

Magazine:	***Motor Trend*** **(August 1962)**
Times:	
0-60 mph (sec):	5.8
0-100 mph (sec):	N/A
¼-mile (sec):	14.4 @ 101 mph
Top speed (mph):	119 (est)
Axle ratio:	3.91:1

AFB carburetors mounted in tandem on a short-ram intake manifold. The Max Wedge used aluminum pistons and a double-breaker ignition system. Its intake and exhaust ports were enlarged 25 percent over the lesser 413 and its tubular cast-iron exhaust-manifold headers measured three inches in diameter. Space for this engine wasn't a problem in the Chrysler New Yorker, but in the Dart, the engineers had to route the headers first up and then back in a ram's-horn sweep. *Motor Trend* called these exhaust manifolds the "most efficient and beautiful ever put on an American car."

Sources differ on some of the Max Wedge's specifications. For instance, horsepower peaked at either 5400 rpm or 5600 rpm, depending on the authority. And while all sources agree that an 11.0:1 compression was the starting point, there is confusion over whether special pistons available upped the compression to 12.0:1 or to 13.5:1. Finally, there is disagreement over whether the slightly hotter version made 415 or 420 horsepower. Regardless, all were given such an encompassing high-performance rework that even the belt pulleys were deep-grooved for better belt retention at high rpm. A 3.91:1 Sure-Grip rear axle was standard, but available ratios ranged from 2.93:1 to 4.89:1.

Coupled to Chrysler's standard three-speed floor-shift manual or its optional pushbutton TorqueFlite automatic—specially fortified for high-upshift abuse—a Ram-Charger 413 Dart would give fits to anything remotely stock. It was good for quarter-miles in the mid-14s at more than 100 mph—on the primitive street tires of the day. At the strip, 413 Ram-Chargers set four NHRA class records in '62, including Dick Landy's 12.7 ET with a three-speed and Bill "Maverick" Golden's 12.5 with an automatic. The Ram-Charger 413 was available in any Dart except the station wagon. Dodge made it part of a package that also included heavy duty rear springs and listed 14×6.5 rear wheels and 9.00×14 tires as a dealer-installed option. Dodge was able to brag in a 1962 advertisement that a Ram-Charger 413 Dart "has about the best power-weight ratio ever offered on a production car. Now up to one horse for every 8.4 pounds."

MoPar would escalate the displacement war in '63 by boring the 413 to 426 cubic inches, a move that doomed the Max Wedge 413. The 413 wedge-head engine itself continued for several years, with 390-horsepower dual-quad versions available through '64. Its time in the Max Wedge limelight may have been short, but this was the engine that put MoPar muscle in the big leagues.

1963
DODGE
426 RAMCHARGER

Chrysler's knee-jerk response to the escalation of the cubic-inch war was the 426-cubic-inch RB-Wedge V-8. Known as the Ramcharger and immodestly billed as the "hottest performing power plant to come off a production line," this Max Wedge design was the next step up from the 413 V-8 of 1962.

Chrysler's quest for brute horsepower brought more changes than just a displacement boost, however. In essence, Dodge's 426 Ramcharger *was* a 413 V-8, bored from 4.19 to 4.25 inches, though the former 3.75-inch stroke was retained. And except for a color change from Turquoise paint on the 413 to Race Hemi Orange on the 426, the two engines looked identical. But there were many serious changes beneath the surface, including large-port cylinder heads, a forged-steel crankshaft, double shot-peened connecting rods with high-strength bolts, and forged-aluminum high-compression pistons.

Each rod was magnaflux-inspected to detect any hairline cracks or imperfections. Mechanical (solid) lifters were used and a heavy-duty valve train held stiffer springs and retainers to prevent high-speed valve "float." Chrysler said the valve train was stable to 6500 rpm.

To ease airflow, Ramchargers used 2.08-inch intake valves and had exhaust valves that were ¼-inch larger than standard. Port areas of each cylinder head were about 25-percent larger than in the standard 413 to boost volumetric efficiency. An oversized exhaust system used streamlined cast-iron, long-branch exhaust manifolds with three-inch outlet cutouts and

two-inch tailpipes. The dual-point distributor offered full centrifugal advance.

In its initial form, two Carter AFB-3447SA four-barrel carburetors rode atop a short-ram intake manifold. A solid-lifter camshaft with 300-degree duration and .509-inch lift pushed valves toward 81-cc (minimum) chamber heads. Mid-year improvements included larger Carter AFB-3705SA carburetors, higher (.520-inch) valve lift, longer (308-degree) exhaust valve duration, and larger combustion chamber volume. Also added in the modified edition were Tri-Y exhaust headers. Dodge rated the Ramcharger V-8 at 415 horsepower with standard 11.0:1 compression or 425 horsepower with the optional 13.5:1 compression ratio. Most observers believed the true outputs were much higher.

Sending all this horsepower to the back wheels was a special three-speed manual gearbox with floor shift and closely spaced ratios (2.10, 1.44 and 1.0 to 1). A heavy-duty TorqueFlite automatic with pushbutton gear selection also was available and was set to upshift at up to 5600 rpm. A "Sure-Grip" rear axle carried a standard 3.91:1 ratio, but the option lists spanned ratios from 2.93:1 to 4.89:1.

If the regular heavy-duty rear springs weren't sufficient, an optional stiffer right-spring setup delivered even more traction to the standard 7.50 × 14 Tyrex-cord tires. Those who wanted bigger grabbers out back could ask the dealer for 9.00×14 skins.

Its important to remember that this engine was available in

Dodge dubbed its version of Chrysler's 426-cid the Ramcharger (bottom, right). Twin Carter carbs atop short-ram manifold gave 415-425 bhp, depending on tune. Engine could be ordered in the plush Polara (opposite) or sleeper 330 sedan (below). TorqueFlite drag car (bottom, left) was national Top Stock Eliminator.

1963 Dodge Ramcharger 426

Facts At a Glance

Engine type:	V-8/RB-Wedge	V-8/RB-Wedge
Displacement (cid):	426	426
Horsepower @ rpm:	415 @ 5600	425 @ 5600
Torque (lbs/ft) @ rpm:	470 @ 4400	480 @ 4400
Compression ratio:	11.0:1	13.5:1
Bore (in.):	4.25	4.25
Stroke (in.):	3.75	3.75
Valve lifters:	Mechanical	Mechanical
Availability:	Dodge, all except Dart	

Magazine:	*Muscle Car Review* (1987)
Times:	
0-60 mph (sec):	N/A
0-100 mph (sec):	N/A
¼-mile (sec):	12.00 @ 117 mph
Top speed (mph):	120 (est)
Axle ratio:	4.56:1
Engine type:	426 (425-horsepower Lightweight racer)

Polara nose for '63 was distinct (opposite, top). TorqueFlite pushbuttons are left of the steering column in this top-of-the-line '63 Polara 500 cabin (opposite, bottom). The '64 "lightweight" sedan (left) could be ordered with a Hemi, but this one has the Max Wedge (below). Tri-Y headers were a hot factory setup (below, left).

any Dodge except the compact Dart. Its most potent application was in the mid-size Polara range. Stretched three-inches from '62, the 119-inch wheelbase Polara came in coupe, sedan, hardtop and convertible, though serious racers might prefer an innocuous wrapper for their Max Wedge, maybe a nice, base two-door sedan. The Polara had taken on a new shape for '63, with elongated front fenders, twin-set headlamps, and sculptured rear quarter panels. It was similar to the new, smaller compact Dart. Like the former (1962) Dart mid-size, the '63 Polara had a rounded dashboard with pod-style "George Jetson" instrumentation, which appeared as a separate unit. Interior styling was futuristic overall, in fact, like all Chrysler products of the era, with tapered door handles, window cranks, and armrests.

Dodge performance fans had four 383-cubic-inch V-8s from which to choose in '63, including the 383 B-Wedge High Performance V-8 that churned out 330 horsepower via a single Carter AFB or 390 horses with two. Known as the 383 "Polara" in Dodge installations, this smaller-displacement V-8 had good road manners and reliability well ahead of the 426 Ramchargers. The 340-horsepower 413 was the largest engine most buyers considered for the street.

With the 426's brute horsepower came reliability and streetability problems that made it tough to manage for daily use. Even the sales brochure warned that the Ramcharger engine warmed up slowly because it put no heat on the intake manifold. Dodge, in fact, issued a clear warning that the power-packed 426 Ramcharger was "not a street machine." Instead, the brochure added, it had been "designed to be run in *supervised, sanctioned* drag-strip competition by those

qualified....Yet, it is stock in every sense of the word."

Dodge Chief Engineer George Gibson said development lessons learned on the Ramcharger trickled down to other Dodges. A "maximum-performance engine explores new ideas," he said. "It subjects engines, transmissions, and other power-train components to stresses and strains far greater than will ever be encountered in normal driving. And as a result, we learn how to improve lubrication, ignition, carburetion, cooling and heat transfer—just to name a few examples."

On the track, the super-powered Dodge earned instant respect. The potent 425-horse, dual-quad 426 Ramcharger blistered the NHRA record books with quarter-mile times in the 12-second range. In factory lightweight form, wearing an aluminum front-end, the 1963 Dodge tipped the scales at 3200 pounds—not bad for a mid-size with a big block under the hood. With the available aluminum front fenders, hood and front bumpers, and two big air scoops feeding the twin ram-inducted four-barrel carbs, the 1963-64 Ramcharger was the toughest of contenders. The aluminum-component Dodges cleaned up in a special "Limited Production" category.

"When a Dodge loses these days," boasted one MoPar ad, "it's to another Dodge."

During 1964, fans of street muscle could order a detuned version of the Ramcharger with 10.3:1 compression, a milder cam, and no ram-induction setup. That one idled a lot smoother, making it more practical on the street. The revived Hemi V-8 was also waiting in the wings for a early-'64 debut. Still, the all-out 1963 Ramcharger Dodges (and equivalent Super Stock Plymouths) hold special meaning for MoParphiles as key players in the history of early muscle.

1964
DODGE
426 HEMI

Few single developments are significant enough to set the automotive world on its ear. The 426 Hemi did. It debuted at Daytona's Speedweeks in February 1964 and promptly swept the first three places at stock-car racing's biggest event, the Daytona 500. Under the hoods of lightweight Super/Stock Dodges and Plymouths, it quickly went on to dominate its class in professional drag racing. The engine was still a couple of years away from street use, but the mark it made on race tracks in 1964 set the stage for glories to come.

The new 426-cubic-inch Hemi-head V-8 resembled Chrysler's Red Ram (Firepower) hemispherical-combustion-chamber V-8s of the 1950s. But displacement of those engines never exceeded 400 cubic inches. This new and potent edition was based on the RB-Block that began life as the 413 and 426 Wedge.

The reason for reintroduction of a Hemi-chambered V-8 was simple enough: Chrysler wanted to dominate NASCAR, NHRA, and AHRA racing. And another name for winning was Hemi.

The Hemi-head was developed as a means of generating more power from the air/fuel mixture without the drawback of severe knock and ping. Its large, half-arc combustion chambers allowed fuel to burn more quickly and completely with reduced risk of destructive detonation. The design proved outstanding at dissipating heat under peak power conditions, making higher compression ratios possible with marginal-octane fuels.

Before World War II, the hemi concept had seen life mainly in race engines and the rare high-priced imported automobile. Chrysler began to experiment with the hemispherical combustion chamber as early as 1946. By 1949, Chrysler engineers had an operational Hemi-head V-8 shattering the silence of their laboratories. In 1951, the Hemi was a showroom reality in a variety of Chrysler cars. Unfortunately, Hemis were expensive and troublesome to produce, so they disappeared after 1958.

The 1964 Hemi, displacing 426 cubic inches, took a giant leap forward from the original 331-cubic-inch mill of 1951. That one reached its 180 horsepower at 4000 rpm. By 1957-58, Hemi displacement reached 392 cubic inches and up to 390 horsepower was on tap, but the block had reached its growth limit. While rumors of the Hemi's return were rampant in the next few years, engineers had to deal with its basic complexity, heavy weight, and high manufacturing cost.

By 1964, Chrysler had developed a Hemi that generated an advertised 425 horsepower at 6000 rpm, yet weighed only about 67 pounds more than a wedge-chambered 426. Observers at the time noted that Chrysler's horsepower estimates were conservative. Real output might have run closer to 570 horsepower.

Accompanying the hemispherical heads were dual rocker-arm shafts to handle the demands of the canted-valve design. The chain-driven, solid-lifter camshaft activated the complex valve network through longer pushrods. Compression ratios reached down to 10.25:1 for the eventual Street Hemi, but started at 11.0:1 and 12.5:1 for these early racing editions. Huge exhaust ports allowed a short passage for spent gases to exit the valve, breezing through tuned-length exhaust headers. Domed pistons had milled relief areas to clear the valve heads. The big advantage of a Hemi lies in the ability of its free-running valves to gulp in plenty of air at high rpm, so intake valves measured 2.25 inches in diameter (versus 2.08 inches for the 426 Ramcharger Max Wedge).

Though identical in bore and stroke to the Wedge V-8, the Hemi's B-block had to be stronger. Designed to carry a rough load, the bottom end held a forged-steel crankshaft with eight-bolt flywheel flange, heavy-duty connecting rods with floating pins, and cross-bolted four-bolt mains with heavier-than-usual webbing. Chrysler built three versions of this engine for '64: two for the drag strip, another for oval track racing. Not until 1966

1964 Dodge 426 Hemi

Facts At a Glance

Engine type:	V-8/RB-Block/Hemi	V-8/RB-Block/Hemi
Displacement (cid):	426	426
Horsepower @ rpm:	415 @ 6000	425 @ 6000
Torque (lbs/ft) @ rpm:	470 @ 4600	480 @ 4600
Compression ratio:	11.0:1	12.5:1
Bore (in.):	4.25	4.25
Stroke (in.):	3.75	3.75
Valve lifters:	Mechanical	Mechanical
Availability:	Dodge 330/440 and Polara	

Magazine:	*Muscle Car Review*
Times:	
0-60 mph (sec):	N/A
0-100 mph (sec):	N/A
¼ mile (sec):	11.40 @ 125 mph
Top Speed (mph):	130 (est)
Axle Ratio:	N/A
Engine:	426 Hemi (425 hp)
Model year:	1964

Dodge's Super Stock standard-bearer for '65 was the new Coronet intermediate. Factory-built Hemi drag cars like this one used all-steel bodies, but had two inches trimmed from the stock 117-inch wheelbase. Removing the air cleaner reveals the Hemi's dual quads and ram-tuned magnesium manifold (above).

was a Street Hemi officially available.

The Dodge in which the Hemi saw service most frequently in '64 was the mid-size 330/440/Polara. These cars had been given new front-end styling that year. Their large headlamps and toothy grille showed the influence of the 1963 experimental Chrysler Turbine car. As in 1962-63, the mid-size Dodge had a pod-style instrument cluster and lean interior appointments. Futuristic door handles, panels, and armrests carried on Chrysler tradition, but oil pressure and alternator gauges replaced the former "idiot lights."

For NASCAR, the 426 Hemi used a single Holley four-barrel carburetor atop a dual-plane high-rise intake manifold. Dodge and Plymouth earned the top seven starting positions at the '64 Daytona 500. Junior Johnson won the pole in a Dodge, setting a new qualifying record at 170.77 mph. A young racer named Richard Petty actually won the race in a Hemi Plymouth, his first Daytona 500 victory.

For the strip, the Hemi's ram-tuned aluminum induction system held a pair of Carter AFB four-barrel carburetors.

The 426 Hemi came standard with the new heavy-duty, side-loading Chrysler four-speed manual gearbox or optional three-speed Torqueflite transmission. This was the final season for the pushbutton-operated Torqueflite. While wedge-powered Ramchargers used twin hood scoops, the Hemi had a wider single air scoop on its hood.

At mid-year, Dodge began offering factory-built race cars built on the Hamtramck, Michigan, assembly line. Called the Maximum Performance Package and intended specifically for sanction drag racing, these Polara-family intermediates were powered by the new Hemi and used aluminum for the hood, front fenders, doors, and some minor body panels. A lightened front bumper and magnesium front wheels also were standard. The cars had no radio, no heater, no back seat or carpet, no sound deadening material. The bucket seats, taken from a Dodge van, weren't adjustable. Side windows were plastic, and the battery rode in the trunk.

Early Hemis weren't so easy to get, even for "official" race drivers, and ordinary folks would have to wait another two years for the "street" edition. But King Kong had arrived.

1965
DODGE CORONET
426 STREET WEDGE

Dodge put a new name on the street in 1965, the Coronet. It was a new intermediate, built on a 117-inch wheelbase and available in hardtop, sedan, convertible and wagon body styles. Now that Detroit had shifted its performance emphasis to the mid-size range, Coronet would be the focus of Dodge's hottest street and strip efforts.

The finest of them all, of course, was the mighty 426 Hemi. Dodge offered this engine in the Coronet for '65, but only in highly strung 12.5:1 compression race tune. It wasn't very streetable, it was very expensive, and few found their way off the drag strip. But there was another 426 that took to the street with impact and aplomb in the '65 Coronet. In its mildest incarnation, it used a single four-barrel carburetor, hydraulic lifters, and a 10.3:1 compression ratio to churn out 365 horsepower at 4800 rpm and 470 pounds/feet of torque at 3200. Known popularly as the 426 Street Wedge, this was the "optional powerplant for true enthusiasts," Dodge's brochure said. "It leaves nothing to the imagination."

The 426 Street Wedge performance package added $513.60 to the base $2674 base price of a Coronet 500 hardtop. Gone were the flamboyant ram's-horn exhaust headers of 413 Max Wedge fame, but while the 426 Street Wedge didn't look as wild, it was just as potent. *Motor Trend* saw 0-60 mph in 7.7 seconds and a 15.7-second quarter at 89 mph in a '65 Street Wedge Coronet.

For those who could imagine more, Dodge had a 426 Max Wedge in an even higher state of tune, which the automaker called the Ramcharger V-8. This one was rated at 425 horsepower at 5600 rpm and 480 pounds/feet of torque at 4400. It had a 12.5:1 compression ratio, solid lifters, and factory exhaust headers. It even looked intimidating with its Race Hemi Orange paint, Ramcharger graphics, and two Carter AFB four-barrel carburetors mounted in tandem. This was basically the same mill as the 425-horsepower 426 Max Wedge that had been known as the Stage III engine in MoPar's 1964 ultra-performance lineup. The so-called 426 Stage II, which was rated at 415 horsepower on an 11.0:1 compression, was not offered for '65.

Behind the 426s stood a choice of Chrysler four-speed manual or TorqueFlite transmission. The standard rear-axle ratio was 3.23:1, but optional choices ranged from 2.93:1 to 4.89:1 and included the Sure-Grip diffential. Only a handful of Coronets received the 426 Street Wedge and fewer still the Ramcharger engine. These 426s eventually would grow into the 440-cubic-inch V-8s that vied for top dog on the street and strip. But '65 was their last hurrah. Chrysler retired them after this year, and a whole generation of muscle fans would begin to forget that "426" once meant something other than Hemi.

Street Wedge was most frequently found in 365-bhp tune (above right), though less-tractable 425-bhp variant was offered. Chrome air cleaner and valve covers were standard. Coronet 500 had center console standard, but floor-mounted automatic shifter was optional (above).

1965 Dodge Coronet

426 Street Wedge

Facts At a Glance

Engine type:	V-8/RB-Wedge
Displacement (cid):	426
Horsepower @ rpm:	365 @ 4800
Torque (lbs/ft) @ rpm:	470 @ 3200
Compression ratio:	10.3:1
Bore (in.):	4.25
Stroke (in.):	3.75
Valve lifters:	Hydraulic
Availability:	1965 Coronet

Magazine:	*Car Life* (May 1965)
Times:	
0-60 mph (sec):	7.9
0-100 mph (sec):	21.4
¼-mile (sec):	15.4 @ 89 mph
Top speed (mph):	120
Axle ratio:	3.55:1
Engine type:	426 (365 hp)

1965-66
DODGE
DART GT 273

As unlikely as it may seem, the humble Dodge Dart of the mid-1960s is a centerpiece of a cult-car movement. The Slant Six Club of America, for example, celebrates these and other MoPars that used Chrysler's 170-cubic-inch six-cylinder engine. Slant-six Darts were durable, modest compacts with surprisingly balanced performance and affectionate styling. Not that any self-respecting muscle-enthusiast of the time would be caught dead in one. That's okay, because there was a Dart or two for this crowd, also.

Dodge had offered its 273-cubic-inch V-8 in the 1964 Dart, but only with a two-barrel carburetor. With 180 horsepower, it was quicker than a slant six, but it still didn't win many stop-light Grands Prix. For '65, Dart got an updated hood, grille, and tail, and could be ordered with a 273 in a potent new form that helped the diminutive Dodge earn a name for itself in the junior muscle arena.

Introduced in 1964, the 273 was a new engine that ultimately led to a series of V-8s known as the "LA" family. With standard two-barrel carburetion, the 273 produced 180 horsepower.

For 1965, Chrysler added a four-barrel intake manifold with a Carter AFB carburetor. This $99.40 option helped squeeze out 235 horsepower at 5200 rpm and 280 pounds/feet of torque at 4000. The 273 had 3.625-inch bores, but with a short 3.31-inch stroke, it had the ability to rev quite freely.

Its most inviting Dart wrapper would have been the GT, a dressed up Dart 270 with bucket seats, console, and attractive chrome appointments. Built on an 111-inch wheelbase, it was

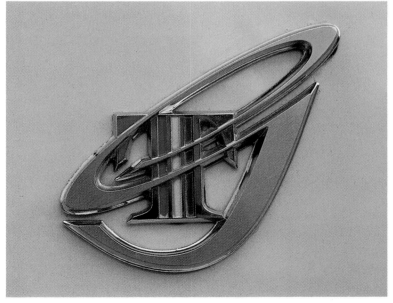

Dodge Dart was a stout compact that turned quite sporty in GT guise (above). Bucket seats, console, extra chrome, and stylized GT badge were included. MoPar's four-barrel 273-cid V-8 gave it a nice kick.

available in hardtop and convertible bodystyles. Dodge's Dart GT was the division's sportiest small car, though over at Plymouth, the Barracuda, with its 106-inch wheelbase and fastback styling, also was available with the optional 273 four-barrel V-8.

Standard behind the 273 V-8 was a three-speed manual transmission, with optional four-speed or TorqueFlite automatic. Axle choices were modest: 3.23:1 standard, 2.93 or 3.55 optional.

A typical 273 Dart GT hardtop could run 0-60 mph in the low-nine-second range and turn the quarter in the mid-16s. *Car and Driver* called the 235-horse Dart's performance "interesting, if not stunning," adding that Dart GT's Torqueflite was "one automatic transmission that can actually be shifted," giving it "overwhelming superiority over manual units in super stock drag racing."

The ultimate racing Dart for '65 would have been one in which its steel body panels were replaced with fiberglass ones made for Dodge by a company called Fibercraft. The switch would have saved 400 ET-robbing pounds.

The 235-horsepower 273 option returned for '66 and Dart was restyled. Interior appointments included a new optional center console.

During '66, Chrysler introduced a specially modified 273 V-8 as a limited-production option for the Dart. At 275 horsepower, it was one of the few engines of the period to pass the magical one-horsepower-per-cubic-inch threshold.

Called the D package, after the D/Stock racing class for which it was tailored, its heart was a 273 that used a radical Camcraft camshaft, solid lifters, special 700cfm Holley 4160 four-barrel carburetor, and free-flow tubular exhaust headers by Doug of California. A full-breathing intake manifold that incorporated a special low-restriction air cleaner also were D items.

A four-speed manual transmission with Weber clutch, and a Sure-Grip 8¾-inch rear with a heavy duty 4.86:1 axle ratio also were part of the D package. A heavy-duty suspension and 6.94×14 tires rounded out the menu on cars that came to be called the D/Dart. Owners of ordinary Darts were advised that they could contact Chrysler's Parts Division to convert to D spec.

Dodge called the D/Dart a "regular production line" car, but cautioned that "Due to the expected use of these vehicles, no warranty coverage applies." Darts at this time also were campaigned in road racing and rallies. Weighing just 2946 pounds, the D/Dart was a contender in not only drag competition, but in a host of other events.

Priced well under $3000, a 273 Dart GT of this period was a great buy, and just might be worthy of a little cult of its own.

1965-66 Dodge Dart GT 273

Facts At a Glance

Engine type:	V-8/LA-Block	V-8/LA-Block*
Displacement (cid):	273	273
Horsepower @ rpm:	235 @ 5200	275 @ NA
Torque (lbs/ft) @ rpm:	280 @ 4000	300 @ 4500
Compression ratio:	10.5:1	10.5:1
Bore (in.):	3.625	3.625
Stroke (in.):	3.31	3.31
Valve lifters:	Hydraulic	Mechanical
Availability:	1965-66	1966

*High Performance

Magazine:	*Car and Driver* (Feb. 1965)
Times:	
0-60 mph (sec):	8.2
0-100 mph (sec):	27.5
¼-mile (sec):	16.9 @ 87 mph
Top speed (mph):	120
Axle ratio:	3.23:1
Engine type:	273 (235 hp)
Model year:	1965

Four-barrel carb option on 238 (left) cost $99.40, dressed up engine, and boosted horsepower from 180 to 235. Note generous size of chromed exhaust outlet (opposite, top). Dart GT on this page is a '65; Cragar mag wheels are classic aftermarket items.

1966
DODGE
CORONET HEMI

Introduced in 1965, the Coronet would carry much of
Dodge's performance banner through the balance of the
decade. A cleanly styled mid-size on a 117-inch wheelbase, its
most distinguishing design cue was a rear roof pillar on the
sedans and hardtops that was wider at the top than at the
bottom. MoPar enthusiasts warmed to the Coronet right away
when they noticed the options list included the 365-horsepower
426 street wedge. For those who searched a little deeper, there
was the mighty 426 Hemi V-8 on the list of extra-cost
powerplants. "Our new 426 Coronet ought to have its head
examined," one ad for the '65 Coronet slyly stated. What Dodge
didn't make clear was that this was the race Hemi, with a
volatile 12.5:1 compression ratio that made it ill-suited for
street use.

That changed in 1966—the year of the Street Hemi. *Hot
Rod* magazine called it "one of the fastest and most fantastic
sedans ever."

Unlike the race Hemi that snuck under some 1965 Coronet
500 hoods, this one had a more tolerable 10.25:1 compression,
achieved by the use of pistons with lower domes. A milder
camshaft was installed and a heat chamber was added to
manifolds so the engine would warm up properly. Basically a
detuned edition of the earlier race Hemi, this street version
carried cast-iron heads and exhaust manifolds—considerably
quieter than the tubular steel headers in race Hemis. Twin
progressive-action Carter AFB four-barrel carburetors sat atop
an aluminum dual-plane intake manifold. One carburetor gained
a choke, and an inline carburetor configuration replaced the
race-oriented ram induction. Otherwise, the two powerplants
were similar, built tough to handle a wallop of torque. They

looked tough, too, with black-crackle valve covers astride the
bright-Hemi-orange block.

Dodge rated the result at 425 horsepower at 5000 rpm and
490 pounds/feet of torque at 4000. Pure stock, it would blast the
3400-pound unibody Coronet to 60 mph in 5.3 seconds and
through the quarter in 13.8 seconds at 104 mph. The
acceleration, said *Motor Trend*, was "absolutely shattering."

Hemi-powered Coronets added an extra leaf to the rear
springs. Those equipped with Chrysler's A-833 four-speed
manual gearbox got a Dana rear end with the biggest ring gear
on the market at 9¾ inches. A variety of axle combinations was
available, but for street/strip use, the TorqueFlite automatic
with the 3.54:1 Dana Sure-Grip was a good compromise.

Part of Chrysler's motivation for bringing the Hemi to the
boulevards was to certify it once again for NASCAR racing by
building at least 500 streetable examples. The Hemi had
dominated NASCAR in 1964 and, deciding it wasn't sufficiently
a production engine, NASCAR banned it for the 1965 stock-car
season. (This prompted the unlikely sight of oval-king Richard
Petty campaigning a Hemi-powered drag racer in '65. Fittingly,
his Super Stock Barracuda was called "Outlawed.")

For '66, the engine was made available at Dodge in the
Coronet and in the new fastback Charger, which was basically a
rebodied Coronet. Many street racers opted for the
less-expensive Coronet, even though the Hemi added nearly
$1000 to the most modest Coronet's $2705 base price. Still, even
with optional bucket seats and console, a Coronet was less flashy
than the Charger. And without the scoops and stripes that
would become fashionable just a few years down the road, the
guy in the next lane wasn't likely to know what lurked beneath

Simple, strong lines of the '66 Coronet made an appropriate host for the debut of the Street Hemi. The 425-bhp 426-cid powerhouse added nearly $1000 to the car's price, but responded with quarter-miles in the high 13s at more than 103 mph. The Hemi Coronet may have been understated, but it was not timid.

1966 Dodge Coronet

Street Hemi

Facts At a Glance

Engine type:	V-8/RB-Block/Hemi
Displacement (cid):	426
Horsepower @ rpm:	425 @ 5000
Torque (lbs/ft) @ rpm:	490 @ 4000
Compression ratio:	10.25:1
Bore (in.):	4.25
Stroke (in.):	3.75
Valve lifters:	Mechanical
Availability:	Coronet, Charger

Magazine:	*Car and Driver*
Times:	
0-60 mph (sec):	5.3
0-100 mph (sec):	12.8
¼-mile (sec):	13.8 @ 104 mph
Top speed (mph):	130
Axle ratio:	3.54:1

Pillared coupe was the lightest body style and was the logical choice for a Hemi Coronet drag car (below, right). Coronet 500 hardtop (bottom) was more stylish. Street Hemi (below) used inline twin four-barrels, as did drag Hemis; NASCAR allowed only one four-barrel.

your Coronet's hood until you were long gone. About the only external clue was a discrete Hemi badge on the front fender.

Any Coronet could be ordered with a Hemi engine, though fewer than 1000 '66 models had it. That total includes just 27 convertibles, and amazingly, two four-door sedans.

"You know what a Hemi is," taunted one Hemi Coronet ad. "It's that wailing stocker that's about a car length ahead at the end of the quarter....If you insist on playing fair, forget it. But if you have just a trace of mean in your make-up...by all means, get one."

1966-67
DODGE
CHARGER HEMI

Though Plymouth was first on the domestic scene with a modern fastback in its 1964 Barracuda, beating Ford's '65 Mustang 2+2 to the market by about two weeks, it took Dodge until '66 to join the fastback fray. But when it finally jumped in, Dodge did it with muscle the other fastbacks could only dream about.

Based on the 117-inch-wheelbase Coronet, the Charger complemented its raked roofline with headlamps hidden in the grille and a single taillamp that stretched across the stern. Inside, bucket seats and space-age styling teamed with full instrumentation—including a 150-mph speedometer and 6000-rpm tachometer, a center console, fold-down rear seat, and chrome appointments for one of the most dazzling cabins of the period.

Under the hood, a 318-cubic-inch V-8 was standard; optional engines included 361- and 383-cubic-inch V-8s, and, Chrysler's new 426-cubic-inch Street Hemi.

"The Hemi was never in better shape," went one Dodge advertising tag line beneath a picture of the rampaging new Charger.

As in the '66 Coronet and Plymouth Belvedere/Satellite applications, Charger's Hemi was a detuned version of the 426 Hemi race motor. The compression ratio was lowered from 12.5:1 to 10.25:1, a milder camshaft was fitted, and a heat chamber was added to the manifolds so the engine would warm up properly. The street version carried exhaust manifolds of cast iron—considerably quieter than the tubular steel headers in race Hemis. Twin progressive-action Carter AFB four-barrel carburetors sat atop an aluminum dual-plane intake manifold.

Charger bowed as a mid-size fastback in '66, just in time to welcome MoPar's mighty 426 Hemi to the streets. King Kong added about $900 to the car's $3128 base price. Car pictured is a limited-edition factory NASCAR replica. Wheels are the same as those used on the race cars.

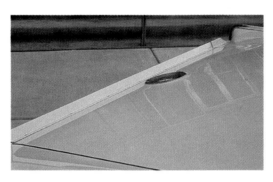

One carburetor gained a choke, and an inline carburetor configuration replaced the race-oriented ram induction. Dodge rated the Street Hemi at 425 horsepower at 5000 rpm and 490 pounds/feet of torque at 4000. Real-world estimates for a stock Hemi ran around 500 horses.

With a Hemi, the 1966 Charger could blister the quarter-mile in less than 14 seconds at speeds of over 100 miles per hour. Zero-to-sixty times were in the six-second range, depending on axle ratio. For a relative heavyweight riding a 117-inch wheelbase, those were impressive figures.

Hemi Chargers got stiffer springs and bigger (11-inch) brakes than usual, along with 0.92-inch torsion bars and a link-type sway bar. The Hemi Charger wore Blue Streak nylon tires, and disk brakes were optional. The TorqueFlite automatic was set for full-throttle shifts at 5500 rpm.

For 1967, the Hemi Charger was unchanged except for a shorter console that allowed five-passenger seating instead of the previous four spots. Dodge also modified the rear seat area to include a fold-down armrest for two-passenger use. Exterior refinements were minimal and horsepower ratings remained the same. Driveline choices still included a Chrysler four-speed or TorqueFlite, both with Sure-Grip.

Of the 37,344 Chargers built during 1966, just 468 were equipped with the Hemi. The total dropped to 118 for 1967, out of a total of 15,788 Chargers.

Moderately priced at $3128 for the base model in 1966, the Hemi added at least $877.55 to the total cost. But this was clearly not an engine for the masses. Chrysler was well aware of its intended use. Besides offering only a 12-month/12,000-mile warranty on the Hemi (other Charger engines were covered for five years/50,000 miles), the automaker stipulated that even this warranty was good only "provided the car is not subjected to any extreme operation [i.e. drag racing]...."

"The 426 Hemi is unquestionably the king of the of the muscle cars, both for its speed and for its defiance," wrote *Car and Driver*'s Patrick Bedard in a January 1990 retrospective of his all-time 10-best muscle cars. "The 'Street Hemi' was a class act," he wrote, "very smooth, quiet at idle, tractable in traffic....Chrysler did the job right...."

The '66 on this page is one of only 85 Chargers delivered with a NASCAR-replica package that included a special cowl-induction air cleaner and a rear spoiler. Engine itself is stock Street Hemi, though the replicas had Mallory ignition and an extra NASCAR-style motor mount. Interior also is stock and came with the folding rear seats. Charger was changed little for '67 (opposite), though the optional front console was shortened to allow seating for five. Street Hemi engine (opposite, bottom) is a vision of power in chrome and orange.

The Charger quickly moved into the professional drag ranks, with the altered-wheelbase "Color Me Gone" entry among the fastest and most popular. For '67, Hemi Chargers came standard with a small rear lip spoiler (below).

1966-67 Dodge Charger Hemi

Facts At a Glance

Engine type:	V-8/RB-Block/Hemi
Displacement (cid):	426
Horsepower @ rpm:	425 @ 5000
Torque (lbs/ft) @ rpm:	490 @ 4000
Compression ratio:	10.25:1
Bore (in.):	4.25
Stroke (in.):	3.75
Valve lifters:	Mechanical
Availability:	1966-67

Magazine:	Car & Driver (April 1966)	Car Life (February 1967)
Times:		
0-60 mph (sec):	5.3	6.4
0-100 mph (sec):	12.8	16.4
¼-mile (sec):	13.8 @ 104 mph	14.16 @ 96.15
Top speed (mph):	130	130
Axle ratio:	3.54:1	3.23:1
Engine type:	426 Hemi	426 Hemi
Model year:	1966 Satellite[1]	1967 Charger

[1]Test of equivalent Plymouth Satellite with same engine/transmission as Charger.

1967-70
DODGE
CORONET R/T 440

I n the heart of the 1960s one thing was certain: there was no substitute for *more* cubic-inches. Chrysler's philosophy was to keep those lightweight unibodies in play, give them plenty of displacement, horsepower, and torque—then stand back and watch 'em pick off the competition.

That philosophy was expressed to a T in the 1967 Coronet R/T. Its initials stood for Road and Track and indeed, performance fans found it one of the best double-duty Dodges ever.

Coronet styling changed little for '67, but as a new model, the R/T got its own cosmetic signature with a handsome grille that resembled the Charger's—except the R/T used four exposed headlights. R/T badges, a small non-functional hood scoop, and optional narrow side stripes were the only clues to the power that lurked within.

"Enter the Big Bore Hunter" was how one Dodge ad introduced the Coronet R/T. "It speaks softly, but carries a big kick," warned another. The reference was to the R/T's standard 440-cubic-inch Magnum V-8.

More flexible, less expensive, and easier to maintain than the King Kong 426 Street Hemi—which was a $907.50 Coronet R/T option—the 440 was an ideal street-racer's powerplant. It was rated at 375 horsepower at 4600 rpm, down some from the Hemi's rating of 425 at 5000, but the 440's torque, 480

Dodge debuted its high-performance R/T designation on the '67 Coronet. Standard was the untemperamental but energetic 375-bhp 440 Magnum. Pictured is one of only 628 '67 convertibles built. Non-functional hood scoop was an R/T standard; mag-type steel wheels were optional.

pounds/feet at 3200 rpm, was a match for the Hemi's 490 pounds/feet, especially since the larger engine reached its torque peak at 3200 rpm, 800 rpm sooner than the Hemi. Capable of quarter-miles in the low 14s right out of the box, the 440 R/T was fast enough to threaten the Hemi in most everything but all-out sanctioned drag racing. At $3199 for the two-door hardtop and $3438 for the convertible, the 440 R/T was, as *Super Stock* magazine called it, "one of the best all-around performance packages being offered."

The R/T's wedge-chambered 440 traced its roots to the tall-deck, B-Block 413-cubic-inch V-8 that had done well in NASCAR and NHRA starting in 1961. In 1963, Chrysler bored the 413 mill to 426 cubic-inches to create a legendary series of engines, the Ramcharger V-8s.

For 1966, Chrysler bored the 426 an extra .060-inch to arrive at 440 cubic inches. The 440 was at first reserved for the full-size Dodge, Chrysler, and Plymouth cars. Equipped with the venerable Carter AFB four-barrel carburetor it churned out 350 horsepower. For '67, Chrysler bestowed it upon the Coronet R/T and its corporate cousin, the Plymouth Belvedere GTX. A longer-duration cam profile, larger exhaust valves, Carter AFB carburetion with twin-snorkel intake, 10.1:1 compression, and free-breathing exhaust manifolds upped its horsepower to 375. Not a temperamental powerplant, the Magnum was reasonably well-behaved in traffic, excellent for the open road.

Standard was a four-speed manual transmission; the TorqueFlite automatic was optional. The standard 3.23:1 Sure-Grip differential served as an excellent street/strip axle ratio. Also standard were 11-inch front and 10.5-inch rear drum brakes; power front discs were optional. Chrysler equipped the R/T with a heavy-duty suspension that included stiffer sway and torsion bars, a front anti-sway bar, heavy-duty shocks and 7.75×14 Goodyear Red Streak tires.

The performance public responded well to the Coronet R/T, with 10,181 produced for '67; 628 were ragtops and 283 carried Hemi power.

1968

New sheet metal and a budget performance Coronet were the big news for Dodge's 1968 intermediates. The 117-inch wheelbase was retained, but the all-new body gained a flowing new roofline, a new grill, and rear fenders that swelled around the wheelwells then tapered to a create a modest spoiler effect at the tail. Dual "bumblebee" stripes to encircle the tail were optional.

Again offered as a hardtop or convertible, the R/T continued as Coronet's best-equipped high-performance choice. The seat design was new and optional color-keyed headrests could be fitted to both front and rear seats. R/T powertrains were unchanged, with the 440 Magnum standard and the 426 Hemi an option. Air conditioning was available only on the 440-engine car and only with the TorqueFlite automatic trans. Once again, Dodge didn't advertise the 440-cubic-inch displacement on the car's exterior; only the R/T badges and a new-for-'68 hood bulge were telltales.

The only other Coronet on which the hood bulge appeared was the new Super Bee. This was a stripper Coronet two-door sedan that came standard with the 335-horsepower 383-cubic-inch V-8 (the Hemi was optional) and was Dodge's answer to Plymouth's Road Runner.

1969-70

Coronet R/T returned for 1969 with a revised grille and taillamps, but few other alterations. The 440 Magnum continued as standard; the 426 Hemi was again optional. Power ratings were unchanged. A Ramcharger fresh-air induction package

Street Hemi (above) was the only optional R/T engine. It cost $907 and was ordered on just 283 '67 Coronet R/Ts. Mid-size Plymouths got a new skin for '68 (top and opposite) and the R/T was marketed under Dodge's new "Scat Pack" performance umbrella. A hood bulge was added, but instrumentation (opposite) was virtually standard-issue Coronet unless the extra-cost round-gauge Rally dash was ordered. A console was optional when a floor shift was specified.

A Ramcharger fresh-air induction package was a new option with the 440-cid R/T for '69 (above). It included functional hood scoops and was carried over for '70 (right), when the Coronet got a new grille and decorative side scoops. R/T was offered with or without bumblebee tail stripes at no extra cost. Among the options for '70 was a high-rise manifold and matching carb under the cleverly named "Bee-Liever" kit.

1967-70 Dodge Coronet R/T

Facts At a Glance

Engine type:	V-8/RB-Block/Wedge	V-8/RB Block/Hemi
Displacement:	440 Magnum	426
Horsepower @ rpm:	375 @ 4600	425 @ 5000
Torque (lbs/ft) @ rpm:	480 @ 3200	490 @ 4000
Compression ratio:	10.1:1*	10.25:1
Bore (in.):	4.32	4.25
Stroke (in.):	3.75	3.75
Valve lifters:	Hydraulic	Mechanical
Availability:	Standard	Optional

*9.70:1 (1970)

Magazine:	Muscle Car Review (Feb. 1967)	Hot Rod
Times:		
0-60 mph (sec):	6.0	6.3
0-100 mph (sec):	14.0	N/A
¼-mile (sec):	13.86 @ 98.36 mph	14.91 @ 93.16 mph
Top speed (mph):	N/A	N/A
Axle ratio:	N/A	3.23
Engine type:	440 Magnum	440 Magnum
Model year:	1968	1967

Magazine:	Car Life (April 1968)	Motor Trend (June 1967)
Times:		
0-60 mph (sec):	6.6	6.8
0-100 mph (sec):	15.0	N/A
¼-mile (sec):	14.69 @ 97.4 mph	15.0 @ 96 mph
Top speed (mph):	123	N/A
Axle ratio:	3.23:1	3.23
Engine type:	440 Magnum	426 Hemi
Model year:	1968 convertible	1967

was a new option with the 440 V-8, standard with the Hemi, and included a hood with two scoops. Chrysler refined axle ratios into performance packages, with components designed to work together in harmony. The Performance Axle Package put 3.55:1 gears in a Sure-Grip differential with the Hemi Suspension Handling Package and an upgraded cooling system. The Track-Pak offered a 3.54:1 Dana axle, Sure-Grip differential, dual-point distributor, heavy-duty four-speed with Hurst shifter, and heavy-duty cooling system. Other packages included 3.91:1 and 4.10:1 axle ratios. Fifteen-inch cast-aluminum road wheels were optional in place of the standard 14-inchers. R/T sales fell by more than 3000 in '69, though Super Bee production rocketed to 28,000.

New front-end styling was the big story for the '70 R/T. The grille was split in two, the rear flanks gained nonfunctional scoops, and the taillamps were revised.

Standard equipment included the 440 Magnum, again with 375 horsepower, but compression was down to 9.70:1. R/T sales fell to a paltry 2615, and, just 13 came equipped with the optional Hemi.

In retrospect, the 1967-70 Coronet R/Ts balanced luxury appointments with the brute performance of Chrysler's RB-Block 440 Wedge or 426 Hemi. A cut above the Super Bee, they offered more creature comforts for less than the cost of a Charger.

1968 DODGE CHARGER R/T 440

oPar fans still bristle at the thought of Steve McQueen and his Mustang getting the drop on the bad guys in their '68 Dodge Charger R/T with its 440 Magnum V-8. Still, it was a great duel while it lasted, those two hot Detroit numbers bounding over the San Francisco hills, engines howling, suspensions crashing. Producers of the film *Bullitt* knew what they were doing when they chose the '68 Charger R/T as McQueen's foil. The car had star quality.

Dodge, in fact, touted its fully restyled Charger as "piece of sculpture...from the long, low-hung, clean snout rolling inquisitively along the ground to the impertinent flip of the spoiler on the rear deck, you wouldn't change a line of it if you could." *Car and Driver* wasn't far behind in its praise: "...the new Charger is beautiful...all guts and purpose, and unlike the Mako Shark-inspired '68 Corvette, it's completely fresh and unexpected."

The brainchild of Dodge chief of design, Bill Brownlie, the Charger was one of the styling high points of the muscle-car era.

An unbroken blacked out grille with hidden headlamps introduced a body that bulged around the front wheels, then narrowed to a pinched waist before swelling again in the rear quarters and finally tapering to fold around a tail that kicked up into a tasteful little spoiler. Four round taillamps were recessed in a flat black escutcheon panel. A semi-fastback roof perched upon the body like the cockpit of a fighter plane, its keynote the handsome flying buttress C-pillars and recessed rear window. The look was clean, voluptuous. Chrome was kept to a minimum, giving strength to design details like the scallops in the hood, which were repeated in the doors, and the bright, racer-style quick-fill gas cap atop the left rear fender.

Compared to the space-age cabin of the previous-generation Charger, the '68 was quite plain, but functional. A matt-black dashboard featured six businesslike round gauges, including a 150-mph speedometer. Thumbwheels controlled the radio, and the doors even had map pockets. Dodge said the Charger had bucket seats, but the front ones really were more of a split bench

Dodge's resculpted second-generation Charger ranks among the best-styled muscle cars. In R/T trim, it was among the fastest, too. This is one of just 475 '68s equipped with the 425-bhp 426 Hemi engine. Black vinyl top and red-line tires were a boss look in '68.

separated by a console. Among the new options was cruise control fitted to the turn-signal lever and an AM radio/eight-track stereo tape player with three speakers mounted in the instrument panel.

Starting at $3014, the Charger came standard with the 318 V-8; two 383s were optional, a 290-horsepower two barrel and a fine 330-horse four barrel. But the hot performance ticket was the R/T. The R/T badge, for Road and Track, debuted on the '67 Coronet and was brought forward to the Charger as a package that upped the price to $3480. For that you got a 375-horsepower 440 Magnum V-8 with high-flow unsilenced air cleaner, high-upshift, competition-type TorqueFlite three-speed automatic transmission, dual exhausts with chrome tips, heavy duty brakes, R/T handling package, and F70×14 Red Streak or white sidewall tires. A bumblebee-style racing stripe encircling the tail was standard with the R/T, but could be deleted on the order form. Like the Coronet R/T, the Charger R/T could be ordered with the 426 Hemi engine. A four-speed manual transmission with Hurst Competition-Plus floor shift also was optional.

Most customers opted for the 440 Magnum and the automatic, which was no penalty on the street, seeing as how the 440 pounded out 480 pounds/feet of root-rousing torque at just 3200 rpm. Though very quick, the 440 had excellent road manners, able to idle in traffic and deliver smooth performance.

R/Ts got a sixth leaf installed in their right rear spring and Dodge said the heavy-duty suspension "treats an angled grade crossing in the rain with studied insolence." Charger R/T also offered a Sure-Grip differential and heavy-duty 11-inch brakes; front discs were optional.

The '68 Charger was a smash hit with the critics and the public. Production increased six-fold from '67, with 96,100 Chargers built. No breakdown on how many were R/Ts is available, but just 475 R/Ts were Hemi equipped and only 211 of those had the four-speed box. This was a high-water mark for Dodge style and performance in the late-'60s. Now, if those San Francisco bad guys had just taken a left, then maybe a quick right....

Charger R/T came standard with the fine 440 Magnum (left). It had 375 bhp and tons of torque for a fast tractable, package. Flying buttress rear roof (above) was a Charger trademark. Tires on this car are not original. Dick Landy campaigned a series of Pro Stock Dodges, including this '68 Hemi Charger (opposite).

Dual exhausts and bumblebee striping came standard with the Charger R/T, but stripes could be deleted for credit. Chrome gas cap atop left rear fender was race inspired. The R/T had an upgraded suspension and was the only Charger available with the King Kong Hemi engine.

1968 Dodge Charger R/T

Facts At a Glance

Engine type:	V-8/RB-Block/Wedge	V-8/RB-Block/Hemi
Displacement (cid):	440	426
Horsepower @ rpm:	375 @ 4600	425 @ 5000
Torque (lbs/ft) @ rpm:	480 @ 3200	490 @ 4000
Compression ratio:	10.1:1	10.25:1
Bore (in.):	4.32	4.25
Stroke (in.):	3.75	3.75
Valve lifters:	Hydraulic	Mechanical
Availability:	Standard	Optional

Magazine:	Muscle Car Review	Hot Rod (Oct. 1967)
Times:		
0-60 mph (sec):	6.0	7.2
0-100 mph (sec):	13.3	N/A
¼-mile (sec):	13.54 @ 101 mph	14.4 @ 98 mph
Top speed (mph):	N/A	N/A
Axle ratio:	3.91:1	N/A
Engine type:	426 Hemi	440 Magnum

1968-69
DODGE
DART GTS 340/383

Dart GTS came standard with MoPar's strong 340-cid four-barrel, but could be ordered with the 383. Bumblebee stripes and hood bulges were non-functional standards. GTS hardtops came with bucket seats. Console and TorqueFlite were optional; this one's column-mounted tachometer is an aftermarket item.

Dodge's compact Dart emerged from Chrysler's styling studios with a boxy new shape for 1967. The sportiest version, the GT, could be ordered with the 235-horsepower 273-cubic-inch four-barrel V-8. But because the new Dart was heavier than the 1965-66 model, the 273 was slower than it had been. Things changed in the new Dart's second season, and when Dodge corralled its performance cars under the "Scat Pack" banner the '68 Dart GTS was made a charter member.

Introduced as the top-line Dart, the GTS was the performance version of the Dart GT and came standard with MoPar's hot 340-cubic-inch four barrel V-8. The 340 retained the 273's short stroke, but bore grew by .64 inch, so it was capable of generating an advertised 275 horsepower at 5000 rpm. Unlike Chrysler's smaller V-8s, which used cast crankshafts, the 340 had a stronger forged crank. A Carter AFB carb, a dual-plane free-breathing manifold, and a hot cam with high lift and long duration added to its street-fighting credentials. Like other Chrysler compacts and larger intermediates, the Dart GTS offered either a standard four-speed or optional TorqueFlite transmission. Available axle ratios included 2.76:1, 3.23:1, 3.55:1, and 3.91:1. Sure-grip was optional. Camshaft profiles differed between the manual-shift and automatic-transmission versions, but both 340s were rated at the same horsepower.

Riding a 111-inch wheelbase and weighing in at 3305 pounds, the GTS was fortified with a Rallye suspension that included heavy-duty shocks, sway bar, heavy-duty rear springs, and E70×14 Red Streak wide-oval tires. Best of all, the lightweight 340 engine didn't render it excessively nose heavy, and *Car Life* said it was "more nimble than most U.S. automobiles." With the 3.23:1 axle, the GTS delivered "neck-snapping acceleration plus a top speed of 122 mph." The magazine also sampled a '68 Charger Hemi and a '68 Coronet R/T 440 Magnum convertible and concluded that neither "could equal the Dart's versatility, agility, road-ability, or even its acceleration." The 340 GTS, in fact, edged out the other two MoPars in a quarter-mile run, crossing the finish line in 14.68 seconds. *Car Life* insisted that the new 340 was "as cleverly engineered as the 426 Hemi, just not so fussy." It was a pretty good value, too, at $3163 for the two-door hardtop and $3383 for the convertible.

But, of course, there were those who couldn't be sated by 340 cubic inches. For them, Dodge offered the GTS with an optional 383 High Performance V-8. Along with the Carter AFB four-barrel, the 383 borrowed its cylinder heads, camshaft, and induction system from the 440 Magnum V-8. It was rated at 335 horsepower at 5200 rpm and 425 pounds/feet of torque at 3400. It shared the 340 GTS's transmissions and rear axles choices, and also enjoyed its suspension upgrades.

Dart drivers soon discovered, however, that both the 340 and 383 covered the quarter-mile in roughly the same time. Because the 383 weighed 89 pounds more than the 340—and it was all in front, which hurt traction off the line—the extra horsepower didn't deliver as much value as anticipated. MoPar followers suspect the 340's true horsepower was closer to 330 than to the announced 275, overshadowing the output from the ostensibly more powerful 383. Plus, the 340 car outhandled the 383 GTS.

For 1969, the GTS received a new grille, taillamps, trim, and side-marker lamps. The front seats got headrests. The GTS returned in hardtop and convertible form with the 340 standard and the 383 optional. But there was now another choice among quick Darts, and it turned out to be one of the performance bargains of the late '60s. It was called the Dart Swinger 340. It used the base Dart trim inside and out, but had the 340 four-barrel from the GTS, a Hurst-shifted four-speed manual transmission, and all the other GTS heavy-duty pieces. At 3097 pounds, the Swinger weighed only a few pounds less than the 340 GTS, but with a list price of $2836, it was nearly $400 cheaper. Though not widely publicized, about 600 1969 Dart GTSs were fitted with the 440 Magnum V-8. Most of the installations were performed by Grand Spaulding Dodge, a performance-oriented dealership in Chicago. In 1968, Dodge had also contracted with Hurst Performance to build a handful of Darts with 440 Magnum and 426 Hemi engines, but these were funneled directly to drag racers, with few, if any, showing up on the street.

Production numbers for 1968 are uncertain, but Dodge built 6700 GTS Darts in '69. Low-buck MoPar performance had already begun to focus on the new-for-'70 Plymouth Duster 340. Both the GT and the GTS 340/383 were dropped from the roster for '70, leaving the Swinger 340 as the sharpest Dart in the pack.

This is one of 48 '68 Darts equipped with the 440 Magnum. The engine was installed at Hurst-Campbell Inc. in Michigan and the cars were sold through Grand Spaulding Dodge in Chicago. These drag-prepared cars paved the way for construction of about 600 '69 440 Darts.

1968-69 Dart GTS 340/383

Facts At a Glance

Engine type:	V-8/LA-Block	V-8/B-Block
Displacement (cid):	340	383
Horsepower @ rpm:	275 @ 5000	335 @ 5200
Torque (lbs/ft) @ rpm:	340 @ 3200	425 @ 3400
Compression ratio:	10.5:1	10.0:1
Bore (in.):	4.04	4.25
Stroke (in.):	3.31	3.38
Valve lifters:	Hydraulic	Hydraulic
Availability:	1968-69 GTS	1968-69 GTS

Magazine:	*Car and Driver* (Sept. 1968)	*Car Life* (Sept. 1968)
Times:		
0-60 mph (sec):	6.0	6.3
0-100 mph (sec):	14.5	N/A
¼-mile (sec):	14.4 @ 99.0 mph	14.68 @ 96.2 mph
Top speed (mph):	114	122
Axle ratio:	3.91:1	3.23:1
Engine type:	340	340
Model year:	1968	1968

1969
DODGE
CHARGER 500 HEMI

Charger 500 was a limited-edition model built to qualify its racing sibling for NASCAR. Its grille is from the '68 Coronet and was mounted flush with the nose to improve aerodynamics over the Charger's standard recessed hidden-headlamp grille. Just 52 of the 392 Charger 500s produced had the optional Hemi engine.

Armed with its new aerodynamic body, the 1968 Charger was indeed faster than its predecessor on the big ovals of NASCAR. Unfortunately, the Ford Torino and Mercury Cyclone fastbacks were even faster—partly because NASCAR had forced power-robbing carburetor-restriction plates on Chrysler's Hemi engine.

Detroit's big three were convinced that winning races meant selling cars, so Chrysler wasn't about to sit back and let Ford trounce it before tens of thousands of people who packed the superspeedways each Sunday. Chrysler engineers spent hours in the windtunnel with a scale model of the '68 Charger. They discovered that its stylish recessed front grille and tunnel backlight were major areas of turbulence that slowed the Charger down in the full-throttle 180-190-mph slice and dice of NASCAR competition.

To correct the situation they took a '68 Charger and mounted the Coronet's grille flush with the leading edge of the Charger's nose. This plugged the grille cavity and made it the only Charger with exposed headlamps. Then they eliminated the backlight recess by mounting the rear window even with the top edges of the flying-buttress rear roof pillars. A fiberglass shelf was fitted behind the trailing edge of the rear window to span the distance to the front of the trunk lid. The trunk lid itself was shortened and a new interior backlight shelf was fabricated. The work was not done at the factory, but at Creative Industries, an aftermarket modifier in Michigan.

Dodge named the car the Charger 500. It was based on a '68 Charger, but was sold as a '69 model, used the '69-style

To rid the Charger of speed-eating turbulence, the standard car's recessed rear window was brought flush with the edges of the rear roof pillars (above). Standard power for the Charger 500 was the 440 Magnum V-8 (opposite). The interior was standard-issue Charger. This example has the optional TorqueFlite automatic. Its tires are not original equipment.

horizontal taillamps, and raced in NASCAR during the '69 season. The street version of the Charger 500 came standard with a 375-horsepower 440 Magnum V-8 and either a four-speed manual gearbox or TorqueFlite. As with the R/T Coronets and Chargers, an optional 426 Hemi was available. Front disc and 11-inch rear drum brakes were standard. The suspension was the same as used on the Hemi Chargers. The interior was unaltered from the standard Charger, but a broad racing stripe encircled the tail, broken on the rear fender by a "500" badge.

Normally, NASCAR required that 500 examples of a production car be built before its racing counterpart could qualify for competition. The sanctioning body apparently relaxed this rule for Dodge—some historians say NASCAR didn't want the Fords to make a mockery of the circuit—and only 392 Charger 500s were produced for sale to the public. Just 52 were built with the Hemi option, which added $673 to the car's $3591 base price.

Dodge teased its performance audience by warning ominously in a sales brochure that the Charger 500 would be offered "specifically for the high-performance race track. It is available only to qualified performance participants and is being built to special order on a limited production basis."

Though obviously rare on the street, the Charger 500 had an impact beyond its production numbers. *Car Life* magazine voted the Hemi Charger 500 it supercar of the year. With four-speed gearbox and dragstrip axle, it was the quickest production model *Car Life* had ever tested. The 4100-pound coupe screamed through the quarter-mile in just 13.68 seconds at 104.8 mph. The magazine said the big Hemi idled smoothly and never stumbled, yet "kept the testers pinned to their seatbacks all the way to redline." It also said the engine seemed less temperamental than its predecessors. *Hot Rod* branded the Charger 500 a "Showroom Racer," adding that it was "surprisingly docile on the street circuit."

It was a slightly different story in NASCAR. The Charger 500 was faster than the standard-body Charger. But Ford answered with the Torino Talladega and Mercury Cyclone Spoiler, limited-edition aero-styled intermediates that enabled the blue oval to maintain its NASCAR edge.

A 1970 version of the 500 was produced, but was a pale shadow of the NASCAR original, lacking the aero shape and 440 engine. The Charger 500 is fondly remembered today as a stepping stone to its true successor and the wildest Charger ever, the Daytona.

1969 Dodge Charger 500

Facts At a Glance

Engine type:	V-8/RB-Block/Wedge	V-8/RB-Block/Hemi
Displacement:	440	426
Horsepower @ rpm:	375 @ 4600	425 @ 5000
Torque (lbs/ft) @ rpm:	480 @ 3200	490 @ 4000
Compression ratio:	10.1:1	10.25:1
Bore (in.):	4.32	4.25
Stroke (in.):	3.75	3.75
Valve lifters:	Hydraulic	Mechanical
Availability:	Standard	Optional

Magazine:	*Car Life* (April 1969)	*Car Life* (April 1969)
Times:		
0-60 mph (sec):	5.7	5.7
0-100 mph (sec):	12.3	12.8
¼-mile (sec):	13.68 @ 104.8 mph	13.92 @ 104.5 mph
Top speed (mph):	134	136
Axle ratio:	3.55:1	3.23:1
Engine type:	426 Hemi	426 Hemi

Note: *Hot Rod* (February 1969) testing a Hemi Charger 500 achieved quarter-mile times of 13.48 seconds (109 mph) with four-speed and 4.10:1 axle, and 13.80 seconds (105.01 mph) with automatic and 3.23:1.

1969 DODGE SUPER BEE 440 SIX PACK

Introduced during the 1968 model year as a Coronet offshoot, the Super Bee was Dodge's response to Plymouth's popular Road Runner. In that vein, the Bee was a bare-bones performance car with a 335-horsepower 383-cubic-inch V-8 and a $3037 price tag. "It's the super car for the guy who doesn't want to shy away from GTOs...only their high prices," was how Dodge promoted the Super Bee.

Available initally as a two-door coupe only, the Super Bee was modestly appointed, but loaded with standard performance items such as a four-speed manual transmission with Hurst Competition-Plus floor shift, heavy duty suspension, sway bar and shocks, and the gauge-packed instrument panel from the Charger. Its four-barrel 383 borrowed its cylinder heads, camshaft, and induction system from the 440 Magnum V-8. The 426 Hemi was the only engine option, but at nearly $1000, it ran counter to the Bee's budget appeal.

That the Super Bee was low-priced didn't mean it wasn't high-profile, however. Bumblebee racing stripes ran across the rear deck and down the rear fenders, where a big, fat "Super Bee" emblem hovered. The grille and tail-light panel were finished in black matte, and the hood had a power bulge.

The Super Bee changed little for '69, though a $3138 hardtop model was now offered and some additional bee insignia

adorned the body. The 383 returned and the Hemi was again an option. Then, midway through the 1969 model year, Dodge unleashed a Super Bee that sent advertising copywriters into overtime and muscle fans into the showrooms.

Dodge dropped its 440-cubic-inch Magnum V-8 into the Super Bee's engine bay, bolted on an Edelbrock Hi-Riser intake manifold and topped it off with three Holley two-barrel carburetors. *Voilà!* The Super Bee Six Pack.

Fortified with Hemi valve springs, a low-taper camshaft with flat-face tappets, dual-point distributor, chrome-flashed valve stems, and tough magnafluxed connecting rods, the 440 Six Pack pumped out 390 horsepower at 4700 rpm and 490 pounds/feet of torque at 3200 rpm. The mill was covered by a matte-black removable fiberglass hood pinned down NASCAR style and sporting what probably was the biggest hood scoop ever to gulp air for a production engine. Just for good measure, "SIX PACK" was printed in bright orange block letters on either side of the wholly functional scoop.

A Hurst shifter controlled the manual four-speed gearbox, which had a special 2.65:1 first gear. Standard was a Dana 9¾-inch Sure-Grip axle with 4.10:1 gears; the TorqueFlite three-speed automatic was an option. Goodyear Red Streak G70×15 tires rode black six-inch wheels with chrome lug

Dodge's response to Plymouth's Road Runner was the Coronet Super Bee. This '69 has the riotous 440 Six Pack, a 390-bhp big block topped with three Holley two-barrel carbs. Scoop on the removable black fiberglass hood (bottom) mated with the giant air cleaner (below).

nuts—no hubcaps on the Six Pack. Bucket seats were available in place of the standard bench, and dealers might install a column-mounted tachometer, but air conditioning, disc brakes, and cruise control were scratched from the options list. Hemi Orange and three other "high impact" body colors were available.

But it was the Six Pack that caused the biggest stir. During normal driving, the center Holley proved adequate. Punching the accelerator opened the two outboard carburetors. Activated by vacuum, they filled the 440's induction system with an astounding 1375cfm charge.

Motorcade magazine took one to the Orange County International Raceway for a test published in its July 1969 issue. Equipped with the TorqueFlite and weighing in at 3790 pounds, the Six Pack Super Bee sprinted from 0-60 mph in 6.6 seconds and turned the quarter in 13.65 seconds at 105.14 mph.

Such performance prompted a flood of hype that played upon the six-pack imagery and made liberal use of the lingo of the day. Listen to this factory notice to dealers: "Here's a small deposit, big-return Six Pack that your hot-eyed, Drag-is-my-bag buffs will know they've been thirsting for the minute they hang their lamps on its wicked lines!" Of course, the press got into the act. *Car and Driver* took one of the new Super Bees to the deep South where it was "road tested" through the hollows and over the hills by alleged bootleg liquor runners. The article was titled "A Six-Pack Full of Shine."

The triple-deuce option added $463 to the price of the base Super Bee and 1907 of the high-performance Coronets were built with it. Production in '69 also included 259 Hemi Super Bees out of a total of 27,800 Super Bees built. The 440 Six Pack Super Bee continued for '70, but with the standard Super Bee's steel hood.

Chrysler's triple-quad setup is a grand example of how wild street performance had gotten by that watershed year of 1969. Several other pentastar products would use the arrangement in this period, including the Road Runner, Challenger, and Barracuda. But nowhere was its outrageous spirit more appropriately expressed than in the Super Bee 440 Six Pack.

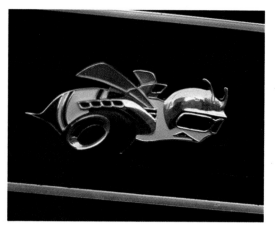

Bee logos swarmed over Dodge's budget-muscle buzz bomb. Super Bee came with a fat stripe on its tail and chrome lug nuts on bare wheels. Bucket seats, center console, and TorqueFlite with floor shift were optional (top); air conditioning wasn't allowed with the Six Pack. The car was offered from '68-70 and could break 14 seconds in the quarter with the 440 or Hemi.

1969 Dodge Super Bee 440

Six Pack

Facts At a Glance

Engine type:	V-8/B-Block/Wedge	V-8/RB-Block/Wedge
Displacement (cid):	383	440 (3x2v)
Horsepower @ rpm:	335 @ 5200	390 @ 4700
Torque (lbs/ft) @ rpm:	425 @ 3400	490 @ 3600
Compression ratio:	10.0:1	10.1:1
Bore (in.):	4.25	4.32
Stroke (in.):	3.38	3.75
Valve lifters:	Hydraulic	Hydraulic
Availability:	Standard	Optional

Magazine:	*Car Life*
Times:	
0-60 mph (sec):	6.3
0-100 mph (sec):	12.5
¼-mile (sec):	13.8 @ 104.2 mph
Top speed (mph):	117
Axle ratio:	4.10:1
Engine type:	440 Six-Pack

Magazine:	*Car and Driver* (Jan. 1969)
Times:	
0-60 mph (sec):	5.6
0-100 mph (sec):	14.1
¼-mile (sec):	14.04 @ 99.55 mph
Top speed (mph):	129 (est)
Axle ratio:	3.55:1
Engine type:	383

1969 DODGE CHARGER DAYTONA

"You may not like it, but you'll never forget it," *Road Test* magazine decreed.

"Nobody, but nobody, walks by without breaking his neck to take a second look," race driver Bobby Isaacs was quoted as saying.

Motor Trend declared it "the fastest collector's item ever built."

They all were talking about the most unrestrained muscle car of an era that brimmed with unbridled muscle cars: the 1969 Dodge Charger Daytona.

This was Chrysler's full-megaton assault on the NASCAR superspeedways. This was the car that took aerodynamics off the high-speed ovals and slammed it down on Main Street America. What made the Charger Daytona the car you couldn't forget, the car you'd break your neck to see, the car you'd break the bank to collect, was its bullet nose and its outrageous high-rise tail wing. Of course, the standard 440-cubic-inch Magnum V-8 or optional 426 Hemi beneath the hood was of interest, as was the flush rear window and huge reverse fender scoops. But it was the snout and the spoiler that made this car really special.

The 1969½ Dodge Charger Daytona was born of Chrysler's desire to regain NASCAR domination. Ford had taken over the stock-car throne with its aero Torino Talladegas and Mercury Cyclone Spoiler IIs. Adding insult to injury, king Richard Petty had abandoned Plymouth in 1969 to race a Ford. Chrysler fought back with the Charger 500, a modified Charger that used a flush grille and flush rear window to correct some of the standard Charger's aero deficiencies. But Ford still won.

Chrysler engineers went back to the wind tunnel in search of a still more slippery shape. Tests showed that at 70 mph, the movement of air created about 180 pounds of front end lift on the standard Charger—enough to elevate the whole nose of the car about ½ inch. To negate this effect and to create downforce, the engineers grafted onto the front of the Charger 500 an 18-inch wedge-shaped steel nose cone and a small lip spoiler. On

Built to pierce the wind and hug the pavement on stock-car superspeedways, the Charger Daytona was among Detroit's wildest creations. Bobby Isaacs (opposite, middle) rode his pure-race version to the '69 NASCAR driving title. Street models (other photos) were mechanically tamer, but looked just as outragous. Only 503 were built. This is one of just 70 equipped with the optional 426 Hemi engine.

the tail, they mounted a huge aluminum horizontal stabilizer that towered some 33 inches over the rear fenders. They found that the proboscis worked to keep air from lifting the front at high speeds and together with the rear spoiler, helped the car cut through the wind with reduced drag and less aerodynamic float.

What got this wondrous package to the street was NASCAR's requirement that a manufacturer build at least 500 versions for pubic sale before the competition counterpart was allowed to race. Chrysler had terminated Charger 500 production at 392 units, just in time to get started on the Daytona. In June 1969, the required number of Charger R/Ts were sent to a Michigan aftermarket modifier, Creative Industries, to be converted into winged Daytonas. Production was a rush job over the summer and was aimed at building 500 Daytonas before the end of the 1969 model year to satisfy NASCAR. The cars were enroute to dealers by early September.

A week later, on September 14, the Charger Daytona made its NASCAR debut at the Talladega 500 in Alabama. Charlie Glotzbach hit 199.466 mph to win the pole, set a new qualifying record, and earned for the Daytona title of the world's fastest stock car. It won races, but too few to carry Chrysler back to the NASCAR manufacturer's title and Ford won it again in '69. But the Charger Daytona proved itself a champion in 1970. Along with its sister ship, the Plymouth Road Runner Superbird, it helped Chrysler recapture the NASCAR manufacturer's title and carried Isaacs to the driver's championship.

Racing Daytonas carried the 426 Hemi. Standard fare for street versions was the 375-horsepower 440 Magnum; the 425-horsepower Hemi was an option. Two 440 Charger Daytonas are known to have been fitted with a three two-barrel-carb setup at the dealership. This was pretty much Charger R/T equipment, with the stock Hemi suspension. A manual four-speed transmission was standard and TorqueFlite automatic optional. Standard final-drive ratio was 3.55:1. On the pavement were F70×14 tires.

Externally, the street Daytona resembled the race version quite closely, with some minor differences. The road cars had fiberglass doors for the pop-up headlamps in their nose, and

Steel nose cone, skyscraper rear wing, and flush backlight were main Charger Daytona cues. Offered for '69 1/2 only, it was more expensive, heavier, and slower than standard Charger with same engine. But what presence!

1969 Dodge Charger Daytona

Facts At a Glance

Engine type:	V-8/RB-Block/Wedge	V-8/RB-Block/Hemi
Displacement:	440 (Magnum)	426
Horsepower @ rpm:	375 @ 4600	425 @ 5000
Torque (lbs/ft) @ rpm:	480 @ 3200	490 @ 4000
Compression ratio:	10.1:1	10.25:1
Bore (in.):	4.32	4.25
Stroke (in.):	3.75	3.75
Valve lifters:	Hydraulic	Mechanical
Availability:	Standard	Optional

Magazine:	Car and Driver (Dec. 1969)	Road Test (Dec. 1969)
Times:		
0-60 mph (sec):	6.0	N/A
0-100 mph (sec):	13.8	N/A
¼-mile (sec):	13.9 @ 101 mph	14.48 @ 96.15 mph
Top speed (mph):	140	N/A
Axle ratio:	3.54:1	N/A
Engine type:	426 Hemi	440 Magnum

though they weren't lowered on their suspension, as were the racing Daytonas, the street cars still carried the rear-facing fender scoops that the competition versions needed for tire clearance and engine-air extraction. The fender scoops on the street car were open, just like the race car's were, however, and were covered with a screen. The race car's rear wing was adjustable for rake, and so was the street version's. Just so you wouldn't mistake this conveyance for anything else, the street cars had a racing stripe that ran up and over the rear wing. The word Daytona was printed in block letters on their rear fenders. Overall length was 226.5 inches, some 20 inches longer than a conventional Charger, and at 3710 pounds, the Daytona was more than 100 pounds heavier than a standard R/T.

Chrysler offered the Charger Daytona during the latter part of the 1969 model year only, though of course, some raced during the 1970 NASCAR season. Chrysler wanted to sell these cars and priced them at $3993, just $300 to $350 over the cost of a Charger R/T with comparable mechanical equipment. Of the approximately 503 Daytonas built, 70 were equipped with the 426 Hemi, which was a $648 option. That was a lot of machine for the money and few vehicles of any sort were likely to draw as much attention. And, as Racer Isaacs pointed out in a Chrysler ad, "You can put down your non-performance friends by pointing out that you have carpeting, disappearing headlights, and a car that you'll never lose in a crowded parking lot."

1970 DODGE CHALLENGER T/A

T/A stood for Trans Am, the race series in which Dodge ran its new Challenger. "340 Six Pak" signified a 340-cid V-8 with three two-barrel carbs. The street version looked much like the competition car, though its engine was larger. Dodge called this color Sublime.

Few racing series so quickly seized fan interest as did the Sports Car Club of America's Trans American Sedan Championship. From its birth in 1966 through 1970, this was the proving ground for America's hottest new automotive segment, the pony car. Chrysler at first was represented by various Valiants and Darts, but they were no match in performance or romance for the Mustangs, Cougars, Camaros, and Javelins that made the series so captivating. So when finally MoPar got legitimate pony cars of its own in 1970, it was a great chance to go Trans Am racing properly. Dodge would campaign the Challenger, Plymouth the Barracuda.

The SCCA required an automaker to build at least 2500 streetable examples of its Trans Am entry in order qualify it for competition. Dodge turned to its own designer, Pete Hutchinson, to come up with the necessary modifications, and to an outside contractor, Autodynamics, to build the car.

Chrysler had watched Ford get an image boost with the Boss 302 Mustang, the street version of its Trans Am racer. Likewise, Chevy had turned its Trans Am offshoot, the Z-28 Camaro, into a respected street machine. Even AMC was getting publicity mileage for its Javelin and AMX via the Trans Am wars. The marketing opportunity was not lost on MoPar, and it took its chance and ran with it. The resulting Challenger T/A was about as high profile as any pony car of the era. Dodge simply put a racing look-alike on the street and even went it one-wilder under the hood.

The street Challenger T/A ran with Chrysler's rev-happy 340-cubic-inch V-8. In its high state of tune, the 305-cubic-inch competition version churned out an estimated 440 horsepower via a single four-barrel carburetor. The street version was rated at 290 horsepower, and while most estimates put its true output closer to 350, its real distinction was its carburetion: three two-barrels. The trio of Holleys sat atop a Chrysler-designed Edelbrock aluminum intake manifold. They were fed

1970 Dodge Challenger T/A

Facts At a Glance

Engine type:	V-8/A-Block/Wedge
Displacement (cid):	340
Horsepower @ rpm:	290 @ 5000
Torque (lbs/ft) @ rpm:	340 @ 3200
Compression ratio:	10.5:1
Bore (in.):	4.04
Stroke (in.):	3.31
Valve lifters:	Hydraulic
Availability:	Challenger T/A and AAR 'Cuda

Magazine:	*Muscle Car Review*
Times:	
0-60 mph (sec):	5.8
0-100 mph (sec):	14.4
¼-mile (sec):	14.3 @ 99 mph
Top speed:	125-plus (est)
Axle ratio:	3.55:1

air via a suitcase-sized scoop molded into a pinned-down, lift-off, matte-black fiberglass hood that was standard on all T/As.

With reinforced main bearing webs, revised pushrods, heavy-duty connecting rods, special cylinder head bolts and adjustable rocker arms, the 340 Six Pack was a potent performance package. Each engine block carried a cast-in serial number that included the "TA" designation. Such foresight for easy verification would make it far more difficult to fabricate one of these limited-production pieces later on.

The Challenger's 340 Six Pack purged spent exhaust gases through a low-restriction dual exhaust system with pipes that exited just in front of the rear wheelwells. Transmission choices were a four-speed manual or the TorqueFlite three-speed automatic. A 3.55:1 rear axle with an 8¾-inch ring gear was standard; a Sure-Grip differential and 3.90:1 axle were available.

The special Rallye Suspension included a rear sway bar, an extra-large front sway bar, heavy-duty shocks and increased camber of the rear springs. The T/A was one of the first production cars equipped with different tires sizes front and rear. It was shod with E60×15 Goodyear Polyglas GTs up front and G60×15 Goodyear Polyglas GTs in back. Power front disc brakes with special semi-metallic pads were standard; the rear brakes were 10-inch drums. Manual steering in a 24:1 ratio was standard, but quicker steering with power assist was an option.

Inside, the Challenger T/A was strictly E-Body MoPar, with pod-style instrumentation, high-back bucket seats, and molded door panels.

With the modified rear-spring camber, required to allow clearance for the tires as well as the side exhausts, the tail of the Challenger T/A was raised about two inches, giving the car a raked, street-racer stance. The custom appearance was enhanced by that wild hood, the chrome-tipped exhausts jutting from beneath the fenders, and a black, "duck-tail" spoiler on the trunk lid. A side stripe with "T/A" in block letters on the cowl and a bright, racer-style fuel cap were icing on the cake.

The Challenger T/A was a quick and well-balanced street machine with rarity and an added dose of the outrageous to bolster its appeal. Dodge zeroed in on its custom appearance in its promotional material. "Challenger T/A," said one ad. "Just the way you'd do it yourself. If you had the time. And the money. Yeah, the money. Frankly, it would probably cost you more to do it yourself. So why bother with do-it-yourself dreams? Check out this bargain for the man who'd rather be moving than building."

The Barracuda version of this car was called the AAR 'Cuda, after Dan Gurney's All American Racers, the team that helped build and race it. The AAR 'Cuda mirrored the Challenger T/A in equipment and race-bred appearance modifications. Neither one, however, was a match for the more established competition, and Ford's Mustang snared the Trans Am title from the Z-28 for 1970. Ford pulled its factory support from Trans Am racing shortly thereafter, and the other automakers followed suit. The series sputtered to a climax without either the Challenger T/A or AAR 'Cuda capturing a championship. Only 2539 Challenger T/As were built before the end of the 1970 model year, but their memory lingers.

T/A body was raked to clear the side exhaust outlets and the rear tires, which were wider than the fronts. Scoop on fiberglass hood fed the 290-bhp 340-cid V-8 (opposite, bottom). Race engine was destroked to 305 cid and used a single four-barrel. Sam Posey drove the race car (opposite, middle), but didn't threaten more established rivals. Note that Posey's racer has a vinyl top! T/A was offered for '70 only.

1970-71 DODGE CHALLENGER R/T

It took Chrysler six years to develop a true pony car and by the time the 1970 Dodge Challenger was introduced, it was difficult to do anything really new with the formula. But Dodge was successful in setting its Challenger apart by offering an astonishing variety of engine choices—nine in all—from a docile slant six to the earth-shaking King Kong Hemi.

Available as a convertible or two-door hardtop, the unibody Challenger was developed along with its Plymouth Barracuda sister ship, though Dodge used a 110-inch wheelbase, two-inches longer than the Barracuda's. This gave the Challenger slightly more rear-seat legroom, but as with any true pony car, there really wasn't much of a back seat. No, this one was faithful to the long-hood, short-deck ethic that had come to define the breed.

Dodge conceived the Challenger as a beefier car than the Barracuda and gave it a more sharply defined body. The rooflines were similar, but the heavier Challenger achieved a more substantial—if busier—look through the use of quad headlamps, a fuller rear fascia, and a character line along each bodyside. The Challenger name itself came from chief Dodge stylist Bill Brownlie, the car's designer, who wanted a nameplate closely tied to that of the popular Charger.

Beyond the 145-horsepower six, the base Challenger and luxury SE model could be ordered with a 230-horsepower 318 V-8, a 275-horsepower four-barrel 340 V-8, or a 383 V-8 with 290 or 330 horsepower. MoPar's fine 340 four-barrel, which brought E60×15 tires as standard, probably created the most balanced performance Challenger. But most muscle buffs were drawn to the R/T label, under which Dodge had corralled an integrated system of go-fast goodies.

Standard Challenger R/T power came from the 335-horse 383-cubic-inch four-barrel V-8. Right on up the options ladder was the 375-horsepower 440 Magnum, the 390-horsepower 440 Six Pack, and the 425-horse 426 Hemi, which had adopted hydraulic lifters for '70. Standard with the 383 was a three-speed manual transmission; a four-speed and the TorqueFlite automatic were optional. The torque-packed 440 engines and the Hemi came standard with the automatic. The four-speed manual was optional with the 440 and Hemi, and ordering it also got you a Hurst shifter and an extra-heavy-duty Dana 60 axle with a 9¾-inch ring gear. All of the four-speeds this year were fitted with a woodgrain pistol-grip shift handle.

Chrysler offered several performance packages designed to enhance any engine's output. If you checked off "A36" on the order sheet, for instance, Dodge shipped the Performance Axle Package that included 3.55:1 Sure-Grip, heavy-duty cooling system, and extra heavy-duty suspension. "A34" brought the Super Track Pak package ($235.65) with the four-speed and 4.10:1 Dana axle and Sure-Grip, dual-point distributor, power front disc brakes, heavy-duty cooling, and heavy-duty suspension. Three other axle packages met a variety of driving conditions.

R/Ts came with a performance hood with dual scoops that were open, but didn't feed directly to the air cleaner. A $97.30 option was the shaker hood scoop, which mounted directly to the air cleaner and stuck up through an opening in the center of the hood. Other options ranged from front and rear spoilers to back-window louvers to a flip-open gas cap. Standard Rallye wheels held F70×14 Goodyear Polyglas GT tires; G60×15s on seven-inch wheels were an option. Many buyers ordered the optional vinyl roof and all could choose between a bumblebee stripe on the tail or a longitudinal tape stripe.

Inside, Chrysler gave the Challenger R/T high-back bucket seats, a console, and full instrumentation. Among the color choices were seven high-impact hues including Hemi Orange, Plum Crazy, and for a short time in the spring, Panther Pink. R/T hardtops also could be ordered in SE guise. Short for Special Edition, this added a vinyl roof with a smaller "formal" backlight, plus leather seat facings, and an overhead console, among other items.

Despite good looks, the Challenger wasn't universally well received. *Car and Driver* rapped Chrysler's knuckles this way: "It's bad enough to be late into the marketplace, but to be late with the wrong kind of car can be fatal." The magazine insisted that "Chrysler doesn't do anything first. Instead, it carefully watches what everyone else in Detroit is doing, and when it sees an area of abnormal market activity, it leaps exactly onto that spot. Because it always leaps late—which is inevitable if it doesn't begin to prepare its entry into the market until someone else already has one—it tries to make up for being late by jumping onto said spot harder than everybody else."

Other critics slammed the poor handling of the big-block Challengers, and most people remarked about a lack of headroom and spotty quality control that resulted in ill-fitting interior panels.

But the R/T was fast. *Road Test* tried one with the Hemi. The engine and attendant heavy-duty hardware added a steep $1227.50 to the $3226 base price. "In return," said the magazine, "you get power that can rattle dishes in the kitchen when you start it up in the driveway." The test car turned the quarter in 14 seconds flat at 104 mph—and got just 6.5 mpg in city driving. *Car and Driver*'s Hemi automatic achieved a 0-60 time of 5.8 seconds.

With Mustang already entrenched and a soon-to-be-classic Firebird and Camaro poised for a 1970½ introduction, Challenger still sold well for '70, and nearly 20,000 of the 83,000

Challenger for '71 sported new graphics (above). Lethal 425-bhp Hemi is shown here without the shaker scoop. "Race-Hemi orange" '70 R/T Six Pack sans vinyl roof (opposite, top) made for a clean machine. Dick Landy's '70 Hemi Challenger was a pro-stock star (opposite, bottom).

built were R/Ts. Only 1070 of the R/Ts were convertibles. Hemis were installed in 356 '70 R/Ts and in only nine convertibles.

The 1971 Challenger R/T was largely a carryover but wore a new recessed split-grille with blacked-out lower section and had new stripes and taillamps. The R/T SE and R/T convertible were dropped. Gone was the 440 Magnum, but the 385-horse 440 Six-Pack remained. The 383 High Performance V-8 was standard, reduced to 300 horsepower. The compression ratio dropped from 9.5:1 to 8.5:1 to accept unleaded fuel.

Challenger sales plummeted 60 percent in '71 and just 4630 Challenger R/Ts rolled off the assembly line; only 71 were Hemi-equipped. The popular new Camaro and Firebird had hurt demand for the MoPar ponies, but so had rising insurance rates and a general cooling of the performance market. By '73, the 340 was the most powerful engine offered with the car and even it died in '74, the last year of Challenger production when just 6063 were built in a shortened model year. Despite what the critics said, Challenger was the right car for 1970. Unfortunately, its time was running out even then.

1970-71 Dodge Challenger R/T

Facts At a Glance

Engine type:	V-8/B-Block/Wedge	V-8/RB-Block/Wedge
Displacement (cid):	383	440 (4v)
Horsepower @ rpm:	335 @ 5200[1]	375 @ 4600
Torque (lbs/ft) @ rpm:	425/410 @ 3400	480 @ 3200
Compression ratio:	9.5:1/8.5:1	9.7:1
Bore (in.):	4.25	4.32
Stroke (in.):	3.38	3.75
Valve lifters:	Hydraulic	Hydraulic
Availability:	1970-71	1970

[1]300 @ 4800 (1971)

Engine type:	V-8/RB-Block/Hemi	V-8/RB-Block/Wedge
Displacement (cid):	426	440 (3x2v)
Horsepower @ rpm:	425 @ 5000	390 @ 4700[1]
Torque (lbs/ft) @ rpm:	490 @ 4000	490 @ 3200
Compression ratio:	10.25:1	10.5:1
Bore (in.):	4.25	4.32
Stroke (in.):	3.75	3.75
Valve lifters:	Hydraulic	Hydraulic
Availability:	1970-71	1970-71

[1]385 @ 4700 (1971)

Magazine:	Car Craft (Nov. 1969)	Motor Trend
Times:		
0-60 mph (sec):	6.0	7.8
0-100 mph (sec):	13.0	N/A
¼-mile (sec):	13.62 @ 104 mph	15.7 @ 90 mph
Top speed (mph):	130	N/A
Axle ratio:	3.23:1	3.23:1
Engine type:	440 Six-Pack	383

1971 DODGE CHARGER HEMI

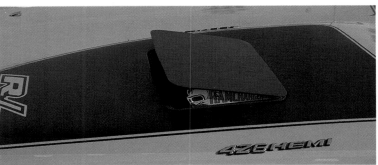

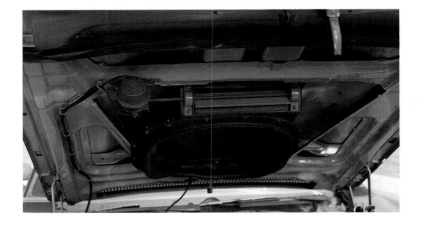

Few would have imagined such a fate. American automakers had been pushing power and big engines for nearly two decades. Now, by 1971, Detroit was *reducing* the power.

Chrysler was holding out, though. One of the last items anyone would have expected on the 1971 Dodge Charger option sheet was the 426 Hemi V-8, but there it was. It wasn't intensely promoted, to be sure, but it was there.

Granted, not many folks ticked the Hemi option: just 85 Chargers were built with it in '71. But if not many Hemis were delivered, that didn't mean the Hemi didn't still deliver. As had been the case since its 1964 debut as a race engine, the Hemi was rated at 425 horsepower and had 490 pounds/feet of available torque. MoPar kept the compression high, too, at 10.2:1.

The legendary engine would fade from the lineup after this year, but the Charger that was its last home was a radically new Chrysler intermediate with an elongated "Coke bottle" shape and a semi-fastback roofline. Wheelbase for once was down, to 115, two inches shorter than the 1970 version. If the Hemi was evidence that Chrysler was holding onto the performance era, the slant-six cylinder engine that came standard in the base '71 Charger was a sure sign that MoPar had glimpsed the end of the muscle age. The base V-8 engine was the 318.

Above the $2707 base Charger was the $3223 500, and $3357 luxury SE. The Super Bee name came to the Charger line for '71 as a basic performance-oriented model with a 275-horsepower 383-cubic-inch V-8 and Rallye Suspension standard. It listed for $3271. A 300-horsepower 383 was the next rung up the V-8 ladder, while the R/T returned with the 370-horsepower 440 Magnum standard. It listed for $3777. The Hemi was available on the R/T and Charger Super Bee models.

All R/Ts received a blackout louvered performance hood, special door skins with simulated air extractors, and Rallye

Charger was "Coke-bottle" shaped for '71. Hemi engine was in it last season and brought with it a standard vacuum-operated hood scoop (opposite, bottom). Just 85 of the 8172 Charger R/Ts and Charger Super Bees built for '71 had the $883 Hemi engine. All R/Ts got decorative door gills. The 440 Six Pack was gone; standard on the R/T (this page) was the four-barrel 440 Magnum. Hood vents weren't functional.

wheels. A colored racing stripe vectored aft from the cowl, following the beltline. Rear deck spoiler and chin spoiler were optional. Hemi Super Bee models were less radical, with fewer door vents, but still striking with their bumblebee graphics.

High-back bucket seats, Slap-Stick or Hurst pistol-grip shifter, console, full instrumentation, trimmed pedals, and a choice of audio options were found inside.

The 426 Hemi cost an extra $883.55 (not including required extras) and was available with standard four-speed or optional TorqueFlite. Sure-Grip differential was a mandatory option. Eleven-inch drum brakes—3 inches wide up front, 2½ inches wide at the rear—were standard in both Super Bee and R/T. Hemi Chargers also had a vacuum-operated hood scoop activated by a dashboard switch. It allowed cold air to reach the twin Carter AFB four-barrel carburetors via the shortest path.

Dodge's Performance Parts Catalog, titled "Hustle Stuff for the Dodge Scat Pack," was one more signal that excitement hadn't been forgotten. The list of available goodies included not only Dodge-brand components but shifters from Hurst, performance cams from Racer Brown and Iskenderian, headers from Hooker, and Edelbrock manifolds.

The 440 Magnum would still give a Hemi—or anything else on the road—a heap of trouble in street racing. One advantage of the 440 had been that it was easier than the Hemi to keep in tune. In 1970, however, Chrysler gave the Hemi hydraulic valve lifters, which helped keep the engine in optimum tune and made it a more viable street sweeper. Quarter-mile times were in the high 13s at more than 100 mph—fine numbers for any era.

Automotive journalist and race driver Patrick Bedard,

listing his personal top-10 muscle cars for the January 1990 issue of *Car and Driver*, remembers how it was: "Hemis were easy to drive in commuter traffic but hard to race from a standing start because of the way the carburetors worked. At light throttle, the engine ran on the front half of the rear four-barrel. As the pedal went down, the primaries of the front four-barrel opened, followed after a bit by both secondaries at once. A good launch required enough wheelspin to get the revs up into the torque range, but it was easy to open too many throttles too soon and burn the tires. The necessary technique was quite challenging with a four-speed. If you were Hemi hunting in a lesser car, you wanted to catch him at a stop. If he fumbled and you were lucky enough to pull out a fender-length on him, you claimed victory early by backing off the power, thereby ending the run. If you were crazy enough to stay on it, the Hemi would take over in short order." Bedard also points out that advances in tire technology by the early '70s helped improve traction and cut quarter-mile times slightly.

With their slick new bodies, Hemi Chargers were again a winning force in NASCAR, and some observers credit Chrysler's drag-racing experience with helping it get the most out of its oval stockers now that NASCAR required them to be closer than ever to production cars.

Dodge sold just 5054 Charger Super Bees and only 3118 Charger R/Ts in '71, and while fewer than 100 were equipped with the Hemi, King Kong would remain a strong presence in all sorts of competitive motorsports for years to come. On the street, however, 1971 was indeed the requiem for this heavyweight.

Slick new Charger body was at home on the NASCAR superspeedways, while Dodge's range of high-impact colors, including extra-cost hues like "Green Go" and "Citron Yella," made it an eye-catcher on the street.

1971 Dodge Charger Hemi

Facts At a Glance

Engine type:	V-8/RB-Block/Hemi
Displacement (cid):	426
Horsepower @ rpm:	425 @ 5000
Torque (lbs/ft) @ rpm:	490 @ 4000
Compression ratio:	10.2:1
Bore (in.):	4.25
Stroke (in.):	3.75
Valve lifters:	Hydraulic
Availability:	1971 Charger R/T and Super Bee

Magazine:	**Muscle Car Review**	**Motor Trend** (Dec. 1970)
Times:		
0-60 mph (sec):	5.8	5.7
0-100 mph (sec):	13.0	N/A
¼-mile (sec):	13.73 @ 104 mph	13.73 @ 104 mph
Top speed (mph):	115	N/A
Axle ratio:	4.10:1	4.10:1

1971
DODGE
DEMON 340

Smaller-sized models with medium-size engines were an interesting subset of the muscle-car market. Their engine compartments could seldom accommodate the big-block motors that made the intermediates so potent, but their compact bodies were lighter and, combined with highly tuned V-8s, presented a tempting power-to-weight ratio for performance buffs on a budget.

Dodge's Dart GTS of 1968 and '69 was a fine example, and equipped with the 383-cubic-inch V-8 or, in very limited numbers, the mighty 440, caught many more overt muscle cars napping.

For '70, Dodge scaled back, offering only the Swinger 340 as its Dart performance entry. Over at Plymouth, the same 340-cubic-inch four-barrel V-8 went into the new Duster, a fresh compact with a strong, simple fastback body. Dodge got its own version of the Duster body for '71 and after rejecting the name Beaver, christened it the Demon.

A near twin to the Duster, the Dodge version differed primarily in its vertically fluted "Frenched" taillamps and louvered grille. They were even less individualized inside, each carrying a dual-pod instrument cluster derived from the 1967-69 Barracuda. High-back bucket seats and console were options. So was a 6000-rpm tachometer and a 14½-inch diameter thick-rimmed, three-spoke "Tuff" steering wheel. Though Demon had no center roof pillar per se, Dodge called this car a coupe because its rear windows opened forward on hinges a couple of inches, rather than rolling down.

Dodge followed Plymouth's successful '70 Duster 340 into the junior-muscle market with the '71 Demon 340. Its high-revving 290-bhp 340-cid four-barrel could jolt the 3200-pound coupe to sub-14-second ETs.

1971 Dodge Demon 340

Facts At a Glance

Engine type:	V-8/A-Block/Wedge
Displacement (cid):	340
Horsepower @ rpm:	275 @ 5000
Torque (lbs/ft)	
@ rpm:	340 @ 3200
Compression ratio:	10.3:1
Bore (in.):	4.04
Stroke (in.):	3.31
Valve lifters:	Hydraulic
Availability:	1971

Magazine:	*Road Test*
	(April 1971)
Times:	
0-60 mph (sec):	7.8
0-100 mph (sec):	N/A
¼-mile (sec):	14.56 @ 96 mph
Top speed (mph):	127 (est)
Axle ratio:	N/A

At just $2721, Demon 340 was a devilish value in mini MoPar muscle. Small-block mill (top) had 10.5:1 compression for '71. Optional hood with non-functional scoops included black-out paint and NASCAR-style tie-down pins (above). Chrome dual-exhaust tips were standard (opposite). Dodge chose the Demon name after rejecting "Beaver."

Demon came standard with the venerable slant six engine. Its base V-8 was the 318 two-barrel. The 340 was yanked from the Dart sedan and coupe and inserted into the new fastback to create the Demon 340. Tipping the scales at just 3165 pounds and starting at only $2721, here was a light, inexpensive performance alternative.

Its MoPar small block delivered 275 horsepower at 5000 rpm. With a 10.5:1 compression ratio, dual exhausts, hydraulic lifters, and a hot cam, the 340 churned out a healthy 340 pounds/feet of torque at 3200 rpm. A fully synchromesh three-speed manual transmission was standard; a New-Process four-speed or TorqueFlite automatic was optional. Buyers could choose from a wide range of axle ratios—2.94:1, 3.23:1, 3.55:1, 3.91:1, or 4.10:1—and a Sure-Grip differential also was available. The standard Rallye suspension included heavy-duty front torsion bars and rear springs, rear anti-sway bar, and oversize shock absorbers. The drum brakes were larger than those on other Demons and so were the E70×14 Goodyear Polyglas GT tires.

"It's a tough little devil," declared the Dodge performance brochure for 1971. And while Dodge promised that "the performance is a lot more than painted on," the Demon 340 did look the part. Chromed tips decorated the dual exhaust outlets. A twin-scoop black-out hood was optional, as were handsome Rallye wheels and spoiler packages.

Driven with skill, a three-speed-manual Demon 340 with one of the performance axle ratios could turn the quarter in

13.98 at 100 mph, though most ran in the high 14s at around 95 mph with their four-speeds and automatics.

Road Test tagged Demon as a car that "will change personality in an instant. When you stomp on this one, hang on and look out!"

Marketed as part of the Dart line, Dodge's '71 Demon sold well. With 69,861 base Demons and 10,098 Demon 340s built, it accounted for 32 percent of Dart-series sales.

Dodge carried the Demon name into 1972, again with optional 340 four-barrel V-8. The compression fell to 8.50:1, however, and atop the 340 for this, its fourth year, was the new Carter Thermo-Quad four-barrel. Because of the carb's plastic body, fuel was less affected by engine temperature.

For 1973, Dodge exorcised the Demon designation, turning to "Dart Sport" until the design expired after 1976. A Dart Sport Rallye model with a four-speed manual, 318 V-8, handling suspension, and front disc brakes was introduced in mid-'73, and for '74, the 340 was bumped to 360-cubic-inches, though the car was heavier by that time and the 360 never became the street threat a good 340 was.

In the big picture, Chrysler had the right car at the right time with the Duster and Demon. The Duster for a while was Plymouth's best seller and the Demon, even in 340 and 360 form, sold well also. One key was the styling, another was the genuinely spirited performance, especially at a time when high insurance rates and general public criticism were taking a big bite out of big-block muscle-car sales.

1962
FORD
406

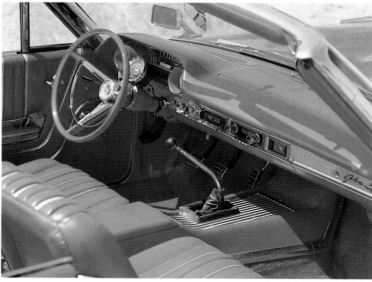

At the dawn of the muscle-car era in the late 1950s and early '60s serious factory performance was reserved for the full-size models. Thundering big-block power, went the prevailing wisdom, needed a big chassis and a long wheelbase. A big body could shift more weight to the rear axle under heavy acceleration for better traction. And on America's new superhighways, there was no substitute for big-car ride and big-cube performance.

At Ford, the name of the game was simple: how to tweak more horsepower out of the FE-series big-block V-8 for the big Fords. From its birth as a 332-cubic-inch V-8 for 1958, and quick expansion into a longer-stroke 352, the FE-series big-block grew into a bored-and-stroked 390 cubic inches for 1961. FE, by the way, was the manufacturer's code for this family of engines; Ford scholars today are in disagreement over what it might actually have stood for. Known as the Thunderbird 390 Special because of its introduction in the 1961 T-Bird, the third-generation FE solid-lifter big-block developed as much as 401 horsepower with a factory Tri-Power setup.

But Ford needed something to meet the 400-cubic-inch-plus challenge being mounted by General Motors and Chrysler. Luckily, a man who was destined to make a lot of automotive news in the decades to come had taken over as Ford Division General Manager in 1960: Lee A. Iacocca. Iacocca was ready to toss the Ford Division head first into the high-performance '60s. He pioneered the springtime introduction as a way to generate showroom traffic long after the fall rush was over and holiday expenses were but a memory. Iacocca's influence at Ford first became evident with a lineup of sporty 1962½ entries.

Ford's theme for '62 was the "Lively Ones," and the exciting mid-year debuts included the all-new downsized Fairlane 500 Sport Coupe and Galaxie 500XL. The "500" designation stood for the exhausting 500-mile trek around a

Ford crossed the 400-cid barrier in '62 with its 406 V-8. Its most glamorous host was the new-for-'62 Galaxie 500XL (opposite page). Note optional stainless steel fender skirts. Tri-carb (left) brought 405 bhp to make plainer Galaxie 500 (below) a very potent sleeper.

NASCAR oval. Toss in a Falcon Futura (which first appeared a year earlier), and you get a diverse trio to whet the appetites of customers across the spectrum.

The spotlight shone brightest on the Ford Galaxie and Galaxie 500XL. After all, that's where the horsepower could be found in a variety of packages and these were the cars that set the stage for those "Total Performance" years to come. While engines as modest as a 223-cubic-inch-six could be had for the full-sized Fords, most customers opted for the lineup of FE-series V-8s: the 352, 390, and now, the 406.

Ford listed the 406 as a factory option at the beginning of the '62 model year; how far into the model year it actually became available isn't known. It basically was a 390 bored to 406 cubic inches. It had a .080-inch larger bore but retained the 390's 3.78-inch stroke. The 406 represented a new era beyond 400 cubic-inches for Ford performance—and an answer to Chevy's soon-to-be-legendary 409.

Even though Ford underplayed the 406 in its sales brochure by listing it as just another engine option, customers with an eye for performance weren't fooled. With a 4.13-inch bore, 3.78-inch stroke and 11.4:1 compression, the 406 was a screamer. This new Thunderbird High-Performance mill, made 385 horsepower with a single Holley four-barrel carburetor or 405 horses with the optional Super High-Performance Tri-Power setup of three Holley two-barrels. One horse per cube was big news in 1961.

Enhancing the 406's breathing potential were factory cast-iron exhaust headers with low-restriction dual exhausts. Behind other powerplants stood the popular Cruise-O-Matic three-speed automatic transmission, but those who chose a 406 had to shift for themselves with a Borg-Warner T-10 four-speed gearbox. A four-speed manual had been offered as a dealer-installed option in '61, but this was the first time Ford

A standard Galaxie with the base 385-bhp four-barrel 406 and four speed was early Ford muscle at its purest, though this one has A/C. "Thunderbird" was stamped on its valve covers, but the 406 wasn't offered in the T-Bird.

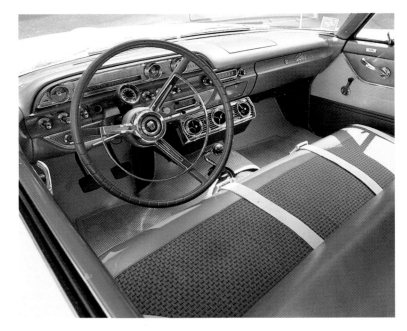

1962 Ford 406

Facts At a Glance

Engine type:	V-8/FE Series	V-8/FE Series
Displacement (cid):	406 (4v)	406 (3 × 2v)
Horsepower @ rpm:	385 @ 5800	405 @ 5800
Torque (lbs/ft) @ rpm:	444 @ 3400	448 @ 3500
Compression ratio:	11.4:1	11.4:1
Bore (in.):	4.13	4.13
Stroke (in.):	3.78	3.78
Valve lifters:	Mechanical	Mechanical
Availability:	Ford Galaxie, Galaxie 500, Galaxie 500 XL (except station wagons)	

Magazine:	Hot Rod (1962)	Motor Trend (March 1962)
Times:		
0-60 mph (sec):	7.1	6.5
0-100 mph (sec):	N/A	N/A
1.4-mile (sec):	15.3 @ 93 mph	15.6 @ 92 mph
Top speed (mph):	N/A	140 (est)
Axle ratio:	3.50:1	3.50:1
Engine (cid/bhp):	406/385	406/405

fans had a chance to run through four gears rather than three in a trans from the factory. Rear-axle ratios as hot as 4.11:1 could replace the standard 3.50:1.

The 406 engine package cost $378.70 (or $379.90, depending on the historical source consulted), and required the four-speed and oversize (6.70 or 7.10) 15-inch tires instead of the usual 14-inchers. The package also included heavy-duty shock absorbers and springs, fade-resistant drum brakes, bigger fuel line, heavier clutch, a stabilizer bar, and a larger-capacity radiator. Among the dealer-installed options were muffler-bypass "power pipes."

Ford made the 406 available in any Galaxie except the station wagons. By far the most popular 406 was the top-of-the-line Galaxie 500XL with bucket seats, console, and striking hardtop styling. Sharpest of the lot were the 500XL Victoria hardtop coupe and Sunliner convertible. "Powered by one of the optional Thunderbird 406 High-Performance V-8s," read Ford's sales brochure, "Sunliner moves with a nimbleness and flight-like quality rivaled by only one other...the Thunderbird itself!" Ford's big sedans had a 119-inch wheelbase and curb weights typical of their ilk. The XL convertible, for example, weighed 3831 pounds and the hardtops were in the 3600-3700-pound range. Lightest of the crew was a base Galaxie sedan, at 3554 pounds, and with the 406 under the hood it was a real sleeper—especially equipped with standard hubcaps. About the only clue to its true nature would be the gold "406" bird emblems on the front fender (the 390 used silver emblems).

Despite the valuable first impression made by the 406, racers soon discovered that its connecting rods were notoriously weak and that its crank shafts and other bottom-end components were prone to failure due to relatively fragile castings and the need for engineering refinements. Ford responded with heavier main webs and four-bolt main bearing caps.

There were other barriers to eking the most out of the new 406. The poor aerodynamic qualities of the '62 Galaxie's notchback roofline proved to be a setback for Ford on the superspeedways. Ford designed a removable "Starlift" fastback roof for convertibles to be used in NASCAR competition. Only two were built and it didn't take long for NASCAR officials to suspend the use of this removable hardtop. Ford would soon remedy this ill with another of Iacocca's mid-year introductions.

But for '62, a 406 Galaxie was about as bold a statement as an enthusiast could make on the street. As Roger Huntington wrote in *Motor Trend*, "For the man who just wants a hot road machine" a 406 will deliver "something like Ferrari performance at a fifth of the price." Not a bad formula, then or now.

1963-65 FORD 427

Aerodynamic shortcomings caused by the Galaxie's notchback roof followed Ford into 1963, and though the problem was felt mostly in NASCAR competition, its solution would have an impact both on the superspeedways and in the showroom.

Carrying through on the mid-year introduction it found so successful in 1962, Ford in February '63 introduced a Galaxie with a fresh new fastback roofline. With the SportsRoof body style, a Galaxie 500 or 500XL was two inches lower than its notchback counterpart and enjoyed a tremendous aerodynamic advantage in NASCAR competition.

But Ford didn't stop with just the SportsRoof. It put its money where its "Total Performance" slogan was and unveiled yet another new engine, the 427. The No. 2 automaker took its 390/406 FE-series engine and opened the bores an additional .010 inch. Interestingly, Ford's 427 didn't actually displace 427 cubic inches; it really displaced 425.

Like the 406 a year earlier, the 427 was a mid-year introduction and a natural for the new 1963½ Galaxie fastback coupe. The new engine was available in two forms. Both were iron-block powerplants with a crankshaft and connecting rods of forged steel and cross-bolted main bearing caps. They could survive forays into the 7000-rpm-range thanks to their lightweight valvetrain and mechanical high-lift camshaft. An oval air cleaner sandwiched an exposed filter element between its aluminum top and bottom sections. Ford also used streamlined cast-iron exhaust manifolds.

The strongest 427 had a pair of 652cfm Holley four-barrel carburetors to help generate 425 horsepower at 6000 rpm and 480 pounds/feet of torque at 3700 rpm. A second version used the same 11.5:1 compression ratio and also had an aluminum intake manifold, but mounted a single 780cfm Holley. It was rated at 410 horsepower at 5600 rpm and 476 pounds/feet at 3400.

Chrome valve covers were standard equipment on both 427s for that dressed-to-thrill look and ordering one brought beefed up suspension, rear axle and rear brakes, and a heavy-duty driveshaft and universal joints. Wheels were 15 inchers, compared to 14s on lesser Galaxies.

The base 427 four-barrel V-8 was a $405 option. With it, buyers had to order a four-speed—a mandatory 427 option. For that same $405 package price ($56 more for the twin four-barrel edition), Ford included heavy-duty suspension, larger drum brakes, and appropriate tires.

The FE-series Ford big-block was suddenly ready to take on Detroit's Woodward Avenue or Daytona's high-banked oval. NASCAR became its domain. Chevy's new 427 Mark IV V-8s actually made the Impala faster in qualifying, but when it came to the checkered flag, Ford Galaxie fastbacks cleaned house. They took 23 Grand National wins to runner-up Plymouth's 19. The highlight of the year was a sweep of the first five places at Daytona

Sales of the new Galaxie 500XL two-door fastback far surpassed those of the more traditional two-door notchback.

But, despite Ford's new cockiness on the street and in NASCAR, its Galaxies still couldn't win consistently on the drag strip. The problem was weight. The 427 engine itself was a match for anything the competition had, but Pontiac, Chevy, Dodge, and Plymouth all fielded cars that tipped the scales at around 3200 pounds, some 300 pounds less than the Galaxie.

Ford's solution was the "Lightweight," a series of 50 Galaxie SportsRoofs built specifically for drag racing and not intended for street use. Front fenders, hood, bumpers and, in some instances, doors were made of fiberglass instead of steel. The cabin was stripped of all but the bare necessities. Specially manufactured bucket seats weighing about 10 pounds each,

Both the Ford 427-cid V-8 and Galaxie fastback-style roofline debuted in mid-'63. The hot new engine and aerodynamic roof were an inspired duo in stock-car racing and carried Ford to the '63 NASCAR title.

rubber floor mats over bare metal and only one sun visor were used. The radio, heater, clock, and all sound deadening was omitted.

The 'Glass Galaxies used a 427 with twin four-barrel carbs on an aluminum high-rise manifold and a 12.0:1 compression for a factory-rated 425 horsepower. Aluminum was used for the four-speed manual transmission's case and for the bell housing. Ford had gotten the weight down to 3425 pounds. Running mostly in the Super Stock class, the best of these cars turned the quarter in 12.07 seconds at 118 mph. Good, but not good enough. No Lightweight ever won a major NHRA title, but few Galaxies are more prized today by collectors.

1964

Galaxie's big news for '64 was attractive new styling. Ford retained only the fastback roof from the '63½, giving the '64 all-new body panels. The 119-inch wheelbase remained, but the rounded sheetmetal was a logical extension of the handsome '63 fastback.

Changes under the hood were less dramatic. The Thunderbird 427 Super High Performance V8 retained its 425 horsepower, the 410-horsepower 427 was unchanged, and the engine appearance package and associated heavy-duty hardware were continued. Street Galaxies were turning 0-60 times in the low 7-second range and a good one could run the quarter in the high 14s. Ford's purpose-built drag-racing 427s used a high-rise manifold that elevated the air cleaner above the stock hood line. This necessitated a tear-drop-shaped bubble hood that later became a popular Ford street-racer accessory. The Lightweight '64 Galaxies had the fiberglass bubble hood and also used unique grille slots as special engine-air intakes.

Time was running out on full-size performance cars in 1964, both a among serious street racers and on the nation's drag strips. Galaxie 427s did no more than hold their own in quarter-mile competition, but excelled in stock-car racing, where their bulk was less of a handicap. Galaxie again led the NASCAR circuit in '64, with 30 victories.

With the SportsRoof now available for a full model year, Ford sold 265,000 fastback Galaxies, a big jump from '63—though only a small percentage had the 427.

1965

Ford not only sent Galaxie styling in a new direction in '65, it thrust itself into automotive folklore with some legendary engineering achievements.

Galaxie dropped its rounded lines for a body that boasted sharp creases, vertically stacked dual headlamps, and rectangular taillamps. Exterior dimensions were altered little, but some revolutionary changes took place beneath the skin.

A redesigned front suspension—employing tricks learned in stock-car racing—resulted in the strongest production-car front end ever. The design proved so sound that all NASCAR racers, regardless of the make or the body, used it through the 1970s.

The new heavy-duty differential also made a name for itself; it was called the Ford nine-inch and went on to become the standard in high-performance production units.

Galaxie started '65 with a flagship 427 engine that was virtually indistinguishable from its '64 low-riser counterpart. In mid year, however, Ford unleashed yet another legend: the side-oiler 427. Racers had found that the peculiar oil routing of Ford's 427s decreased engine life under the rigors of competition. In response, Ford engineers specified a new block with a large oil gallery on its lower left side. Called the Thunderbird 427 Super High Performance V-8, it was the ultimate Galaxie go option for '65. The side-oiler sported dual 652cfm Holleys on a medium-rise aluminum manifold, 11.1:1 compression, an ultra high-lift mechanical camshaft, and such improvements as stronger connecting rods and hollow-stem valves. It was rated at 425 horsepower at 6000 rpm and 480 pounds/feet of torque at 3700.

If that wasn't enough, Ford had yet another legend to spring on the automotive world. Prodded by the pounding it was taking from Chrysler's 426 Hemi, Ford developed a 427 with hemispherical-shaped combustion chambers. But the blue-oval boys upped the performance ante by fitting their new heads with overhead camshafts.

The resulting SOHC 427 was available only as a $2500 option installed at the dealership. At an astonishing 616 horsepower with a single four-barrel carb or a 657 horsepower with dual quads, it was the most powerful production engine ever offered. NASCAR, however, deemed that it was not a true production powerplant and banned it from its tracks. That didn't chill participants in other forms of competition, principally drag racing. Ford's SOHC 427 went on to power scores of winners in everything from funny cars to factory experimental stockers. Few made it onto the street, however. So radical were its cams that the engine couldn't generate enough vacuum to supply such production-car necessities as power steering or power brakes. Besides, street racers were turning increasingly to lighter-

1963-65 Ford 427

Facts At a Glance

Engine type:	V-8/FE Series	V-8/FE Series
Displacement (cid):	427 (4v)	427 (8v)
Horsepower @ rpm:	410 @ 5600	425 @ 6000
Torque (lbs/ft) @ rpm:	476 @ 3400	480 @ 3700
Compression ratio:	11.5:1	11.5:1
Bore (in.):	4.23	4.23
Stroke (in.):	3.78	3.78
Valve lifters:	Mechanical	Mechanical
Availability:	1963-65 Custom, Galaxie, Galaxie 500, Galaxie 500 XL (except station wagons)	

Engine type:	SOHC V-8/FE	SOHC V-8/FE
Displacement (cid):	427 (4v)	427 (8v)
Horsepower @ rpm:	616 @ 7000	657 @ 7500
Torque (lbs/ft) @ rpm:	515 @ 3800	540 @ 4000
Compression ratio:	12.1:1	12.1:1
Bore (in.):	4.23	4.23
Stroke (in.):	3.78	3.78
Valve lifters:	Mechanical	Mechanical
Availability:	1965-67 Custom, Galaxie, Galaxie 500, Galaxie 500 XL (except station wagons)	

Magazine:	*Motor Trend* *(Feb. 1964)*
Times:	
0-60 mph (sec):	7.4
0-100 mph (sec):	N/A
¼-mile (sec):	15.4 @ 95 mph
Top speed (mph):	N/A
Axle ratio:	4.11:1
Engine (cid/bhp):	427/425
Model year:	1964

Dual-quad 427 (opposite page in a '63) made 425 bhp. Oval air cleaner and chrome valve covers were standard. "Lightweight" '64s (this page) used fiberglass front end to slim down for drag racing. High-rise manifold required special bubble hood. Few were seen on the street.

weight mid-size cars.

Even without the overhead-cam heads, Ford's 427s dominated NASCAR once again, winning 48 of the 55 races they entered, including the 1965 Daytona 500.

But despite its superior front end, its side-oiler engine, and its other achievements, the performance bloom was off the Galaxie. Pontiac's 1964 GTO had changed the face of Detroit muscle with its big-engine/small-body ethic, and Ford and Chrysler had no choice but to follow suit.

The 427 could still be ordered through 1967, and buyers could get the SOHC version as a factory option that year. But in 1966, Ford had begun to spell big-block Galaxie power "7-Litre." The race-bred 427's big-bore, short-stroke design made it a performer at high revs but found it short on torque at low rpm. Ford needed a quiet and reliable long-stroke engine, an excellent mid-range, high-torque powerplant tailor-made for big cars loaded with accessories. The "7-Litre" was it. Interestingly, Ford said the 7-Litre displaced 428 cubic inches, but in fact, it was a 427.

The 427 Galaxie left behind some fond memories of Ford's fight in the early muscle years.

Bare-bones cockpit of '63½ "Lightweight" used special seats that weighed 10 pounds each (top). At the other end of the 427 spectrum was the luxurious 500XL convertible (middle). Removing the air cleaner exposed the two Holley 652cfm four-barrels and the aluminum manifold.

1964 FORD THUNDERBOLT FAIRLANE 427

Even in Lightweight guise, the big Ford Galaxies were no match in the quarter-mile for the lighter-still Dodges and Plymouths with their 426 Max Wedges and Hemis. Even the older full-size Chevy 409 Z-11 and 421 Pontiac proved stiff competition, while on the street the new General Motors intermediates used their 300-plus-cubic-inch mills to shame Ford drivers.

The blue-oval crew had a mid-size, the Fairlane, but its engine bay would accommodate nothing larger than the 289 V-8, which was overmatched even in its 271-horsepower high-performance guise. The solution was obvious: find a way to get the bulky high-riser 427 into the Fairlane. Clearly, a wholesale reworking of the production car was untenable. So Ford trained its sights on a limited-volume version of a two-door Fairlane 500 sedan. It would be called Thunderbolt and it would finally capture for Ford some drag strip glory. Just as significantly, you could trot over to your friendly Ford dealer, slap down an order for a Thunderbolt, and take delivery of a street-legal—though not exactly streetable—race car.

The task of building the Thunderbolt fell to Dearborn Steel Tubing, a Ford contract car builder. The stock 115-inch wheelbase was unchanged, but extensive front suspension modifications were necessary to custom-fit the 427. Installing the eight equal-length exhaust headers created a snake's nest of pipes coiling through the suspension components.

Weight-shedding revisions included a switch to fiberglass

Ford finally had a drag-racing winner in its 427-powered Fairlane Thunderbolts. In race tune and on slicks, the 425-bhp T-bolts ran in the high 11s/low 12s and won six of seven NHRA division titles in '64.

for the pinned-down bubble hood, the front fenders and doors, and to Plexiglas for rear and side windows. The front bumper was fiberglass on early models, aluminum on later ones. Anything not vital to a quarter-mile assault was removed, including the sunvisors and rear-view mirror. Thunderbolts had no sound-absorbing material, no armrests, no jack or lug wrench. The standard rear bench seat was retained, but lightweight front buckets were appropriated from the police package. An oil pressure gauge was plugged into the dash and a tachometer strapped to the steering column.

The same 427 used in the Lightweight Galaxies was employed. Atop the engine stood a high-rise aluminum intake manifold with pressure-equalizing box sporting twin Holley four-barrel carburetors. Machined combustion chambers and domed pistons teamed up for a volatile 11.5:1 compression ratio. A forged-steel crank shaft turned in a 10-gallon oil pan. Inner headlights of the Fairlane's quad setup were replaced by screened ram-air intakes to feed the carburetors via two six-inch-diameter flexible ducts.

Behind the hand-built 427 went a choice of two transmissions: a Hurst-shifted aluminum-case T-10 four-speed with a 4.44:1 final drive; or the PCA-F automatic from the Lincoln, which employed a 4.58:1 gear. Amazingly, the Ford nine-inch differential used with the 289 Hi-Po was strong enough to survive the cut. Thunderbolt's rear springs used three leaves on the right, two on the left. Huge traction bars also were added and a 95-pound bus battery rode in the right-rear of the trunk.

At around 3225 pounds, the Thunderbolt actually weighed about 300 pounds more than a stock Fairlane 500 two-door sedan. But as a race car, it was just 25 pounds over its

1964 Fairlane Thunderbolt 427

Facts At a Glance

Engine type:	V-8
Displacement (cid):	427
Horsepower @ rpm:	425 @ 6000[1]
Torque (lbs/ft) @ rpm:	480 @ 3700
Compression ratio:	11.5:1
Bore (in.):	4.23
Stroke (in.):	3.78
Valve lifters:	Mechanical
Availability:	1964 Fairlane 500 Two-Door Sedan

[1]Stock (announced) figures; estimates of actual output reached 500-550 horsepower.

Times:

¼-mile (sec):	11.76 @ 122.78 mph[1]

[1] Achieved by Butch Leal at the 1964 NHRA Nationals in Indianapolis. Gas Ronda managed 11.60 seconds (124.38 mph) at 1964 NHRA Winternationals.

Most Thunderbolts were run by pro drag racers (opposite page, top), but they also could be bought through dealers for street use (black car and white car). All had a lightweight front end that included a bubble hood to clear the 427's high-rise intake manifold (above). Screened inner headlight bezels were engine-air intakes (above, left).

NHRA-class minimum. One Thunderbolt was built in 1963, 100 were built in '64, and two were constructed in '65; 59 had the automatic transmission, 41 the 4-speed.

Even though the package came close to doubling the $2365 base price of an everyday Fairlane, all it took was $4000 ($100 less with manual shift) to purchase a new, ready-to-race Thunderbolt 427 from your local Ford dealer. An elite band of private racers, called the Ford Drag Council, was favored by the factory with a special price on a Thunderbolt: $1.

These cars were an unbeatable deal for the enterprising weekend racer but, as *Hot Rod* warned, "not suitable for driving to and from the strip, let alone on the street in everyday use."

Thunderbolt at the ready, Ford scurried after the 1964 NHRA crown. Now it was Ford's turn to crow. Gas Ronda's Thunderbolt snared the S/S Winternationals crown with a blistering 12.05-second effort at 120.16 mph. Butch Leal followed up with a NHRA Nationals S/S title at Indianapolis with a 11.76/122.78 pass in his Thunderbolt. When the season was over, the Thunderbolt had helped earn Ford the 1964 Manufacturer's Cup and Ronda the NHRA Top Stock points crown.

Total Performance was Ford's battle cry in the mid-'60s and no where was it stated with more authority than in a modest mid-size-sedan-turned-storm-trooper, the Thunderbolt.

Thunderbolt was a bargain at around $4000, but made for a brutal street machine. Weight transfer and reduction were essential to low ETs so a 95-pound bus battery was mounted in the trunk (top, left) and lightweight seats were borrowed from the police package (above).

1965-66
FORD MUSTANG
HIGH-PERFORMANCE 289

Ford's Mustang burst upon the public like Secretariat springing from the gate at Churchill Downs. Introduced on April 17, 1964, at the New York World's Fair, the sporty four-seater ignited a showroom stampede, trampling sales records with 418,812 sold in the first 12 months. Ford's launch had been expertly conceived and skillfully executed, but it was the car itself that spelled success.

Though based on the mundane mechanicals of the compact Falcon, Mustang broke from the herd with styling that gave the masses the long-nose/short-rear-deck previously reserved only for the most exotic sports cars. Then there was the price: the 1964½ hardtop started at just $2368; the convertible began at $2614. What sealed the deal for many buyers was that Ford made available such a wide array of options it was easy to tailor a Mustang to virtually any taste or budget.

The place to begin was the engine bay. A 101-horsepower 170 cubic-inch Falcon six was standard initially, replaced in September '64 by a 120-horsepower 200-cube six. At the same time, a 164-horsepower 260-cubic-inch V-8 borrowed from the Fairlane was replaced as the next-biggest engine choice by a 289-cubic-inch V-8 rated at 200 horsepower. Ford had offered a 289 from the start; it made 195 horsepower with a two-barrel carburetor and 210 if you paid an extra $158 for a four-barrel. When the 289 became the base V-8, output of the four-barrel was boosted to 225 horsepower. But there was still another 289, this one called the Hi-Performance 289, and it's the one that really put the spurs to the pony.

The 289 Hi-Po had made its debut in the 1963 Fairlane intermediate, and continued as a Fairlane option for 1964. This

Mustang was one of history's most influential cars, but it took the optional High-Performance 289-cid V-8 to make it a fast car. This '64½ convertible looked much like any other Mustang ragtop from the outside, but it packed the potent solid-lifter 271-bhp four-barrel (above).

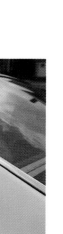

1965-66 Mustang 289 High

Performance

Facts At a Glance

Engine type:	V-8/Windsor
Displacement (cid):	289
Horsepower @ rpm:	271 @ 6000
Torque (lbs/ft)	
@ rpm:	312 @ 3400
Compression ratio:	10.5:1
Bore (in.):	4.00
Stroke (in.):	2.87
Valve lifters:	Mechanical
Availability:	1965-66 Mustang, Mustang GT

Magazine:	***Sports Car Graphic***
	(Aug. 1964)
Times:	
0-60 mph (sec):	7.5
0-100 mph (sec):	21.5
¼-mile (sec):	15.7 @ 89 mph
Top speed:	117
Axle ratio:	4.11:1

potent 271-horsepower V-8 wasn't available to the public in a Mustang until June 1964. A $328 option, Ford said the Hi-Po 289 was tailor made "for the true driving enthusiast who wants sports car performance to complement Mustang's sports car styling."

Equipped with solid lifters and a pleasantly radical high-lift camshaft, plus header-style exhausts and four-barrel carburetor, the Cobra 289 Hi-Po was a high revving, free spirited small-block producing its peak horsepower at a healthy 6000 rpm. Torque was rated at 312 pounds/feet at 3400 rpm. With heavier connecting-rod bolts, thicker main bearing caps, and a hand-selected nodular iron crankshaft, the 289 High Performance V-8 was designed to withstand abuse. Up top stood special cylinder heads (same ports as the 289 two- and four-barrel engines) with screw-in rocker-arm studs and cast-in-valve spring rockets for stability at high revs.

Ordering the Hi-Po 289 meant you also had to take the extra-cost four speed gearbox (an automatic transmission wasn't available with this engine until 1966). It also was the only Mustang engine offered with the optional 3.89:1 and 4.11:1 rear-axle ratios. Despite Ford's liberal linking of the terms sports car and Mustang, a garden-variety Mustang would wallow through dips and leaned hard in the turns, no matter the engine. The Hi-Po 289 was much better mannered thanks to its handling suspension and 5.50/5.90×15 Firestone Super Sport Tires.

Straight-line performance was respectable, but not astonishing. *Sports Car Graphic* ran a '65 Hi-Po hardtop with 4.11:1 gears to a 15.7-second quarter-mile at 89 mph. But Jerry Titus, who drove one for the magazine lauded its all-around performance. "The car goes, and damned well...the stability is excellent and you can honk around most any corner at racing velocity well under control," he said.

Paul O'Shea road tested a Hi-Po Mustang for *Hot Rod* and

pronounced it "one of the most forgiving cars I have ever driven."

Car and Driver had criticized the Mustang as "a car designed by committee to offend as few people as possible." But the magazine nonetheless recognized that "the high-performance version of the 289 V-8 is more closely comparable to a full-house Corvette than anything else in the Ford stable," noting that driving the first-year ponycar was "a sensational—if noisy—experience."

For those who wanted more, there was a twin-carburetor induction kit ($245), special camshaft ($75.10), or heavy-duty distributor ($49.80). Owners were encouraged to contemplate the wonders of four Weber carbs and 343 horsepower with the proper bolt-on components.

On April 17, 1965, Ford celebrated the Mustang's first anniversary by introducing a brace of desirable options, including the GT Equipment Group, Interior Decor Group (Pony Interior), and styled steel wheels. And in September 1965, a fastback 2+2 body joined the original notchback coupe and convertible.

Records of how many early Mustangs were ordered with the Hi-Po 289 are sketchy, through only 472 were so equipped in '67. That was the Hi-Po 289's final year in the lineup and big-blocks were in vogue. Nonetheless, this was the engine that helped cement the Mustang as a genuine performance car. It laid the foundation for all those high-protein muscle lightweights that would follow. And it served as the platform for the 1965-67 Shelby GT-350s Mustangs. Not a bad legacy.

Unique 289 fender badge identify this '64½ convertible as one of the Hi-Po crowd. The original 271-bhp solid-lifter V-8 was a $328 option and the extra-cost four-speed manual was mandatory. Mustang quarter-mile times were in the mid-15s with this engine.

1965-66 SHELBY MUSTANG GT-350

Mustang already was an unprecedented showroom blockbuster, but Ford chief Lee Iacocca wanted more. He decreed that it should beat the Corvette in Sports Car Club of America competition, establishing the new pony as an image leader as well as a sales champion.

He turned to race-car-driver-turned-race-car-builder Carroll Shelby, a hell-bent-for-leather Texan who had installed a Ford V-8 into the British AC roadster to create the legendary Ford AC Cobras. Immediately apparent to the team Shelby had assembled was the stock Mustang's milquetoast performance, even with the top-rung 271-horsepower four-barrel 289 V-8. The suspension was mushy and the brakes surrendered without a fight at the first hint of high-speed application. The factory Mustang wallowed through turns with the driver sawing away at the grossly inadequate manual steering. The optional Special Handling Package eased the suffering a little, but still would be no match for the rigors of war in SCCA B-Production.

The needed transformation began with a lowering of the Mustang's upper control arms to raise the front roll center. The spring rates were stiffened and Koni adjustable shocks added. A one-inch front sway bar was installed along with over-the-axle traction bars. Shelby also swapped the standard manual steering box with its 22:1 ratio for a power-steering-compatible unit and a longer Pitman arm, which narrowed the ratio to 19:1.

On to the brakes. Shelby chose larger Kelsey-Hayes 11-inch ventilated front discs with DS-11 composition pads. In back went 10-inch drums borrowed from the big Ford station wagons, with 2.5-inch wide metallic linings. Out went the Mustang's standard 14-inch wheels, replaced by 5.5×15-inch steel station wagon wheels sporting 7.75×15 Goodyear G-8 Blue Dot tires rated to 130 miles per hour. Five-spoke 6×15-inch Cragar wheels would be offered as an option.

Shelby stiffened the structure by installing the brace used on exported Mustangs and Falcons. This V-shaped metal arm ran from the firewall to the shock towers. For good measure, he added a Falcon-derived Monte Carlo bar, a steel tube that anchored the inner fenders just ahead of the air cleaner.

The Mustang's 289 High Performance V-8 earned a big boost to 306 horsepower at 6000 rpm via an aluminum high-rise intake manifold, and a center-pivot 715cfm carburetor made especially for Shelby by Holley. Finned cast-aluminum valve covers were emblazoned with "Cobra-Powered By Ford." Special Tri-Y headers were manufactured for Shelby by Belanger and Cyclone and routed to exhausts that exited just in front of the rear wheels. Shelby discarded the stock five-quart oil pan in favor of a 7.5-quart unit of finned cast aluminum. The pan was shaped as an inverted "T" and kept plenty of lubrication on hand during high revs and hard cornering. All of this was covered by a pinned-down fiberglass hood with center air scoop. A Borg-Warner close-ratio aluminum T-10 four-speed gearbox reduced weight and smoothed shifts. Out back was a nine-inch Ford Galaxie rear end with 4.11:1 gears in a Detroit Locker differential.

The cabin was decked out racer-style: three-inch-wide competition seat belts, tachometer and oil pressure gauge mounted at eye level on a stock Mustang dash, and a flat, wood-rim racing-type steering wheel. Omitting the back seat enabled the GT-350 to run as a sports car rather than as a

One of the most charismatic cars of the '60s, the Shelby Mustang GT-350 was a racer for the street, with razor-sharp reflexes and a raucous 289-cid V-8. Above is a '66 in classic Shelby white and blue.

1965-66 Shelby Mustang GT-350

Facts At a Glance

Engine type:	V-8/Windsor
Displacement (cid):	289
Horsepower @ rpm:	306 @ 6000
Torque (lbs/ft) @ rpm:	329 @ 4200
Compression ratio:	10.5:1
Bore (in.):	4.00
Stroke (in.):	2.87
Valve lifters:	Mechanical
Availability:	1965-66 GT-350

Magazine:	**Car and Driver (May 1965)**
Times:	
0-60 mph (sec):	6.5
0-100 mph (sec):	17.0
1.4-mile (sec):	14.9 @ 95.0 mph
Top speed (mph):	119 (est)
Axle ratio:	3.89:1
Engine type:	289

Magazine:	**Car Life (July 1966)**
Times:	
0-60 mph (sec):	6.2
0-100 mph (sec):	16.8
1.4-mile (sec):	14.0 @ 92.0 mph
Top speed (mph):	127
Axle ratio:	3.89:1
Engine:	289 Paxton supercharger

"sedan" under SCCA rules. In place of the rear seat was a fiberglass pan to which was bolted the spare tire. For those who occasionally needed "+2" seating, Shelby offered a kit with a small rear bench that put the spare back in the trunk.

As for naming this creation, legend has it that old Shel' himself grew weary of an all-day meeting on the topic held at his small shop in Venice, California. He is said to have asked how far it was to the engineering building across the street. An associate paced it out and came up with approximately 350 feet. Presto: the GT-350.

Final specifications for the GT-350 were determined by fall 1964 and a dozen 2+2s were built by hand at the Venice plant. All were completed by Christmas. Meantime, Ford's San Jose, California, assembly plant had shipped another 100 white fastbacks for conversion. The car's public unveiling came at Riverside Raceway on January 27, 1965. All 1965 models were painted white; no other colors were available. All Ford and Mustang insignias had been removed, but blue rocker-panel stripes displayed the GT-350 name. Most early Shelbys also got the matching, extra-cost 10-inch-wide twin "Le Mans" stripes that ran from hood to rear deck over the top.

Two versions of the GT-350 were planned from the start: a full-house GT-350R model for competition and a GT-350S street version, which was simply a more tractable derivative of the competition car. Advertised as dyno-tuned and race-ready, the race engine was fully balanced and blueprinted. Horsepower was estimated at 360. Curb weight was only 2500 pounds, versus 2800 for the GT-350S. The GT-350R was homologated for SCCA B-Production, which meant it would compete against small-block Corvettes, Sunbeam Tigers, Jaguar E-Types, and the occasional Ferrari or Aston Martin. Out of 562 GT-350s completed as 1965 models, no more than 30 were built to racing specifications. However, all the special parts were available over the counter, so anyone could turn a street car into the racing version by simply removing and/or substituting components. Sold through a select group of Ford dealers, the street GT-350 listed for $4547, about $1000 over the cost of a standard 289 Hi-Po fastback and about $1000 less than a Corvette. The ready-to-race GT-350R cost $6950.

With 0-60-mph times averaging 6.5 seconds, a top speed of 130-135 mph, and race-car handling and braking, the street GT-350 drew rave reviews.

Helping fuel the fire was the GT-350's success on the track. It notched three class wins in its very first outing in February 1965. The cars went on dominate to the SCCA's B-Production, claiming the National Championship for the next three years.

1966

An exciting, hairy-chested performer, the '65 Shelby-Mustang was by nature a raw machine. Its noisy, lurching, Detroit Locker rear end howled and clunked at low speeds; its

side-exit exhaust was not only loud but illegal in some states; and the policy of "any color you want, so long as it's white" was an obvious sales limitation. From Ford came a demand for something a little tamer—and a little more cost-effective. Thus did the Shelby Mustang begin evolving away from Carroll's original concept and toward something with broader market appeal—a car more like the standard Mustang and less like the semi-tamed racer it started out to be.

As a limited-production manufacturer, Shelby didn't always incorporate specific changes with the first car of a new model year. So there's no clear distinction between the 1965 and 1966 GT-350. The first 250 or so '66s were in fact leftover '65s with Plexiglas rear quarter windows and all the new-model cosmetic changes, including a revised grille and side scoops. When actual '66 production began, color choices expanded to red, blue, green, and black, all set off with white or gold racing stripes. At the same time, the Mustang fastback's extra-cost fold-down rear seat became a Shelby option as well and almost all the '66s had it.

Heavy-duty Ford-installed shock absorbers were retained, as were the special Pitman and idler arms that gave the '65 its sharp steering. All '65 and early '66 cars had rear traction bars running from inside the chassis rails to the top of the rear axle; later '66s were fitted with Traction Master underride bars. Early cars also had lowered front A-arms, which altered the steering geometry for improved cornering, but this was deemed to be uneconomical and was eliminated on later '66s.

Engines stayed mostly the same, but the Detroit Locker rear end was made an option—as was automatic transmission. Like the '65s, all '66 Shelbys had front disc brakes and large rear drums with sintered metallic linings. These were high-effort binders, but they just didn't fade, even though cooling area diminished somewhat with a switch to 14-inch wheels. The wheels were either chrome styled steel or cast-aluminum alloy at the buyer's option. If the '66 Shelby wasn't as loud or fierce as the '65, Carroll kept things interesting with a Paxton centrifugal supercharger as another new option. Sold factory-installed at $670 or as a $430 kit, the blower was said to boost horsepower by "up to 46 percent"—to beyond 400—which potentially cut 0-60-mph times to a mere five seconds. Few cars were so equipped, however.

Shelby also sold the Hertz rental-car company on the idea stocking its rental fleet with 1000 specially trimmed GT-350s. Called the GT-350H, these models were finished in black or red with gold stripes and could be rented from Hertz at major airports throughout 1966.

Total 1966 Shelby-Mustang production was 2380, including 936 Hertz models and six specially built convertibles that Shelby gave to friends. No racing cars were constructed, though a few '65 leftovers were registered as '66s. Shelby Mustangs continued to race and win that season, but were essentially the same cars that had run the year before.

Shelby's '66 GT-350s are identified externally by the side air scoop and the rear-quarter windows (opposite page). A Paxton supercharger was a '66 option (above, left). It boosted 306-bhp engine (above, right) to over 400 bhp. Cabin of this '65 shows pod-mounted gauges.

During 1966, Hertz stocked 1000 '66 GT-350s as rental cars. They were black or red with gold stripes and bore the GT-350H label. Hood tie-down pins were standard. Many of these cars were returned to Hertz bearing evidence of race-track use. Rental deal was offered during '66 only.

1966-67
FORD
427 FAIRLANE

The Thunderbolt Fairlane had defended Ford's honor against the nation's best drag racers in 1964 with a radically lightened body and a 427-cubic-inch V-8 under its fiberglass hood. It was only a matter of time before its thunder would be heard in an intermediate aimed at the street.

The 427 had already earned a place in performance-car history under the hood of Carroll Shelby's AC Cobra and of the big Ford Galaxie. What better choice for its mid-size debut than beneath the bonnet of the 1966 Fairlane?

Clad in fresh skin with a revised chassis for '66, the new Fairlane was Ford's answer to the pace-setting General Motors' intermediates. Gone was Fairlane's previous chunky styling. New quad headlamps stacked vertically in a restyled grille combined with simpler, wind-swept styling for the most attractive Fairlane yet. But the best news for performance buffs was that Ford's mid-size finally was available with big-block power.

During 1962-65, Fairlane had been saddled with a series of small-block Windsor Ford V-8s, of 221-, 260- and 289 cubic-inch displacement. None presented a serious challenge to the GM or Chrysler big-block intermediates. The 1964 Thunderbolt Fairlane 427 had been Ford's best shot in the hotly contested mid-size arena, but only about 100 had been built and few made it to the street, where it was ill-suited to daily driving, anyway. Here, then, was a new opportunity for Ford's intermediate to make a name for itself.

Ford's best shot at a truly dominating street racer might have been the new-for-'66 Fairlane with the optional 400-bhp-plus side-oiler 427 (above). Fiberglass hood with functional scoop identified the '66. Only about 70 were built.

Shining star for the 1966 Fairlane was the 335-horse 390-cubic-inch High Performance V-8 with hydraulic valve lifters. Anyone opting for the 390 could order the GT Equipment Group with Special Handling Package and attractive GT graphics.

Though the 390 with 401 horsepower had been a big gun in Ford's arsenal in the early '60s, its hydraulic lifters and milder camshaft profile—coupled with tougher emission standards—made for a rather "vanilla" 390 in 1966, even with 335 available horsepower. It didn't leave much of an impression against the likes of Pontiac's 389 Tri-Power, Chevy's SS 396 Chevelle, and Chrysler's 426 Street Wedge.

So Ford turned to the 427. Available in the two-door sedan and hardtop body, this was the famous side-oiler 427, so named for the oil gallery on the left side of its block. Officially known as the 7-Liter Cobra High Performance engine, the race-bred 427 made 410 horsepower at 5600 rpm and 476 pounds/feet of torque at 3400 rpm with a single 780cfm Holley four-barrel. Most, however, were equipped with dual 652cfm Holley quads for 425 horsepower at 6000 rpm and 480 pounds/feet of torque at 3700. Compression ratio was 11.1:1.

The added weight of the 427 made necessary larger front coil springs and its bigger size called for relocation of the Fairlane's shock towers. Free-breathing cast-iron exhaust headers, a low-restriction dual exhaust system, and Ford's top-loader four-speed manual gearbox completed the powertrain.

The 427 Fairlanes used a fiberglass hood with a scoop that fed fresh air to the air cleaner. The hood had no hinges and could be lifted off once a quartet of tie-down pins were released. A Special Handling Package, manual front disc brakes, longer rear leaf springs, and larger bias-belted blackwall tires also were part of the package.

While honor on the street was surely a goal, Ford felt it could get the most publicity mileage out of its 427 Fairlane by campaigning it in professional drag racing. It needed to build only 50 to make it eligible for the Super Stock drag class and though it bettered that figure by about 20 units, this limited production meant the 427 Fairlane was a rare site around the hamburger stand on a Saturday night, where it might finally have earned Ford some street-racing respect.

1967

All Fairlanes got some cosmetic alterations inside and out for 1967, but the biggest change for the 427 Fairlane was that it was made a regular production option. That meant it wasn't quite as rare as a '66, but still, fewer than 200 1967 427 Fairlanes are believed to have been built. The engine choices and power ratings remained unchanged, though the fiberglass hood was made an option.

It took several years for the 427 Fairlane to finally meet Ford's expectations in professional drag racing, partly because the National Hot Rod Association kept switching it into classes where it ran into faster MoPars and even some 427 SOHC Mustangs. Stock car racing was a different story, however. The 427 Fairlanes Ford was running in NASCAR weren't exactly stock, with a Galaxie front suspension assembly and non-street-legal tunnel-port heads being just a few of the modifications. Still, when Parnelli Jones won the Motor Trend 500 at Riverside in one, Ford marketing people quickly jumped at the opportunity. They ran an add that showed Jones' NASCAR Fairlane with its big No. 115 on the door; beneath it was a photo of a street model. "The 427 Fairlane," read the copy, "is also available without numbers." The high point was Mario Andretti's Daytona 500 victory in a Holman & Moody prepared 427 Fairlane.

The Fairlane's 427 would remain a rare, limited production option through the end of December 1967, though it's uncertain whether any '68 Fords actually were built with one. Mercury produced a few hundred Cougar GT-Es with the 427 in 1968, though it was pealed back to 390 horsepower by hydraulic lifters and exhaust-emissions hardware.

On the street, where muscle-car reputations are made, Ford never seemed to have the right equipment at the right time. Perhaps no blue-oval offering ever came closer to putting these two elements together than the 427 Fairlane, which makes its unfulfilled promise all the more painful for Ford fanatics.

1966-67 Fairlane 427

Facts At a Glance

Engine type:	V-8/FE Series	V-8/FE Series
Displacement (cid):	427 (4v)	427 (2x4v)
Horsepower @ rpm:	410 @ 5600	425 @ 6000
Torque (lbs/ft) @ rpm:	470 @ 3700	480 @ 3700
Compression ratio:	11.1:1	11.1:1
Bore (in.):	4.23	4.23
Stroke (in.):	3.78	3.78
Valve lifters:	Mechanical	Mechanical
Availability:	Fairlane, Fairlane 500, and 500 XL	

Magazine:	Car & Driver (March 1966)
Times:	
0-60 mph (sec):	N/A
0-100 mph (sec):	15.0
¼-mile (sec):	14.26 @ 99.0 mph
Top speed (mph):	N/A
Axle ratio:	3.89:1
Engine type:	390/335[1]

[1]Performance times for 427-cid V-8 not available, but *Hot Rod* magazine estimated ¼-mile time at about 14.5 seconds and 100 mph.

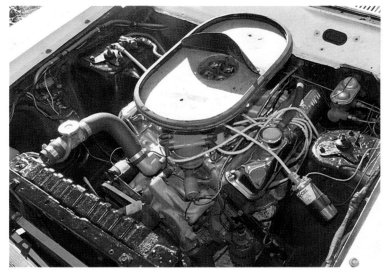

The 427 was a successful stock-car-racing engine, but it also powered Super Stock drag cars like this '67 (top row, both pages). Opposite page middle is a rear view of the '66 427. Blue Fairlane on this page is a '67, Stock hood was used this year. With air cleaner off, dual-quad 652cfm Holleys are exposed (left). The 427 was a regular production option for '67, but fewer than 200 Fairlanes were ordered with it.

1967-68 SHELBY MUSTANG GT-350/GT-500

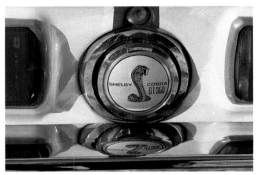

The Shelby Mustang was changing, drifting steadily away from its original market—not unlike the basic Mustang itself. The original GT-350 had been a rough riding, thundering bundle of steel and fiberglass. For '67, customers and dealers still wanted the Cobra aura, but in a more civilized high-performance Mustang. At the same time, Ford had revamped its Mustang, making it slightly longer and wider—in large measure to accommodate the company's FE-series big-block V-8s. Now the 390 High Performance V-8 could be fitted and it gave the Mustang 320 horsepower with a single four-barrel Holley carburetor.

Bigger things, however, were in store for the Shelby Mustangs: a longer-stroke, larger-bore 428-cubic-inch "Police Interceptor" powerhouse, rated at 355 horsepower. Shelby called this car the GT-500. The GT-350, meanwhile, continued with the 306-horsepower 289 V-8. As for the GT-500 name, just as Shelby's choice of "350" to designate the 289-powered car was apparently quite arbitrary, so was the decision to tag the 428 car a "500." Both numbers sounded hot and tough.

The 1967 GT-350 and GT-500 were the first steps in a transition of the Shelby Mustangs from road racers to touring GTs. In fact, Ford's advertising slogan for the '67 Shelby Mustangs was "*The* Road Cars...." Unlike their 1965-66 predecessors, the 1967 models offered such options as factory air conditioning and power steering. Standard was the Mustang's optional Interior Decor Group in brushed aluminum with molded door panels and courtesy lamps. Shelby added a

wood-rimmed Shelby steering wheel, Stewart-Warner oil and amp gauges mounted at mid-dash, and full instrumentation, including an 8000-rpm tachometer and 140-mph speedometer. All GT-350s and GT-500s had the standard Mustang fold-down rear seat, but Shelby added a padded roll bar as standard equipment. Two interior colors were available: black and parchment.

it was a year earlier. Standard was a Toploader four-speed and 3.89:1 Traction-Lok gears; optional was Ford's C-4 Cruise-O-Matic automatic with a 3.25:1 rear end. As before, the 289 High Performance V-8 was topped with a cast-aluminum Cobra high-rise intake manifold, 715cfm Holley carburetor with center pivot float, open-element air cleaner, and cast-aluminum valve covers with solid lifters. Gone were the Tri-Y tubular headers of 1965-66, replaced by 289 Hi-Po cast-iron exhaust manifolds.

The 428 Police Interceptor was equipped with a cast-aluminum "427" medium-riser intake manifold supporting a pair of 600cfm Holley four-barrel carburetors that operated via a progressive linkage and vacuum-activated secondaries. Unique to the Shelby big-block were the special oval finned aluminum open-element air cleaner and cast aluminum valve covers. The 428 came with either a Toploader four-speed or optional C-6 Cruise-O-Matic. Axle ratios ranged from 3.50:1 to 4.11:1.

A handful of 1967 GT-500s received the 427-cubic-inch medium-riser V-8 engine instead of the 428, either during manufacture or through the dealer.

Shelby Mustang suspension remained very similar to that of the 1967 Mustang GT/GTA, with a 15/16-inch front sway bar,

All '67 Shelby Mustangs were 2+2s modified with a shark-like front fascia that included an air scoop beneath the grille and a new hood with a ram-air openings. GT-350 (opposite page) continued with 306-bhp 289 V-8. GT-500 (below) bowed with the 355-bhp dual-quad 428. Center-mounted lights were moved outboard on some cars to meet laws in certain states.

stiffer springs on all four corners, and shock absorbers with more controlled damping rates. Shelby replaced his Mustangs' Koni Shocks with less expensive, adjustable units made by Gabriel. On the pavement, choices included stock steel wheels with wheel covers, 15×7-inch Kelsey-Hayes MagStars, or cast-aluminum Shelby 10-Spokes. Tires grew to E70×15.

1968

Some Shelby purists say Ford Division's heavy involvement in the 1967 Shelby Mustangs marked the end of the true Shelby Mustang. That's open to debate, but there's little doubt that in 1968, the car lost a vital part of its unique identity.

The Shelby Mustang had been a custom built, limited-production, competition-bred car built at Shelby's own facilities in California. In '68, however, production was moved to Michigan.

Ford wanted more control over the cars, and Carroll Shelby was increasingly occupied with Ford's international racing program. Plus, Shelby American's lease on its shop near Los Angeles International Airport had expired. Cars destined for Shelby-ization were shipped by rail from Ford to an A.O. Smith Company facility in Ionia, Michigan, for the transformation.

The 1968 Shelby GT-350 and GT-500 had a new fiberglass fascia and redesigned hood with air scoops placed at the leading edge for enhanced ram effect. The center-mounted high-beams were supplanted by fog lamps at the outboard edges of the grille. As in 1967, a fiberglass rear decklid remained, coupled with a revised rear panel that included the pop-open Shelby gas

cap and (except in California) 1965 Thunderbird sequential taillights. Shelby had built a few convertibles for special customers, but '68 marked the first year a Shelby Mustang drop top was offered as part of the regular lineup. Finally, all these cars were rechristened the Shelby Cobra, though the GT-350 and GT-500 designations were retained.

Under the GT-350's hood went Ford's new 302-cubic V-8 with a Holly 600cfm four barrel on a stock cast-iron intake manifold, hydraulic lifters, and 250 horsepower. Behind the 302 sat a choice of Toploader four-speed or C-4 Cruise-O-Matic transmissions. Axle ratios ranged from 2.79:1 to 4.30:1. This milder GT-350 was in response to more stringent exhaust-emissions standards.

As in 1967, GT-500 meant big block. For 1968, the 428 Police Interceptor included a single 650cfm Holley four-barrel carburetor, but horsepower was up slightly to 360 at 5400 rpm. With the 428 came the choice of two transmissions, a Toploader four-speed or C-6 Cruise-O-Matic. Rear-end choices ranged from 3.25:1 to 4.30:1, with the more extreme ratios dealer-installed.

On April 1, 1968, Ford introduced the 428 Cobra Jet V-8 and it proved a turning point for Shelby muscle. This variant of the 428-cubic-inch Police Interceptor sported "427" medium-riser heads, a nodular iron crankshaft, heavy-duty connecting rods, dished pistons for reduced compression and valve clearance, and a 735cfm Holley carburetor. The result was 335 advertised horsepower, though a more realistic figure was 400.

With the new Cobra Jet V-8, big-block Shelby Mustangs changed from the GT-500 designation to GT-500KR; the KR

141

First regular-production Shelby Mustang convertible was the '68 (below). The GT-500's 428 used a single four-barrel this year, but horsepower was up to 360 (bottom, left). GT-350 (opposite page) switched to Ford's new 302-cid Windsor tuned to 250 bhp. Note new hood design. These were the first Shelby Mustangs not built at Shelby's California plant.

standing for "King of the Road." Transmissions and rear-end ratios were the same as the GT-500, though the car was considerably quicker. *Hot Rod* turned the quarter-mile in 14.01 seconds at 102.73 mph in a GT-500KR fastback with manual shift.

Inside, the 1968 GT-350 and GT-500 received the Mustang's optional Interior Decor Group as standard. Shelby graphics were added, as was a special console that included oil and amp gauges. Available in Black and Saddle, the Shelby Cobra cabins had woodgrain appointments. Prices for the GT-350 and GT-500 were up only slightly from '67; the GT-500KR coupe sold for $4473. The convertible was available in all GT-350, GT-500 and GT-500KR forms and included a padded roll bar. Prices for the ragtop started at $4238 and went to $4594.

Production for the 1968 Shelby Cobra:
GT-350: fastback, 1253; convertible, 404
GT-500: fastback, 1140; convertible, 402
GT-500KR: fastback, 933; convertible, 318

Significantly, the standard Mustang was available with the 428 starting in mid-year. Though a 427 was offered in the Mustang in '67, introduction of the '68 1/2 428 Cobra Jet Mustang—and the Boss Mustangs that would soon follow— spelled the beginning of the end for the Shelby-inspired versions of Ford's pony car.

Though the Shelby Mustangs started life as well-balanced road-course warriors, '67 production figures show how much the public demanded the sheer brute of cubic inches. Shelby built 1175 GT-350s, but found demand for 2048 GT-500s. Another result of Ford's involvement was a lower price: The '67 GT-350 listed for $3995, down more than $600 from '66. The GT-500 sold for $4195, about $150 less than a contemporary 327 Corvette coupe.

1967-68 Shelby Mustang
GT-350/GT-500

Facts At a Glance

1967	GT-350	GT-500
Engine type:	V-8/Windsor	V-8/FE Series
Displacement (cid):	289	428
Horsepower @ rpm:	306 @ 6000	355 @ 5400
Torque (lbs/ft) @ rpm:	329 @ 4200	420 @ 3200
Compression ratio:	10.5:1	10.5:1
Bore (in.):	4.00	4.13
Stroke (in.):	2.87	3.98
Valve lifters:	Mechanical	Hydraulic
Availability:	GT-350	GT-500

Magazine:	N/A (April 1967)	Motor Trend
Times:		
0-60 mph (sec):	7.1	6.2
0-100 mph (sec):	N/A	N/A
¼-mile (sec):	15.3 @ 91 mph	14.52 @ 101.35 mph
Top speed (mph):	129	120
Axle ratio:	3.89:1	3.50:1
Engine type:	289	428

Magazine:	Motor Trend (May 1967)	Car and Driver (Feb. 1967)
Times:		
0-60 mph (sec):	7.8	6.5
0-100 mph (sec):	N/A	16.6
1.4-mile (sec):	15.9 @ 90 mph	15 @ 95 mph
Top speed (mph):	N/A	N/A
Axle ratio:	N/A	3.25:1
Engine type:	289	428

1968	GT-350	GT-500
Engine type:	V-8/Windsor	V-8/FE Series
Displacement (cid):	302	428
Horsepower @ rpm:	250 @ 4800	360 @ 5400
Torque (lbs/ft) @ rpm:	318 @ 2800	420 @ 3200
Compression ratio:	10.5:1	10.5:1
Bore (in.):	4.00	4.13
Stroke (in.):	2.87	3.98
Valve lifters:	Hydraulic	Hydraulic
Availability:	GT-350	GT-500

Magazine:	Muscle Car Review
Times:	
0-60 mph (sec):	7.5 (est)
0-100 mph (sec):	N/A
¼-mile (sec):	13.93 @ 95.44 mph
Top speed (mph):	N/A
Axle ratio:	3.50:1
Engine type:	428 (GT-500)

1968	GT-500KR
Engine type:	V-8/FE Series
Displacement (cid):	428
Horsepower @ rpm:	335 @ 5200
Torque (lbs/ft) @ rpm:	440 @ 3400
Compression ratio:	10.6:1
Bore (in.):	4.13
Stroke (in.):	3.98
Valve lifters:	Hydraulic
Availability:	GT-500KR

Magazine:	Car Life (Oct. 1968)
Times:	
0-60 mph (sec):	6.9
0-100 mph (sec):	14.6
1.4-mile (sec):	14.57 @ 99.55 mph[1]
Top speed (mph):	130
Axle ratio:	3.50:1
Engine type:	428 (GT-500KR)

[1]Hot Rod magazine's testers went through the quarter-mile in 14.01 seconds, reaching 102.73 mph, in a GT-500KR fastback with manual shift.

1969
FORD
FAIRLANE COBRA 428

Nothing represented the muscle-car ethic at its purest better than the low-buck, big-cube intermediates of the late 1960s and early '70s. Instead of fancy bucket seats and flashy wheels, these cars cut to the quick with taxi-cab interiors and fleet-grade hub caps; the only bells and whistles were under the hood. The '68 Plymouth Road Runner—335-horsepower for $2896—was the prototypical example. Ford saw the light in '69 with the Fairlane Cobra.

These were dressed-down Torinos, with the grille blacked out and exterior ornamentation confined to little more than chrome wheel-lip moldings. Plain vinyl bench seats and a four-speed manual were standard. The package was available in either the sedan or SportsRoof fastback body style. But about the only obvious clue to the car's true nature was on the front fenders and rear panel, where Ford pasted decals of a stylized Cobra snake aboard racing slicks. Its fangs were bared, its wheels trailed flames.

Under the hood was Ford's 335-horsepower Cobra Jet 428-cubic-inch V-8, and it was backed by a passel of serious performance extras. Both body styles listed for under $3200. "Bargain day at the muscle works," was one Ford advertising slogan for these cars.

The 428 sported a 735cfm Holley four barrel and got new cast-iron exhaust headers and bigger intake and exhaust ports for '69. Horsepower was unchanged from the year before, but peak output was now 5200 rpm instead of 5400. Torque was unchanged, at 440 pounds/feet at 3400 rpm. A $133.44 Ram-Air option brought a hood scoop that fed fresh air to the air cleaner at full throttle. Engines with this advantage were called CJ-R and ordering one required the buyer to purchase extra-cost wide-oval raised-letter tires, a 6000-rpm tachometer ($47.92); and bucket seats ($120.59). The CJ-R engine added no horsepower to the advertised figure.

Backing up the Ford big-block was a choice of four-speed manual or C-6 SelectShift Cruise-O-Matic transmissions. Plenty of axle ratios were available, including standard 3.25:1 as well as optional 3.50:1, 3.91:1, and 4.30:1, the latter being a bulletproof Detroit Locker. Both the 3.91:1 Traction-Lok and 4.30:1 Locker were special options that required race-prepared components, such as an engine oil cooler, for more reliable operation. Later, in 1970, both the 3.91:1 and 4.30:1 would become part of the "Drag Pack" option.

Ford raced into the budget-muscle market with its '69 Fairlane Cobra. It had low price, big-block power, beefy suspension, and low-key interior. Hardtop body or, as here, the SportsRoof, were offered.

1969 Fairlane Cobra 428

Facts At a Glance

Engine type:	V-8/FE Series
Displacement (cid):	428
Horsepower @ rpm:	335 @ 5200
Torque (lbs/ft) @ rpm:	440 @ 3400
Compression ratio:	10.6:1
Bore (in.):	4.13
Stroke (in.):	3.98
Valve lifters:	Hydraulic
Availability:	Fairlane Cobra SportsRoof and Hardtop (notchback)

Magazine:	*Car & Driver* (January 1969)	*Car Life* (January 1969)
Times:		
0-60 mph (sec):	5.6	7.3
0-100 mph (sec):	14.0	15.5
¼-mile (sec):	14.04 @ 100.61 mph	14.9 @ 95.2 mph
Top speed:	129 (est)	125.5
Axle ratio:	3.50:1	3.50:1

Ram-Air option for 428-cid V-8 (above, right) force fed the four-barrel carb at full throttle through a functional hood scoop. Fast, strong, and reliable, these were among the very best Ford muscle cars.

The Cobras also included as standard a competition suspension with staggered rear shocks, F70×14 tires on six-inch rims, and hood lock pins. Styled steel wheels were among the options and later in the year, the Cobra decals were changed to smaller metal emblems of a similar design.

In a *Motor Trend* comparison of six contemporary muscle cars, a CJ-R Cobra with the locking 3.50:1 gears turned a 0-60-mph time of 6.3 seconds and ran the quarter in 14.5 at 100 mph. That was slower than a duet of 440 MoPars, a Plymouth GTX (5.8; 13.7/102.8) and a Dodge Charger R/T (6.1; 13.9/101.4). But it was faster than a Chevelle SS 396, Pontiac GTO, or Buick GS 400. The icing on the cake was that at $3945 as tested, the Cobra was the least expensive of the bunch and was, according to *Motor Trend*, the most solidly built.

Ford had set out to create a budget screamer and, for once, had accomplished its objective.

1969
FORD TORINO
TALLADEGA 428

R ace on Sunday, sell on Monday isn't just a catchy cliche, especially in the world of stock car racing. With NASCAR enjoying the full force of factory participation in the 1960s, the public's allegiance to a racing Ford, Chevy, or Pontiac was especially fierce. Fans who wanted to drive the same make of car as their hero accounted for a lot of automobile sales.

Thankfully, NASCAR rules required automakers to offer to the public cars very similar to the ones they supplied to the racers. Occasionally, the rule inspired Detroit to offer something really wild to the public. Probably the best example would be the Dodge Charger Daytona and Plymouth Road Runner Superbird with their drooping snouts and outrageous rear wings.

At Ford, the 1969 Torino Talladega holds the honors for NASCAR-inspired flamboyance and is today one of the rarest and most historic of the blue-oval muscle cars.

Its story begins with the heated rivalry between Ford and Chrysler for NASCAR dominance. The racing arms of the two manufacturers had produced engines—Chrysler's Hemi, Ford's Wedge—that could dominate on any given Sunday. That left the racer's edge to the body design that cut through the air with the least wind resistance. Dodge announced in the fall of 1968 that it would campaign in 1969 the Charger 500, an aerodynamically modified Charger hardtop with a flush grille, fixed headlamps, and a flush semi-fastback rear window.

Ford knew it had to counter with a similar plan for its SportsRoof Torino. Dearborn and its racers came up with a design and christened it the Talladega, after the small Alabama town that would soon become the location of NASCAR's biggest superspeedway. Ford shut down the Atlanta, Georgia, assembly plant where Torinos and Fairlanes were assembled for two weeks in January 1969 to devote all efforts to the production of these limited-edition intermediates. NASCAR rules at the time required that at least 500 streetable production units be assembled for public sale before the car could be certified for racing.

Ford put a sloped nose on the stock-car-racing version of its 1969 Torino to help its aerodynamics on NASCAR superspeedways. Rules required Ford to build at least 500 street versions. Hence, the Torino Talladega.

To keep costs respectable, Ford started with a base Fairlane Cobra SportsRoof. During assembly, the rocker panels were rerolled so Ford could legally lower the bodies. The standard SportsRoof was 53.5-inches tall; the Talladega would be 52.6. From that point, the cars were virtually hand built. Front fenders were extensively modified at the bottoms to match the rerolled rocker panels. Front aero extensions were welded to each fender for improved aerodynamics and to match actual NASCAR Talladegas. This tapered nose added 5.9 inches to the length of a stock Torino.

The Fairlane grille had to meet flush with the leading edges of the fenders, exactly like their racing brethren, and include a header panel between the hood and grille. Poor lead joints during assembly required Ford to "repair" dozens of front fenders before the Talladegas could be released and shipped to dealers. The front bumper was actually a Fairlane rear bumper cut into three pieces, narrowed to fit, then welded and rechromed for installation.

Ford went on to build 754 street Torino Talladegas, including prototypes. All were equipped with the 335-horsepower 428 Cobra Jet V-8 with a single Holley 735cfm four-barrel carburetor, C-6 Cruise-O-Matic with column shift, and 3.25:1 nodular iron Traction-Lok differentials. Underneath, the Talladegas were equipped with the Competition Handling Suspension and staggered rear shocks.

Because the Talladega was a budget exercise, only three colors were available on the street cars: Royal Maroon, Presidential Blue, and Wimbledon White. The hoods were painted matte black. A Bright Yellow preproduction unit also was built and delivered to Ford Motor Company President Semon "Bunkie" Knudsen.

Inside, the Torino Talladegas were as taxicab-oriented as the garden variety Fairlanes, equipped with bench seats and standard instrumentation. Knudsen's car, however, had a white interior, bucket seats, and even air conditioning; all others had black interiors.

Ford wanted to power its racing Talladegas with its Hemi-head Boss 429 V-8. NASCAR demanded 500 streetable Boss 429 engines in completed vehicles before they would certify the Hemi/Talladega combination for competition. But NASCAR didn't require the manufacturer to certify the engine in the same car in which it would race. For some reason, Ford decided to install 500 of the 429s in Mustangs, and thus was born the legendary Boss 429 Mustang.

To make things more complicated, those Boss 429 Mustangs weren't completed in time for the 1969 NASCAR season, so the first racing Talladegas had to run with the 427 Tunnel Port FE-series wedge, which hadn't been offered in a street Fairlane since 1966. The 429 finally was certified part way through the '69 season and was raced by the Talladegas and the Cyclone Spoiler II, Mercury's Talladega-style clone. When it was over, Ford had captured 26 wins to earn the NASCAR Manufacturer's Cup.

Back on the street, Ford was giving its limited-production Torinos very little publicity. Even the car itself was devoid of Talladega nameplates, save for a plate on each interior door panel. A dummy gas-cap emblem on the rear panel and insignias above the exterior door handles, all with the letter T, were the only external indications.

The Torino Talladega wasn't offered to the public after '69. though it proved more aerodynamic than the restyled 1970 Torinos and so was campaigned again in NASCAR. As it turned out, 1970 was the last year of Ford's full factory participation in stock car racing, so the slick 1969 Torino Talladega was not only a unique muscle car, but one that closed an historic chapter in Dearborn's history.

1969 Torino Talladega

Facts At a Glance

Engine type:	V-8/FE Series
Displacement (cid):	428
Horsepower @ rpm:	335 @ 5200
Torque (lbs/ft)	
@ rpm:	440 @ 3400
Compression ratio:	10.5:1
Bore (in.):	4.13
Stroke (in.):	3.98
Valve lifters:	Hydraulic
Availability:	1969 Torino Talladega

Magazine:	***Special Interest Autos* (Feb. 1986)**
Times:	
0-60 mph (sec):	6.8
0-100 mph (sec):	N/A
¼ mile (sec):	14.2 @ 101 mph
Top speed (mph):	130
Axle ratio:	3.50:1

Ford named the Talladega after the site of NASCAR's biggest track. It built 754 of them, all with the 335-bhp 428 Cobra Jet (top). Air cleaner, polished valve covers, and beer can are non-factory items.

1969-70
FORD
MUSTANG BOSS 302

Nearest thing to a Trans-Am Mustang that you can bolt a license plate onto," claimed Ford ads for the 1969 Boss 302. For once, they weren't kidding.

"Without a doubt," proclaimed *Car and Driver*, "the Boss 302 is the best handling Ford ever to come out of Dearborn and may just be the new standard by which everything from Detroit must be judged...." Tall praise for a Mustang. But the Boss 302 was some machine, with power, grace, style, and balance way beyond the grasp of most American sporty cars of the time.

The Boss 302 story begins with Semon E. "Bunkie" Knudsen and his surprise shift to Ford from arch-rival General Motors in February 1968. Knudsen was a car guy who cranked the performance spirit into the Pontiac Division in the late 1950s and early '60s.

The other side of the Boss 302 equation concerns the Mustang's success in Sports Car Club of America B-Production competition on the strength of its Hi-Performance 289-cubic-inch

Perhaps the most appealing factory high-performance Mustang ever was the
Boss 302. A bare-knuckle fighter on the street, it blended power, style, and
handling. Below is '70 model; '69's had four headlamps.

V-8. Rival Chevrolet was coming on strong with the 1967 Z-28 Camaro, which had a short-stroke 302 cubic-inch small-block screamer.

During 1968, Ford's engineers found that with some modifications, the big-port cylinder heads from their upcoming 351-cubic-inch Cleveland V-8 would fit the Windsor-based 302 Tunnel Port V-8. The combination seemed a perfect way to wring more horsepower from the Windsor small-block while staying within the Trans-Am displacement limit of 305-cubic inches.

Knudsen saw an opportunity to create a hot new street Mustang, a Z-28 fighter. Ford engineers went to work detuning the racing 302 for public consumption. Knudsen had brought from GM the talented Larry Shinoda, who was named chief of Ford's Special Design Center. Since the early '60s, Shinoda had designed wind-cheating shapes such as the original Sting Ray, Corvette Mako Shark, Monza GT, and Corvair Super Spyder. Shinoda was fond of aerodynamic aids—spoilers, low noses,

airfoils, front air dams and the like—and some of these would appear on later Mustangs and other Ford models. Shinoda promptly went to work on the Mustang, cleaning up the SportsRoof body by removing the quarter-panel insignias and fake air scoops. Because Shinoda often referred to Knudsen as "Boss," legend has it that the name found its way to the 302 Trans Am and 429 NASCAR packages.

The 1969 Boss 302's blacked-out headlamp doors and rear panel, front and rear spoiler, and rear backlight sports slats were all Shinoda concepts. The C-stripes on its sides were inspired by the LeMans-proven Ford GT-40s. Inside, the 1969 Boss 302 remained much the same as a garden-variety Mustang SportsRoof, except for full instrumentation and a four-speed.

Under the hood, the 302 engine was a Windsor block derived from the 221/260/289/302 series of small V-8s. Vital differences included a heavier casting in critical areas and the use of four-bolt main caps to contain the high-revving forged steel crankshaft, plus forged-aluminum pistons for 10.5:1 compression. Up top, modified 351 Cleveland cylinder heads with larger ports and canted valves improved flow at high rpm. In the racing spirit, an aluminum intake manifold carried a 780cfm Holley carburetor with manual choke. The result was excellent high-rpm performance. The engine was rated at 290 horsepower at 5800 rpm.

All 1969 Boss 302 Mustangs held Ford Toploader four-speeds in either close- or wide-ratio format, with a 10.5-inch conventional clutch. As with the 289 High-Performance Mustangs of 1965-67, a Ford nine-inch removable carrier

differential was incorporated with a choice of 3.50:1, 3.91:1, or 4.30:1 gears. The first two were Traction-Lok, while the 4.30:1 was a Detroit Locker. Handling was the province of heavy-duty front coil and rear leaf springs, stiffer shock absorbers, a heavy-duty (15/16-inch) front stabilizer bar, and staggered rear shock mounts to dampen and eliminate wheel hop under torrid takeoffs. The wheel openings were widened to make room for the F60×15 fiberglass-belted tires and the steering was quickened. Power front-disc brakes were added.

Put simply, the 1969 Boss 302 Mustang represented a race-car attitude adjusted for street use. Yet it was not without reliability problems. Because disconnecting the rev-limiter was a simple route to higher rpm, piston failures on production models gave Ford a distressing share of warranty headaches.

Introduced on April 17, 1969, Mustang's fifth anniversary, the Boss 302 cost $3588 and won immediate accolades.

"It's what the Shelby GT-350's and 500's should've been but weren't," said *Car and Driver*. Most testers criticized the extremely stiff ride, but the majority agreed it was worth it to achieve such great handling. "It simply drives around the turns with a kind of detachment never before experienced in a street car wearing Ford emblems." said *Car and Driver*.

Pitted against a '69 Z-28, which cost about $3700 but wrung 350 horsepower from its 302, most testers found the Boss a trifle easier to drive on the street because its engine was less peaky than the Chevy. *Car Life* turned identical 14.85-second quarter-miles in the two rivals, but the higher-horsepower Z-28's 101-mph trap speed was nearly five mph faster than the Ford's.

As for 1969 Trans Am season, the Boss 302s of Parnelli Jones just couldn't overtake the Mark Donohue Z-28s. In 12 races, the Fords managed just three wins. But the lucky few who snapped up the 1934 Boss 302s built for the street considered themselves winners all the way.

1970

Here was the Mustang to have "when you like it quick," purred the promotional copy. "All-out performance for adventurous souls who want to rule the road," it said. And if the Boss's ferocious performance didn't attract enough attention, maybe one of the Grabber colors (Calypso Coral, Wimbledon White, bright yellow, Acapulco Blue) with new "hockey stick" side striping would. The small-block Boss got a T-handle for its Hurst shifter, while the options list ranged from slats for the tinted backlight to a rear spoiler and Magnum 500 wheels.

For 1970, the Boss 302 Mustang received visual updates that mirrored those of the other Mustangs. The twin-set headlamps of 1969 were shelved in favor of single units positioned inside the grille. False air intakes in fender extensions helped create a shark-like appearance. The Boss's rear panel and taillight bezels were blacked out to aid identification.

Under the hood, the Boss 302 engine received slightly smaller valves for improved driveability and emissions, a revised water pump, cast-aluminum valve covers (formerly chromed steel), and improved pistons. Horsepower remained at 290, but price was up to $3720.

By the time production ended in the summer of 1970, 6319 '70 Boss 302 Mustangs had been assembled for a total of just 7103 in its short lifespan. But the car went out in a blaze of glory. Running against an all-out assault by Pontiac, Plymouth, Dodge, American Motors, and Chevrolet, the Boss 302s recaptured for Ford the SCCA Trans Am title. Parnelli Jones piloted the Boss 302 to five wins and George Follmer drove it to four.

Shaker hood scoop was standard on '69 Boss 302s, but was an option on '70s like these. Backlight slats and hood-mounted tach also were optional. Strong 302-cid V-8 was underrated at 290 bhp. Boss 302's racing counterpart won the '70 Trans Am title for Ford.

1969-70 Boss 302 Mustang

Facts At a Glance

Engine type:	V-8/Windsor (Cleveland heads)
Displacement (cid):	302
Horsepower @ rpm:	290 @ 5800
Torque (lbs/ft) @ rpm:	290 @ 4300
Compression ratio:	10.5:1
Bore (in.):	4.00
Stroke (in.):	3.00
Valve lifters:	Mechanical
Availability:	Boss 302 Mustang

Magazine:	*Car Life* (Sept. 1969)	*Motor Trend* (April 1970)
Times:		
0-60 mph (sec):	6.5	8.1
0-100 mph (sec):	17.0	N/A
¼-mile (sec):	14.85 @ 96.15 mph	15.8 @ 90 mph
Top speed (mph):	118	111
Axle ratio:	3.91:1	3.91:1

Magazine:	*Car Life* (Sept. 1969)
Times:	
0-60 mph (sec):	6.9
0-100 mph (sec):	N/A
¼-mile (sec):	14.9 @ 96 mph
Top speed (mph):	118
Axle ratio:	3.91:1

1969-70
FORD
MUSTANG BOSS 429

The Boss 429 resides at the summit of Mustang lore, though it never was meant to dominate the streets, and it didn't. This is a '70 model. All were SportsRoofs reworked to accept Semi-hemi 429-cid V-8.

BOSS 429

You're not likely to find a car that incited more lust in Ford fanatics than the 1969-70 Boss 429. Oddly enough, the passion is born more of what the car promised than what it delivered.

Like so many street muscle cars, its origin could be traced to the race course, this time, the high-speed ovals of NASCAR. The tale begins with the FE-series, wedge-head 427 V-8 and its eclipse in NASCAR by Chrysler's rampaging 426 Hemi. The fallout was felt not only in the winner's circle, but in Ford showrooms. Dearborn's answer was to take full advantage of the upcoming 385-series lightweight big-block engine—in both 429- and 460-cubic-inch displacement.

Ford quickly learned that the 429 Wedge wasn't as fast as the FE-series 427. However, with semi-hemispherical combustion chambers and a good cross-flow design, the 429 suddenly came alive with horsepower and torque that surpassed the 427. It was FoMoCo president Semon "Bunkie" Knudsen himself who decided to push the 429 Semi-hemi into action.

NASCAR required production of at least 500 streetable units to qualify the engine for racing. Knudsen ordered work to begin on at least that many street-ready Boss 429s—but tucked into the new 1969 Mustang SportsRoof body, not the fastback Torinos that Ford would campaign in stock-car racing. NASCAR rules allowed such a switcheroo.

Ford's Kar Kraft plant in Brighton, Michigan, had to alter the Mustang's shock towers extensively to accommodate the massive semi-hemi-head Boss 429 V-8. Front fenders and rear wheelwell lips had to be modified to handle much wider tires. Kar Kraft also revised the Mustang's suspension to handle the added engine weight up front and had to find room for such items as oil and power-steering fluid coolers.

Its heart, of course, was the Boss engine. This was a tough character, with four-bolt main bearing caps and a forged steel crankshaft. A 735cfm Holley four-barrel carburetor sat atop a cast-aluminum high-riser manifold and was fed by a huge ram-air hood scoop. The semi-hemi-heads and the valve covers also were made of aluminum. A heavy-duty Toploader four-speed and Traction-Lok 3.91:1 gears were standard. Like the Boss 302, its big brother carried a full complement of suspension goodies: large front anti-sway bar, stiffer front coil and rear leaf springs, stouter shock-damping rates, and staggered rear shocks to eliminate wheel hop. Tires were F60×15 Goodyear Polyglas bias-belted on Magnum 500 wheels. A 65-amp alternator, 85 amp-hour trunk-mounted battery, and full instrumentation that included an 8000-rpm tachometer were part of the package.

Aesthetically, the Boss 429 was refreshingly simple, with the only real hint of its true nature being the tasteful "BOSS 429" decals on the front fenders. For what amounted to a factory drag racer, the Boss 429 was surprisingly lush inside, however. Each one left Kar Kraft with the Decor Group that was optional on other Mustangs, along with high-back bucket seats, deluxe seatbelts, center console, and woodgrain dash trim. Ford also threw in the optional Visibility Group, comprised of parking brake warning lamp, glovebox lock, and lights for luggage compartment, ashtray, and glovebox. Automatic transmission and air conditioning, however, weren't available even as options.

At $4798, the Boss 429 was the costliest non-Shelby Mustang to date.

Of course, neither the Boss 429 nor the Boss 302 was intended to make money; these were, instead, specialty models that had to be built to appease racing authorities. *Car Life* magazine tested both Bosses and found the little guy quicker to 60 mph—6.9 seconds versus 7.2. But the 302 lost in the quarter-mile at 14.85 seconds and 96.14 mph compared with

14.09 seconds and 102.85 mph for the 429. Top speed for both was shown as 118 mph. Obviously, the 429 was potent, but its chassis was simply overwhelmed in standing-start acceleration. As a starting point for those who wished to modify for the strip, it was fearsome, but on the street it was something of a disappointment. In fact, the Mustang 428 Cobra Jet Mach 1 was almost always quicker on the street.

Fact is, Ford never intended the Boss 429 Mustang to rule the street. Roy Lunn, who oversaw Ford's Boss 429 Mustang program, is quoted in *Mustang! The Complete History of America's Pioneer Ponycar:* "There was no incentive to make the package a complete racing car as delivered. It was really just a hairy, crazy road machine for people who like that sort of thing...and a means of keeping competitive in stock-car racing."

1970

The Boss 429 Mustang went unchanged mechanically for 1970, though its styling did follow changes to the other Mustangs: The headlamps were moved inside the mouthy grille and the taillights were now one-piece units. The price was unchanged, but just 498 were built to 1970 specs. A tamer 429 then became a regular Mustang option, only to disappear after a single year.

In retrospect, the Boss 429 Mustang was a flare that burned brightly just before Ford's factory-backed racing program flamed out in August of 1970. It is revered today as much for its light as its fire.

Mustang needed much modification to accept the NASCAR-bred 375-bhp big-block (above). Battery was trunk mounted (opposite page, top); there was no room in engine bay and it helped balance weight a little. Boss 429 exterior was free of geegaws; hood scoop is functional.

1969-70 Boss 429 Mustang

Facts At a Glance

Engine type:	V-8/385 Series (semi-hemispherical head)
Displacement (cid):	429
Horsepower @ rpm:	375 @ 5200
Torque (lbs/ft) @ rpm:	450 @ 3400
Compression ratio:	10.5:1
Bore (in.):	4.36
Stroke (in.):	3.59
Valve lifters:	Mechanical[1]
Availability:	1969-70 Boss 429 Mustang (and Cougar Eliminator)

[1]Early examples had hydraulic lifters.

Magazine:	*Car Life* (July 1969)
Times:	
0-60 mph (sec):	7.1
0-100 mph (sec):	13.6
¼-mile (sec):	14.09 @ 102.85 mph
Top speed (mph):	118
Axle ratio:	3.91:1

1969-70
SHELBY
MUSTANG GT-350/GT-500

Shelby Mustangs were back for 1969 in fastback and convertible body styles in GT-350 and GT-500 form. They were differentiated from the production Mustang by a three-inch-longer hood, reshaped front fenders, and a new nose with a big loop bumper/grille (all made of fiberglass to hold down weight). The Shelby also had a clipped tail with a lip spoiler and Cougar sequential turn signals. Scoops were everywhere—five NACA ducts on the hood alone—and wide reflective tape stripes ran midway along the flanks.

As in 1968, Shelbys shared the Mach 1's Knitted Vinyl Sports Interior. Two basic colors were offered, Black and Parchment; but Red, Saddle, and Blue interiors have also have been unearthed. A special Shelby console held oil and amp gauges. Both convertibles and SportsRoofs contained roll bars. An 8000-rpm tachometer and 140-mph speedometer were part of the Shelby package. On the ground, mag wheels became standard equipment and they wore F60×15 Goodyear Polyglas bias-belted tires. The look was macho and mean.

Said *Car and Driver's* Brock Yates: "I personally can't think of an automobile that makes a statement about performance...any better than [this Shelby]."

But brag is one thing, fact another. And the fact was that greater weight and stiffening emission controls rendered the '69s a lot tamer than any previous Shelby. Yates derisively described the '69 GT-350 as "a garter snake in Cobra skin."

The 428 Cobra Jet returned for 1969 in the GT-500, but without the "KR" designation. Horsepower was again advertised at 335 at 5200 rpm. Some historians say actual output was down an estimated 25 horses; others insist the engine still made at least 400 horses or more. In any case, finned-aluminum "Cobra" valve covers and intake manifold were performance

Last of the Shelby Mustangs were tough—and tough looking—but had rivals even within regular Mustang ranks. GT-500 used Ford's 428 Cobra Jet, the GT-350 its 351 Windsor. Mustang Mach 1 held either engine for less money, but also with less distinction. These are '69 models.

Ford added a chin spoiler and hood stripes to leftover '69 Shelby Mustangs and called them '70 models (both pages). Stylish Shelby mags with F60×15 Goodyear Polyglas GTs were standard. GT-500 again used 335-bhp Ram-air 428 (opposite page). This was the last Shelby Mustang.

1969-70 Shelby Mustang

GT-350/GT-500

Facts At a Glance

	GT-350	GT-500
Engine type:	V-8/Windsor	V-8/FE Series
Displacement (cid):	351	428
Horsepower @ rpm:	290 @ 4800	335 @ 5200
Torque (lbs/ft)		
@ rpm:	385 @ 3200	440 @ 3400
Compression ratio:	10.7:1	10.6:1
Bore (in.):	4.00	4.13
Stroke (in.):	3.50	3.98
Valve lifters:	Hydraulic	Hydraulic
Availability:	GT-350	GT-500

Magazine:	*Car Life*
	(Feb. 1969)
Times:	
0-60 mph (sec):	8.0
0-100 mph (sec):	21.6
1.4-mile (sec):	15.59 @ 89.09 mph
Top speed (mph):	119.2
Axle ratio:	2.75:1
Engine type:	351 (1969 Mustang)

Magazine:	*Car Life*
	(March 1969)
Times:	
0-60 mph (sec):	5.5
0-100 mph (sec):	12.8
1.4-mile (sec):	13.9 @ 103.32 mph
Top speed (mph):	121
Axle ratio:	3.91:1
Engine type:	428 CJ (1969 Mach 1)

assets, topped with a ram-induction air cleaner and 735cfm Holley four-barrel.

The GT-350 received a larger powerplant—Ford's new 351-cubic-inch Windsor four-barrel V-8 rated at 290 horsepower. Shelby's 351 Windsor enjoyed the benefit of a cast-aluminum intake manifold topped by a 470cfm Autolite four-barrel carburetor. This engine was standard in the new Mach 1 fastback, which cost much less than the Shelby, though finned-aluminum valve covers were a Shelby exclusive. Either engine could be backed by a four-speed manual or a C6 automatic.

But if the magic was gone part of the problem was that Carroll Shelby had long ceased to be involved with his cars. The '69s, in fact, were built at Ford's Southfield, Michigan, plant right alongside box-stock Mustangs. With design now being determined by production economics and marketing studies, proposed features like fuel injection, moonroof, and reclining seats didn't stand a chance.

The other part of the problem was new competition from the Mustang line itself. The Mach 1 was interference enough, but mid-year brought the hot Boss 302, a thinly disguised Trans-Am racer for the street, and the Boss 429 drag racer stuffed full of Ford's potent "semi-hemi" big-block.

Of course, the Bosses were no cheaper or more readily available than the Shelbys. But they were "a curious duplication of effort," as Yates put it, and only dimmed what luster the Shelbys still had. "The heritage of the GT-350 is performance," Yates mused, "and it is difficult to understand why the Ford marketing experts failed to exploit its reputation." But fail they did, and production sank by fully 25 percent, to 3150 units. This left a bunch of 1969 Shelby GT-350s and GT-500s to contend with. Along with a new serial number, each leftover vehicle received hood stripes and a Boss 302 Mustang chin spoiler for a quickie update to "1970" models. Approximately 789 1969 Shelbys were retitled and serial-numbered as 1970 cars, but with that, an era closed.

Curiously, the passing of these very special cars went largely unlamented. The late '60s and early '70s were heady high-performance days. Muscular setups deluged every automaker's showroom. The parade of ever-hotter machinery seemed as if would never end. But it did, and today any Shelby Mustang is respected as a direct link to one of the rare moments when Detroit did not compromise.

1971
FORD
BOSS 351 MUSTANG

A decade of Ford "Total Performance" was drawing to a close. In November 1970, Dearborn announced its pullout from most competitive racing. It also was dialing back its performance offerings for the street in response to tighter emissions rules, growing public criticism of big-cube production cars, and even a shift in the market as baby boomers began to settle down to family life. But as 1971 dawned, something was still kicking in the Ford ponycar stall: the Boss 351.

The 1971 Boss 351 Mustang SportsRoof actually came as an afterthought—a replacement for what was to have been the 1971 Boss 302. At the eleventh hour, Ford shifted gears, incorporating the new 351-cubic-inch Cleveland V-8 into the 1971 performance lineup. Tightening emissions standards helped dictate the larger mill, but so did the Mustang's new heft.

This last-gasp Boss would saddle up Mustang's largest body ever. Though wheelbase was up only an inch, the '71 Mustang ballooned eight inches in overall length, six inches in width, and gained some 600 pounds in curb weight. The styling was broad

Boss 351 brought the curtain down on Mustang's first muscle era with a Cleveland 351 four-barrel. It was a close kin to the '71 351C Mach 1, but was faster, with 330 bhp to the Mach's 285 bhp. The Boss also handled slightly better. ETs were commendable: low 14s at 100 mph.

and horizontal and the car's signature was a sweeping, almost flat fastback roofline. Its full-width grille and Kamm-style back panel had been inspired by the 1970 Shelby Mustangs. The Shelbys were gone now, but the Mach 1 accompanied the Boss into '71. The $4124 Boss in fact took much of its identity from the $3268 Mach 1.

They shared a twin-scoop hood that was optional on other models, a grille with a small running-horse emblem on honeycomb mesh, and horizontal parking lamps styled to look like driving lights. The Mach 1 would later in the year get the Boss's side strips, but the main visual difference was that the Boss used a chrome front bumper instead of the Mach 1's color-keyed one, and of course, it had "Boss 351 Mustang" graphics on the bodyside and rear deck.

In standard form, the Boss 351 came with the everyday Mustang interior, right down to a two-spoke Pinto steering wheel. An optional Interior Decor Group spiced the hot performance package a bit. Full instrumentation was standard,

though, and included a tachometer and an array of vital-function gauges. Bright chrome Ford corporate hub caps with trim rings decorated the Boss wheels, which carried white-letter F60×15 Goodyear Polyglas bias-belted tires on seven-inch wheels. Eleven body colors were available and they included striking green metallic, yellow, blue and lime—the "grabber" hues. A rear spoiler and Magnum 500 wheels were optional.

The Competition Suspension was the same as the Mach 1's and used staggered rear shocks, though the Boss 351 handled slightly better. Some credit goes to its ⅝-inch rear sway bar, which was bigger than the Mach's ½-inch bar. The Mach 1's standard tires also were smaller, at F70×14.

Like the Mach 1's optional 351C engine, the Boss used a 351-cubic-inch V-8 with a four-bolt main block. But the Mach 1's 351C had a compression ratio of 10.7:1, hydraulic lifters, and a 470cfm Motorcraft four-barrel for a maximum of 285 horsepower at 5400 rpm. The Boss's 351 had an 11.7:1 compression ratio, a 750cfm Motorcraft quad, mechanical lifters, and such goodies as

a dual-point vacuum-advance distributor, a special cooling package, and a rev limiter. It was rated at 330 horsepower at 5400 rpm. A Hurst shifter controlled the Toploader four-speed manual transmission, which led to a 3.91:1 Traction-Lok differential.

The Boss 351 ran 0-60 mph in 5.8 seconds and turned the quarter-mile in 14.1 seconds at 100.6 mph for *Car and Driver*. Top speed was 117 mph.

This was the best-balanced high-performance Mustang for '71. Buyers could get more power by ordering a Mach 1 with a 375-horsepower 429 Super Cobra Jet Ram Air mill, but the 429 put more than 850 pounds over the car's front axle—not exactly a boon to handling.

Perhaps the performance-buying public didn't realize this would be the last true Boss; perhaps other realities had finally caught up with the muscle car. Whatever the reason, Ford built just 1806 Boss 351s in 1971, and only now is the car beginning to attract serious collector interest.

1971 Boss 351 Mustang

Facts At a Glance

Engine type:	V-8/335 Series Cleveland
Displacement (cid):	351
Horsepower @ rpm:	330 @ 5400
Torque (lbs/ft) @ rpm:	370 @ 4000
Compression ratio:	11.7:1
Bore (in.):	4.00
Stroke (in.):	3.50
Valve lifters:	Mechanical
Availability:	1971 Boss 351 Mustang

Magazine:	***Car and Driver*** **(Feb. 1971)**
Times:	
0-60 mph (sec):	5.8
0-100 mph (sec):	13.9
¼-mile (sec):	14.1 @ 100.6 mph
Top speed (mph):	117
Axle ratio:	3.91:1

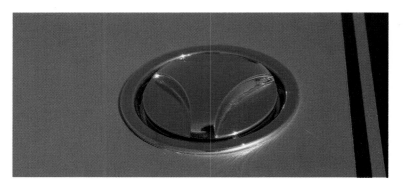

Boss 351 had a chrome bumper and chin spoiler to distinguish it from the lesser Mustang Mach 1, though both had the scooped hood and other '71 Mustangs eventually got similar side stripes. Rear spoiler was optional. Boss 351 was quicker and more tractable than earlier Boss 302, but also had less character.

1966-67 MERCURY COMET CYCLONE GT

Muscle fans can be forgiven for overlooking Mercury in the mid-'1960s. Rarely did it feature anything that couldn't be had for less money over at Ford, and sometimes the hottest Ford pieces weren't even available on the Mercs. But for the buyer who liked performance with a luxury bent, there were some attractive offerings at the sign of the cat.

The 1966-67 Comet Cyclone GT is a good example of all these Mercury strengths and weaknesses. Comet jumped from a compact to an intermediate in '66 thanks to its use of the new Ford Fairlane body shell. The cars shared a 116-inch wheelbase and, for all intents and purposes, had the same silhouette in both convertible and two-door hardtop form.

Despite the absence of an optional 427, the 1966 Comet Cyclone GT was no softy. Beneath the non-functional hood scoops sat Ford's 390-cubic-inch High Performance V-8 with a four-throat Holley carb. As in the Fairlane GT, it was rated at 335 horsepower at 4800 rpm and 427 pounds/feet of torque at 3200 rpm. A 10.5:1 compression ratio and dual exhausts were part of the package, as was a higher degree of reliability than offered by the high-strung 427.

A three-speed manual transmission was standard; optional was a four-speed manual or the C-6 Merc-O-Matic three-speed automatic. New 1-2-D Sport Shift let the automatic-transmission's driver change gears manually. A rear-axle ratio of 3.25:1 was standard, with optional ratios of 3.00:1, 3.50:1, 3.89:1, and 4:11:1 available. Underneath, a heavy-duty suspension operated with stiffer spring and shock damping rates. Up front, a larger sway bar (15/16 inch) helped keep the body stable during hard cornering. Standard GT gear also included sporty stripes and an engine dress-up kit that consisted of a chrome air cleaner and valve covers. The standard tires were 7.75×14 whitewalls on 5.5-inch rims. Mercury offered optional hub caps that looked like chrome wheels without wheelcovers.

The Comet Cyclone GT was about $100 more expensive than its Fairlane counterpart. It had richer interior appointments that included a five-dial instrument cluster, plush bucket seats, and sculptured console. Power steering, power front disc brakes, and factory-installed under-dash air conditioning were optionally available.

Mercury got some valuable exposure for its Comet Cyclone GT when it was chosen as the official pace car of the '66

Comet Cyclone GT was a cousin to the less plush Ford Fairlane, but Fairlane could be ordered with the 427-cid engine. Mercury had to make the most of its 390-cid four-barrel. It was a good performer, but wasn't mean enough to win widespread respect on the street. The '67 pictured has aftermarket mag wheels.

Indianapolis 500. But on the street, where it counted, serious performance enthusiasts were favoring the likes of the Pontiac GTO, Chevy Chevelle SS 396, and big-block Dodge Coronet and Plymouth Belvedere. Actually, the '66 Fairlane was one of the big winners in this segment, though only 37,343 were GTs. Cyclone GT production was 15,970. Pontiac, by contrast, built 96,946 GTOs that year.

1967

Dig hard enough and there will emerge news that Mercury equipped some 50 1967 Comet Cyclone GTs with Ford's thundering 427-cubic-inch engine. But even this is in dispute, and whether any made it to the street is far less certain. So except for 15 fewer horses from the 390 High Performance V-8, minor trim changes, a new grille, and added safety features, the 1967 Mercury Cyclone GT was a carryover.

Two-door hardtop and convertible body styles continued. Safety features included Ford's padded "crash dome" for the steering wheel, and a new dual braking system that provided braking if either the front or rear hydraulic system should fail. Power front disc brakes were made standard on Cyclone GT.

Don Nicholson campaigned a dragster that used a fiberglass Cyclone body—one of the original Funny Cars—to numerous NHRA wins across the country. But once again, the Cyclone GT failed to ignite the passions of street-oriented enthusiasts the way some of its competitors did.

GTO production, for example, was 81,722 that year, while output of the Cyclone GT fell to just 3797. The comparison is apt because both were marketed to slightly upscale performance enthusiasts, and the Mercury, at $3034 for the coupe and $3294 for the convertible, actually cost about $100 more than the GTO. But where the Cyclone GT's 390 made 320 horsepower, the GTO's 389 started at 335 and went up to 360. Even though the GTO weighed more, its approach to performance was much more integrated. Finally, Mercury had its new Cougar pony car to promote for '67, so the Cyclone GT lost out in that department, as well.

The 390-cid V-8 in the '67 Cyclone GT (above) had 320 bhp—15 less than in '66—and also was overshadowed in the showroom by Mercury's new-for-'67 Cougar. About 50 '67 Cyclone GTs are thought to have been equipped with the 427-cid mill.

1966-67 Mercury
Comet Cyclone
Facts At a Glance

Engine type:	V-8/FE Series	V-8/FE Series
Displacement (cid):	390	390
Horsepower @ rpm:	335 @ 4800	320 @ 4800
Torque (lbs/ft) @ rpm:	427 @ 3200	427 @ 3200
Compression ratio:	10.5:1	10.5:1
Bore (in.):	4.05	4.05
Stroke (in.):	3.78	3.78
Valve lifters:	Hydraulic	Hydraulic
Availability:	1966 Cyclone GT	1967 Cyclone GT

Magazine:	*Car and Driver (March 1966)*
Times:	
0-60 mph (sec):	N/A
0-100 mph (sec):	N/A
¼-mile (sec):	13.98 @ 103.8 mph
Top speed:	N/A
Axle ratio:	4.11:1
Engine type:	390
Model year:	1967 Cyclone GT[1]

[1]Test car had stock components, but was not showroom stock.

1969-70 MERCURY COUGAR ELIMINATOR

Cougar Eliminator was Mercury's stab at a high-profile, high-performance pony car. The most interesting version had Ford's Trans Am-racing derived Boss 302 engine. A '70 model is pictured.

Cougar was launched for the 1967 model year as Mercury's version of Ford's original Mustang pony car. In keeping with Lincoln-Mercury's upscale mission, the Cougar rode a Mustang chassis that had been stretched three inches to give the car a 111-inch wheelbase and a more boulevard ride. Additional sound-deadening material and some extra amenities were added in an effort to capture more of a sports-luxury-touring feel.

While the Cougar would always be a beat behind the lighter, more lithe Mustang in all-out performance, that didn't stop Mercury from sharpening its cat's claws. Right from the start, the Cougar GT and XR-7 offered a choice of powerteams that included the 289-cubic-inch two- and four-barrel V-8s, and the 390 High Performance V-8. (The 271-horsepower High Performance 289 V-8 never was available as a Cougar option.)

Cougar bounded into its second season with an array of sporty options that included the XR-7G (Dan Gurney Special) with gold interior appointments. More exotic was the GTE (GT-Eliminator). First equipped with the 427-cubic-inch V-8, then, after April 1, 1968, the 428 Cobra Jet engine, the GTE served as a prelude to the 1969-70 Cougar Eliminators.

For '69, there was a sheetmetal facelift, a subtle refining that produced the handsomest Cougar ever. The grille switched to horizontal ribs—still with hidden headlamps—and the body grew softer and more contemporary. The sharp kick-up behind the door was replaced by a more rounded form and a crease now swept in a gentle arc from the nose to the rear wheelwell.

Mercury was concerned about the tepid reception Cougar was getting in the showroom, however, and so on April 1, 1969, it announced the Eliminator model. This was Mercury's answer

to both the Mach 1 and Boss 302 Mustangs, not to mention the Z-28 Camaro and soon-to-be-released Pontiac Firebird Trans Am.

Because of its midyear introduction and Mercury's somewhat haphazard launch of the Eliminator, there exists today some confusion over which of its announced engines actually made it to the showroom in any numbers. The plan called for its powertrain choices to mirror those of the Mach 1 and Boss 302. Base price was to be $3499.50 for an Eliminator with the standard 290-horsepower 351-cubic-inch Windsor four-barrel V-8. The 290-horsepower Boss 302 V-8 was announced as a $335.50 extra, but some sources indicate production problems limited this engine to only a few cars. The 428 Cobra Jet was also listed as a $283.60 option and finally, Mercury said the 320-horsepower 390-cubic-inch four barrel would also be available.

In any case, the Eliminator featured a nice array of performance and appearance extras. The car was available in such high-impact colors as Bright Blue Metallic, Competition Orange, Bright Yellow, and Wimbledon White. A black stripe ran along the front fenders and doors, culminating in the word "Eliminator" on the rear flanks. A blacked out grille, chin spoiler, and rear-deck spoiler were standard, as was a hood scoop, which was functional only with the optional Ram-Air 428 CJ. Standard styled steel wheels were outfitted with F70×14 Goodyear Polyglas bias-belted tires. A firmed-up suspension with heavy-duty shocks was fitted; the rear shocks were staggered to reduce wheel hop in quick starts. Quick-ratio manual steering and power front disc brakes also were standard.

Inside, the 1969 Cougar Eliminator was all business, with a pinch of luxury. Because it was not an XR-7 model, it received the base Cougar's standard vinyl interior, but its instrumentation included a tachometer.

A four-speed manual transmission was mandatory with the Boss 302 engine. Ford's gutsy C-6 Select-Shift Cruise-O-Matic was optional. Buyers had an array of rear-end choices: 3.25:1; 3.50:1; 3.91:1; and 4.30:1. The 3.25:1 was available only with Cruise-O-Matic. When equipped with the 3.91:1 or Detroit Locker 4.30:1, as part of a Drag Pak or Super Drag Pak option, the Eliminator automatically gained an engine oil cooler for its 428 Cobra Jet.

Since the only major component added to the Cougar line by the Eliminator was the Boss 302 engine, road testers of the time seemed to focus their interest there. Derived from Ford's successful Trans Am racing engine, this was the same mill used in the potent Boss 302 Mustang: a canted-valve, mechanical-lifter small block with 10.6:1 compression and a Holley 780cfm four-barrel.

Critics generally found the Boss 302 Eliminator a willing, well-balanced package, though the small-block was a little overmatched in all-out drag racing by the Cougar's 3600 curb weight. Shifting 200 rpm before the 6000-rpm redline, *Road Test* saw a quarter-mile time of 14.84 at 96.16. But drag racing wasn't the car's forte, the magazine concluded. "On the open road or a relatively quiet freeway it's a joy to play with the smooth gearbox and the responsive engine," wrote its editors. "Throttle and brake are on an even plane so that heel-and-toe operation for hard, fast braking gives a real sports car feel. Third gear is excellent for cruising in traffic. The high revving engine feels under no strain at all and there is ample urge and surge to take advantage of traffic opportunities." As mentioned earlier, not many Boss 302 Eliminators made it into production; fewer than 500 are thought to have been built for '69.

1970

Cougar received mild styling alterations for 1970, the biggest change being at the front, where the grille was split by a nose-like protrusion. Mercury's sales brochure called Eliminator the "road animal," and promoted a series of staged hop-up kits available at dealers: the Impressor, the Controller, and the Dominator.

As in 1969, Cougar 's grille and headlamp doors received a matte black treatment to emphasize the Eliminator's performance profile. Eliminator side stripes moved from the beltline to the upper bodyline, running the full length of the car. Styled steel wheels remained standard, along with the functional ram-air hood scoop with the 428 CJR only.

Changes under the hood for 1970 included the deletion of the 390 Hi-Po engine from the option sheet. Ford's new 351 cubic-inch V-8, known as the Cleveland, replaced both the 390 and the four-barrel 351 Windsor. More powerful than the Windsor, the large-port Cleveland generated 300 horsepower with four-barrel carburetion. Ram Air induction was an option. Transmission choices with the high-tech 351 included a standard three-speed manual, optional four-speed with Hurst shifter, or C-6 Cruise-O-Matic.

For 1970, both the 3.91:1 and 4.30:1 axle ratios earned buyers a Drag Pak option that included the 428 Super Cobra Jet with 335 horses and an engine oil cooler. The Boss 302 also carried an oil cooler. Boss 302 upgrades this year included cast aluminum valve covers and revised cylinder heads for better

1969-70 Cougar Eliminator

Facts At a Glance

Engine type:	V-8/Windsor	V-8/FE Series
Displacement (cid):	351	390
Horsepower @ rpm:	290 @ 4800	320 @ 4600
Torque (lbs/ft) @ rpm:	385 @ 3200	427 @ 3200
Compression ratio:	10.7:1	10.5:1
Bore (in.):	4.00	4.05
Stroke (in.):	3.50	3.78
Valve lifters:	Hydraulic	Hydraulic
Availability:	Standard (1969)	Optional (1969)

Engine type:	V-8/Windsor (Boss 302)	V-8/FE Series (Cobra Jet)
Displacement (cid):	302	428
Horsepower @ rpm:	290 @ 5800	335 @ 5200
Torque (lbs/ft) @ rpm:	290 @ 4300	440 @ 3400
Compression ratio:	10.5:1	10.6:1
Bore (in.):	4.00	4.13
Stroke (in.):	3.00	3.98
Valve lifters:	Mechanical	Hydraulic
Availability:	Optional (69-70)	Optional (69-70)

Engine type:	V-8/Cleveland
Displacement (cid):	351
Horsepower @ rpm:	300 @ 5400
Torque (lbs/ft) @ rpm:	380 @ 3400
Compression ratio:	11.0:1
Bore (in.):	4.00
Stroke (in.):	3.50
Valve lifters:	Hydraulic
Availability:	Optional (1970)

Magazine:	*Car Life* (April 1970)	*Road Test* (Sept. 1969)
Times:		
0-60 mph (sec):	7.6	N/A
0-100 mph (sec):	21.1	N/A
1/4-mile (sec):	15.8 @ 90 mph	14.84 @ 96.16 mph
Top speed (mph):	104	N/A
Axle ratio:	4.30:1	3.91:1
Engine type:	Boss 302	Boss 302

Photos on opposite page show styling differences between the '69 Eliminator on the left, and the '70 model. The best-balanced package had the 351-cid V-8, which had 300 bhp in '70. Boss 302 version (this page) got aluminum valve covers and more low-end torque for '70. The engine was willing, but slightly overmatched by the 3600-lb. Cougar. No drag demon, Cougar Eliminator was instead a comfortable and responsive grand tourer.

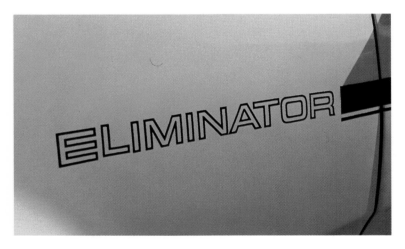

low-end torque and emissions.

The 1970 sales brochure listed the 429 Boss engine, rated 375 horsepower at 5200 rpm, as an Eliminator option. But Ford's Kar Kraft facility, where 1969-70 Boss 429 Mustangs were built, is known to have assembled only two 1970 Cougar Eliminators with Hemi-head Boss 429 V-8s.

Wringing out a '70 Boss 302 Eliminator, *Car Life* came to much the same conclusion as earlier testers. "Like the GTOs we tested," it said, "the Cougar has grown too big and plush to be able to roll up its sleeves and scrap with the new, young tough stuff." *Car Life* found the 302 overmatched by the Eliminator's heft. It also concluded that the big-blocks would do little but add more weight in the wrong place and would spin the tires too much to contribute to really good ETs. So it advised ordering the 351.

Still, not many buyers got the message. Production for 1970 was just 2200 units and the Cougar would grow even larger for '71, abandoning any pretention as a street fighter.

Ohio's Fast Eddie Schartman's '70 pro-stock drag car (top) was one of only two Cougars equipped with Ford's Boss 429 V-8. It turned 10.38-second quarter-miles. A hot street setup was the 335-bhp 428-cid Cobra Jet four-barrel (viewed above in a '69 Eliminator). This version does not have the Ram-Air Cobra Jet option. Color-keyed rear spoiler was an Eliminator standard feature.

1969 MERCURY MARAUDER X-100

Once all muscle cars were full-size models with their maker's biggest engine, but by the late '60s, big-block boats like this 429-cid Marauder X-100 were marketed as prestige specialty models.

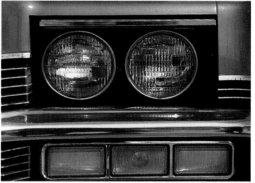

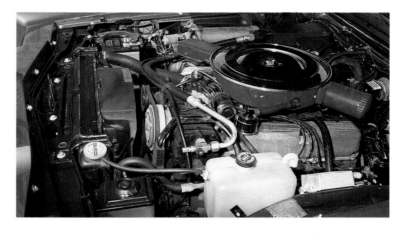

As the 1960s drew to a close, performance came in two basic forms: big engines in small packages and big engines in *big* packages. Typified by the Pontiac Grand Prix, Buick Riviera, and Ford Thunderbird, the latter were considered by the automakers to be prestige specialty cars. At Mercury, the full-size fire-breather for '69 was the Marauder X-100.

The Marauder was a two-door hardtop based on a Marquis chopped in wheelbase by three inches and shortened in the body by about five. The result was a relatively roomy two-door hardtop with a long-hood/short-deck profile on a still-substantial 121-inch wheelbase. Curb weight started at two tons, escalating to 4500 pounds with a full option load. Marauder essentially was the same as Ford's big Galaxie 500XL coupe and its flying buttress roofline and upright, tunneled backlight mimicked the SportsRoof Ford.

X-100 was the costlier of the two Marauders and came standard with rear fender skirts (optional on the base model), as well as "sports tone" matte-black paint on the tunneled rear deck area. The last could be deleted for credit or by ordering the extra-cost vinyl roof. The dash was Marquis to a T, so there really wasn't much sporty about an X-100 inside, even if you ordered the optional buckets and console in place of the plushly padded front bench.

To move this considerable mass, Lincoln-Mercury specified the venerable 265-horsepower, two-barrel, 390-cubic-inch Ford V-8 as base power. Standard for the X-100 and optional on the base model was Dearborn's new 429-cubic-inch V-8 in four-barrel form with 10.5:1 compression, a rated 360 horsepower at 4600 rpm, and 480 pounds/feet of torque at 2800. A three-speed Select-Shift automatic was the only transmission and an Interstate-gulping 2.80:1 rear axle ratio was standard. With the optional 3.25:1 Traction-Lok gears, the X-100 could turn the quarter in the mid-15s at 86-92 mph.

"We realize that this level of performance is perfectly *adequate*, but adequate for whom?" queried *Car and Driver*. Certainly not muscle-car mavens, it concluded. Surprisingly, the X-100 was a pretty competent roadgoer. Though understeer was the rule and the power steering was unnervingly light, roadholding was better than the base Marauder, thanks in part to the X-100's standard Goodyear Polyglas H70×15

1969 Mercury Marauder X-100

Facts At a Glance

Engine type:	V-8/385 Series
Displacement (cid):	429
Horsepower @ rpm:	360 @ 4600
Torque (lbs/ft) @ rpm:	480 @ 2800
Compression ratio:	10.5:1
Bore (in.):	4.36
Stroke (in.):	3.59
Valve lifters:	Hydraulic

Magazine:	*Car and Driver* (Dec. 1968)	*Car Life* (April 1969)
Times:		
0-60 mph (sec):	7.8	7.5
0-100 mph (sec):	22.8	19.9
¼-mile (sec):	16.0 @ 86.0 mph	15.17 @ 92.3 mph
Top speed (mph):	124 (est)	126
Axle ratio:	3.25:1	2.80:1

Marauder used the conservative Mercury Marquis luxury-car dash, but optional buckets and console added a dash of sportiness (top). Ordering a vinyl top deleted the rear-deck black-out paint applied to other X-100s. Mercury built about 8300 X-100s for '69 and '70.

bias-belted white sidewall tires on Kelsey-Hayes "MagStar" five-spoke aluminum wheels. Handling could be further improved by the stiffer springs and shocks offered with the $31.10 optional competition suspension. As a bonus, the X-100's ride was pleasingly firm and its optional $71.30 power-assisted front disc brakes helped produce short, sure stops. Overall, said *Car and Driver*, "it's extremely controllable in a wide range of situations—which is more than we can say for most of its competitors."

With a base price of $4091, the X-100 listed for $700 more than the base Marauder. Toss in such options as air conditioning, power windows, tilt wheel, and remote trunk release, and the X-100 could run $4800 or more. That kind of price didn't stop Mercury from building 14,666 Marauders in '69, 5635 of which were X-100s. The car came back little changed for 1970, and production was down to 6043 Marauders, just 2646 of them X-100s.

That the car didn't sell in huge numbers and wouldn't run with the supercars of the day is not really the point. As a broad-shouldered heavyweight with the biggest engine in the stable, the Marauder X-100 was typical of one branch of the muscle car family.

1969-71
MERCURY
CYCLONE

Despite successes in NASCAR and in selected drag-racing classes, Mercury performance had always played second fiddle to big-brother Ford. Even in expensive and seldom-seen 427 V-8 guise, Mercury's intermediate, the Cyclone, never could climb completely out from under Torino's shadow. But in mid-'68, it got an engine that would help it cast a shadow of its own: the 428 Cobra Jet.

Rated at 335 horsepower at 5200 rpm and 440 pounds/feet of torque at 3400, the 428 was plenty strong and, just as important, blessed with everyday drivability. It used hydraulic lifters, a Police Interceptor manifold with a Holley 735cfm four-barrel, 10.6:1 compression, dual exhausts, and a high-volume oil pump. Ram air induction made it even more potent.

It wasn't until the '69 model year that Mercury set about promoting the 428 Cyclone with any impact. The engine actually was optional in the Cougar, Montego, Comet Sports Coupe, and the Cyclone; it was standard only in the Cyclone CJ. All Cyclones had the fastback SportsRoof bodystyle that year and at $3224,the Cyclone CJ stood apart with its blacked-out grille, engine dress-up kit, competition handling package, and 3.50:1 rear axle. Its styled steel wheels carried Goodyear Polyglas F70×14 bias-belted tires. This stylish intermediate wasn't overwhelmed by the 428 the way the Cougar was and proved to be the engine's most hospitable environment.

Writing in *Car and Driver's* January 1990 issue, Patrick Bedard included the '69 Cyclone CJ among his top-10 all-time muscle cars. "The 428 had an unfashionably long strong and generally uninspiring hardware," he said. "Moreover, it had a

Cyclone carried Mercury's mid-size muscle banner. Spoiler model for '70 (top) had a 370-bhp 429-cid Cobra Jet V-8 standard. Cale Yarborough Special (above) was a limited-edition '69 Spoiler II that celebrated Mercury's NASCAR success. Note its aerodynamic droop nose.

lethargic way about it; it wasn't zingy like a Chevy. But it had earth-mover torque, and it stayed in tune—exactly what street racers needed. It was good with an automatic, too: just punch it and hang on. Which meant that every CJ was a threat no matter what kind of yahoo was in the chair."

Acceleration evidently wasn't its only virtue. "The machine is so nimble in any traffic situation it's in a class by itself," *Motor Trend* bubbled in a road test of a 428 Cyclone. "The power reserve on tap is in the proportion of the Grand Coulee Dam, and if you're worried about stopping, forget it. The gear disc/drum combinations will halt the car on a plumb-line from 60 mph in an abbreviated 124 feet."

Just as Ford turned its NASCAR effort up a notch with the wind-cheating Torino Talladega, Mercury answered the aero challenge in mid-'69 with the Cyclone Spoiler II. Elongating and lowering the Cyclone's front end improved the Mercury intermediate's ability to slice through the wind. On the big NASCAR ovals, the slicker aerodynamics and Ford's 427 V-8 made the difference between 160 and 190 miles per hour and helped Mercury do its part to win for Ford another NASCAR manufacturer's crown. Mercury had to offer 500 street-going versions of these racers in order to qualify it for NASCAR competition. It did this with two take-offs on the car. Sold with the NASCAR droop nose was the Spoiler II; a version with the standard Cyclone nose was sold as simply the Spoiler. Spoiler and Spoiler II came standard with a deck-lid air foil that was not used on the race version. And while all 1969 Ford

Cyclone CJ for '69 came standard with Ford's strong, flexible 428-cid V-8. The CJ pictured has the Ram-Air Cobra Jet engine. This was probably Mercury's finest street racer. It stayed in tune, had tornado-like torque, and was tailor made for the fool-proof automatic tranny. Quarter-miles were in the high 13s at 100 mph.

1969-71 Mercury Cyclone

Facts At a Glance

	1969	1970-71
Engine type:	V-8/FE Series (428 CJ)	V-8/385 Series (429 CJ/SCJ)
Displacement (cid):	428	429
Horsepower @ rpm:	335 @ 5200	370 @ 5400[2]
Torque (lbs/ft) @ rpm:	440 @ 3400	450 @ 3400
Compression ratio:	10.6:1	11.3:1
Bore (in.):	4.13	4.36
Stroke (in.):	3.98	3.59
Valve lifters:	Hydraulic	Hydraulic[2]
Availability:	Cyclone and Cyclone Spoiler[1]	Cyclone, Cyclone GT, Cyclone Spoiler

[1] Not available in limited-production 1969 Spoiler IIs equipped with 290-horsepower, 351 Windsor V-8.

[2] 429 SCJ rated 375 horsepower at 5600 rpm, with mechanical lifters and Holley four-barrel. Standard Cyclone 429 produced 360 horsepower at 4600 rpm.

Magazine:	Car and Driver (Jan. 69)	Motor Trend (August 1968)
Times:		
0-60 mph (sec):	5.5	6.1
0-100 mph (sec):	13.9	N/A
¼-mile (sec):	13.94 @ 100.89 mph	13.86 @ 101.69 mph
Top speed (mph):	116 (est)	N/A
Axle ratio:	3.91:1	4.11:1
Engine type:	428 CJ	428 CJ

Torino Talladegas were equipped with the 428 Cobra Jet V-8, Cyclone Spoilers and Spoiler IIs came standard with the 290-horse 351 Windsor four-barrel V-8 coupled to an FMX Cruise-O-Matic with 3.25:1 Traction-Lok gears. Among the street Cyclone Spoilers and Spoiler IIs were a limited number of blue/white Dan Gurney Specials (sold west of the Mississippi) and red/white Cale Yarborough Specials (sold east of the Mississippi) built to commemorate Mercury's NASCAR successes.

Cyclone was an offshoot of the Montego line and while As many as 519 NASCAR-based Spoilers are said to have been built, but only 300 or so are likely to be Spoiler IIs.

1970

Montego got a smoother new body on a one-inch longer 117-inch wheelbase for '70. Its signature was a protruding nose and some critics characterized it as coffin-shaped. There was a gun-sight grille feature in the center and the new stern held a quartet of hooded taillamps.

With the Cyclone's new body came a number of refinements. The Cyclone GT joined the lineup as a middle-ground alternative for those who wanted something milder than the Spoiler, yet more upscale than the standard Cyclone. The 351 and 390 V-8 engines continued, but the 428 gave way to Ford's new 385-series 429 Cobra Jet V-8 as the top Cyclone mill. It was optional in the Cyclone and Cyclone GT, where it was rated at 360 horsepower, and standard in the Spoiler, where it was rated at 370 horsepower. The Super Cobra Jet ram-air induction version upped output to 375 horsepower.

A Hurst-shifted four-speed manual was the Cyclone standard; the C-6 Cruise-O-Matic was optional. A wide selection of axle ratios was available, ranging from 3.25:1 to 4.30:1. Super Cobra Jet models were equipped with an engine oil cooler in an optional Drag Pak, with 3.91:1 or 4.30:1 axle ratios.

Production remained soft for 1970, with just 1631 Spoilers and 1695 standard hardtops built. Surprisingly, though, 10,170 Cyclone GTs came off the line.

1971

Cyclone's final year was a carryover of 1970 with minimal change, mostly in the grille and graphics. By this time, Mercury was beginning to see that its niche was luxury cars, not race-oriented models. As a result, 1971 was a twilight year for high-performance at Mercury. Still available was the 429 Cobra Jet V-8—this year with a Rochester Quadra-Jet carburetor—and a choice of transmissions and rear axles mirroring 1970. But Cyclone production was only 3084, of which 2300 were GTs. For Mercury, it was over. But unlike some muscle rivals, the Cyclone, especially the 428 and 429 cars, never lost its sense of purpose. *Car and Driver* put it best when it said the Cyclone CJ "can best be described as a gentleman's muscle car." Despite its "competition-oriented external appearance," the editors noted, the Cyclone was "carefully developed for minimum intrusion on the occupants' senses."

The other half of Mercury's '69 NASCAR commemorative Spoiler II set was the Dan Gurney Special (top). It had a 351-cid V-8, aero nose, and rear spoiler. Super Cobra Jet ram-air induction on the '70 Cyclone (above and above, left) upped the 429's output to 375 horsepower.

1964-67 OLDSMOBILE 4-4-2

Oldsmobile in some sense pioneered the muscle car way back in 1949 when it dropped the 135-horsepower Rocket V-8 from its Ninety-Eight series into the new, lightweight Futuramic Seventy-Six chassis. Presto! The Rocket 88. A legend in its time, that car set street-rodders' hearts aflutter and dominated NASCAR for a while, but it would be another 15 years or so before Olds recaptured that Rocket 88 flavor.

In 1964, Pontiac took a page from the Rocket 88 book to create a legend of its own. Pontiac found a loophole in GM's corporate edict against intermediate cars with engines larger than 330 cubic inches. It was able to get its big-car 389-cubic-inch V-8 into its mid-size Tempest by making it part of an option package. Thus, the GTO. Olds was caught a little off guard. Its F-85/Cutlass series shared the Tempest/LeMans platform, but its top engine offering was a 330-cubic-inch V-8 with a two-barrel carb, 9.0:1 compression, and 210 horsepower. Scrambling to its feet, Olds at mid-year extended its Police Apprehender Pursuit package to the intermediate. Onto the 330 V-8 went a four-barrel carb, behind the engine went a four-speed manual transmission, and out back, dual exhausts could be found. From these components Olds derived a name for the option package: 4-4-2. With 10.25:1 compression, the engine now made 310 horsepower at 5200 rpm and 355-pounds/feet of torque at 3600. Available on any F-85 except the station wagon, the $136 4-4-2 package also carried Red-Line tires and heavy-duty chassis components.

Olds used 4-4-2 on its original '64 muscle intermediate (above) to denote a four-barrel carb, four-speed manual transmission, and dual exhausts. Package was based on police equipment and used a 310-bhp 330-cid V-8 in two- or four-door body style.

A reasonably quick runner, this first 4-4-2 was the victim of some muddled marketing. Performance enthusiasts weren't used to looking to Olds for tire-frying power in these years, and while Pontiac conceived and promoted its GTO as a factory hot rod, Olds ads for the 4-4-2 showed a couple of cops behind the wheel of an F-85 four-door sedan under the tag line, "Police needed it...Olds built it...Pursuit proved it!" Not exactly the hippest come-on. Only 2999 Olds buyers ordered the 4-4-2 option its first half-year. Pontiac, by contrast, moved more than 32,000 GTOs in '64.

1965

The F-85/Cutlass series received minor trim and equipment updates for this, its second year as a restyled and enlarged mid-size. The line was becoming a major portion of Oldsmobile's business and sales of the intermediate coupes, sedans, convertibles, and station wagons would total more than 212,000 in '65. Olds refined its 4-4-2 strategy, offering the package only in the sporty two-door versions of the 115-inch-wheelbase pillared coupe, hardtop, and convertible F-85 and its upscale Deluxe and Cutlass siblings.

In the wake of the GTO's phenomenal success, General Motors had eased its corporate ban on big-cube intermediates in time for the 1965 model year. The displacement ceiling was raised to 400 cubic inches. Oldsmobile destroked and debored its 425-cubic-inch V-8 to come up with a 400-cube motor that it offered exclusively in the 4-4-2 package. The name became code for 400-cubic-inch engine, four-barrel carb, and dual exhausts. Now the ads showed a speed-blurred patch of pavement under

the heading "Olds 4-4-2 was here!" At $190.45 on the F-85 and Deluxe and $156.00 on the Cutlass, Olds touted the 4-4-2 as the "lowest priced high-performance car in America!"

Under the hood was that big V-8 with 345 horsepower at 4800 rpm and 440 pounds/feet of torque at 3200. Compression remained at 10.25:1. Transmissions choices were a three- or four-speed manual or Jetaway automatic. Standard 4-4-2 pieces included heavy-duty wheels, shocks, springs, rear axle, driveshaft, engine mounts, steering and frame; stabilizer bars front and rear; fat tires; special exterior and interior trim; 11-inch clutch; and a 70-amp battery.

Performance wasn't a match for all-out boulevard devils like the Dodge Coronet 426 Street Wedge, but 0-60 mph runs of around 7.5 seconds and quarter-mile times in the mid-15s at 85 mph allowed the 4-4-2 to embarrass its share of more overt racers—plus, it lent itself to all the high-performance hop-ups of the day. More important, the car now had an identity of its own.

1966-67

Olds gave its F-85 series new sheetmetal and a slightly wider track for '66 and the car gained a more rounded, heavier appearance. Still available as an option on the F-85 family of coupes and convertibles, the 4-4-2 package was distinguished by its own grille and taillamps and a recessed front fender scoop. Bold "4-4-2" graphics in a multi-hued insignia topped it off. Inside, circular instruments replaced the horizontal-sweep speedometer. Climate controls and the radio now were all contained in the same vinyl cluster. An optional

1964-67 Oldsmobile 4-4-2

Facts At a Glance

Engine type:	V-8/Oldsmobile	V-8/Oldsmobile
Displacement (cid):	330	400
Horsepower @ rpm:	310 @ 5200	345 @ 4800 (1965)
		350 @ 5000 (66-67)
		360 @ 5000 (1966)[1]
Torque (lbs/ft)		
@ rpm:	355 @ 3600	440 @ 3200 (1965)
		440 @ 3600 (66-67)
		440 @ 3600 (1966)[1]
Compression ratio:	10.25:1	10.25:1/10.5:1[2]
Bore (in.):	3.93	4.00
Stroke (in.):	3.38	3.97
Valve lifters:	Hydraulic	Hydraulic
Availability:	1964	1965-67

[1](3x2v).
[2]1966-67.

Magazine:	*Car Life*	*Car and Driver*
	(May 1965)	*(Dec. 1966)*
Times:		
0-60 mph (sec):	7.8	7.8
0-100 mph (sec):	20.1	19.4
¼-mile (sec):	15.5 @ 84 mph	15.8 @ 91 mph
Top speed (mph):	118	130 (est)
Axle ratio:	3.23:1	3.08:1
Engine (cid/bhp):	400/345	400/350
Model year:	1965 4-4-2	1967 4-4-2

Olds upped the tempo on the '65 4-4-2 (opposite), limiting the option to sporty two-door models and convertibles, and installing a 345-bhp 400-cid V-8. Production increased to 28,500, including 3500 ragtops. The '66 4-4-2 (this page) got shapely new sheetmetal and 350 bhp. Engine shown has the four-barrel, but a triple-carb option cost $100 and bumped horsepower to 360.

A hood with functional louvers helps distinguish the '67 4-4-2 (this page). Tri-carb setup was dropped, but the W-30 option returned. It was a civilized muscle car and Motor Trend *said the 4-4-2 proved "that Detroit can build cars that perform, handle and stop without sacrificing road comfort..."*

tachometer pod to the driver's left was a rarely ordered extra. Bucket seats remained a 4-4-2 option and could be enhanced by an extra-cost console for the three- or four-speed manual or automatic transmission.

Still exclusive was the 400 V-8, but its horsepower was kicked to 350 with the standard Rochester Quadra-Jet four-barrel. For another $100 buyers could tick the L-69 box on their option sheet and take home Oldsmobile's first factory tri-carb setup since the J-2 option package of 1957-58. The three Rochester two-barrel carburetors boosted horsepower to 360. Among the most notable of the '66 changes was the introduction of the W-30 option. With fiberglass inner fenders, chrome engine appointments, trunk-mounted battery, cold-air package, radical camshaft, and a choice of either a three-speed manual, Muncie M21 four-speed, or Turbo Hydra-Matic 400, the W-30 was a brute drag-racing package available through Olds dealers. Only 54 were assembled and sold in 1966.

The 4-4-2 option was still a bargain, adding just $185 to an F-85 or $151 to a Cutlass. Olds built 21,997 4-4-2-spec cars in '66, including an estimated 2750 convertibles.

1967

Now in its final season year as merely an option package, the 4-4-2 was confined to the Cutlass line, which gained series status of its own for '67. A new grille sported individual headlamp pods separated by parking lamps and a blacked-out center grille with "4-4-2" insignia. Out back were new split taillamps and Cutlass and 4-4-2 graphics graced the decklid. Opting for the $184.31 4-4-2 package also brought a hood with functional louvers and access to several extra-cost performance items, including UHV transistorized ignition, an engine-gauge package, super stock wheels, front disc brakes, and several special axle ratios.

Horsepower ratings remained the same for 1967, through the optional three-deuce package was no longer available. As in 1966, the W-30 package remained a desirable option for those who could afford it.

"Sedate it ain't," declared one 4-4-2 advertisement for '67. Production was 24,833, with an estimated 3104 convertibles. The 4-4-2 had established itself as a bona-fide muscle car, a street-fighter in spats. But some of the best was yet to come.

1968-72 OLDSMOBILE 4-4-2

Olds stylists came up with a curvaceous new body for the F-85/Cutlass line in 1968. Understated grillework and quad headlamps were fitted to a tapered nose, while thin, horizontal taillamps above a huge chrome bumper made for a tasteful rear view. The profile was bullet shaped and the roof a graceful semi-fastback in this, one of the most enduring GM designs of the period. Wheelbase on the four-door models and wagons was stretched an inch, to 116. Two door models, now on a 112-inch wheelbase, lost three inches. This was the year the 4-4-2 matured into its own series of two-doors and convertibles. Lightest and least expensive was the 4-4-2 Sports Coupe, a 3450-pound post coupe that listed for $3087. Next came the pillarless two-door Holiday Coupe, which weighed 3470 pounds and started at $3150. Top of the line was the 4-4-2 convertible, at 3540 pounds and $3341.

Still exclusive to the 4-4-2 was the 400-cubic-inch Rocket V-8, which retained a four-barrel carburetor, 10.5:1 compression, and dual exhausts. However, the bore/stroke dimensions were altered, the heads were new and had a modified port design, the valve springs were stiffer, and the camshaft more radical. With the standard three-speed manual transmission or optional Muncie M21 four-speed—both of which carried Hurst shifters—horsepower was 350 at 4800 rpm and torque 440 pounds/feet at 3200. Ordering the optional M40 Turbo Hydra-Matic automatic trans cost 25 horsepower. Axle ratios ranged from 2.56:1 to 4.66:1. Heavy-duty springs and shocks, front and rear stabilizers, and F70×14 nylon cord red-line tires were standard.

Performance was in its heyday and Olds jumped in feet first with a host of hot hop-ups. One was the Force-Air induction system, which funneled air to the engine via a pair of discrete scoops beneath the front bumper. It was optional on 4-4-2 and Cutlass S models and boosted the 400's horsepower to 360 at 5400 rpm.

Next up was the optional W-30 package. This was centered around a 400 V-8 with hand-selected parts that made it the closest thing to a blueprinted performance package that anyone could get from the factory. Ordering the W-30 option brought a heavy-duty rear end, heavy-duty cooling system, red plastic inner fenders, cold-air induction, radical camshaft, improved Rochester Quaadra-Jet, and a host of other performance goodies. The usual selection of manual and automatic gearboxes was available with the W-30, though the Turbo Hydra-matic 400 was fortified with a special high-performance converter, high-rpm shift points, and firmed-up shifts. *Car Craft* recorded a 13.33-second quarter-mile pass at 103.56 with a W-30.

The most radical '68 4-4-2, however, came from the Lansing, Michigan, shops of Demmer Engineering, where the Hurst/Olds was assembled. This most special 4-4-2 was originally a one-off custom job built for George Hurst himself. Hurst and his employee, Jack "Doc" Watson, who designed the car, sold Olds on the notion of a limited-run of these hand-built specialty cars. Olds shipped engineless 4-4-2s to Demmer, where a specially built 455-cubic-inch Olds "Toronado" V-8 was installed. Known as the W-46 engine, this 455 four-barrel had a radical camshaft, recurved distributor, Rochester Quadra-Jet four-barrel, and Force-Air induction. The result was 390 horsepower and 500 pounds-feet of torque from a mill that weighed 10-12 pounds *less* than the 400 it replaced.

Of 515 H/Os built that year, 56 were post coupes. Dealers

Olds muscle for '68 was wrapped in a new bullet-shaped body with a fastback roof (above). 4-4-2 was promoted to its own model line and retained exclusive rights to the 400-cid V-8, which had 350 bhp with manual transmission. Base price of this Holiday Coupe was $3150.

had collected 3000 orders for the cars, but the production run was allocated only to key Oldsmobile dealers around the country. The H/O sold for just $434 above the sticker price of a 4-4-2 sports coupe, which sold for $3087, or holiday coupe, which listed for $3150. Production of 4-4-2's rocketed to 33,607—including 5142 convertibles.

1969

Enter the good Dr. Oldsmobile—a sort of mad scientist in a baggy white lab coat, slicked-back hair, and silent-movie handlebar mustache. He was conjured up to personify the division's muscle efforts in 1969 and the cars from his laboratory were more potent than ever. The 1969 4-4-2 received grille and taillamp revisions, including bolder "4-4-2" and "W-30" graphics. Little changed inside, apart from upholstery and door panel revisions. The 400 was again exclusive to the 4-4-2 and came standard with 350 horsepower with manual transmission and 325 with automatic. The Force-Air option brought 360 horsepower again.

Also returning was the Hurst/Olds 4-4-2, but no longer was it remotely low-key in silver and black. "Firefrost Gold" striping accented its white paint, a dual-snout air scoop was on the hood, and an air-foil spoiler stuck up from the decklid. The engine was again the 455-cubic-inch V8. It was detuned slightly to 380 horsepower, but still churned out 500 pounds/feet of torque.

Testers saw 0-60 mph in 5.9 seconds and the quarter in 13.98 at 101.3 with the '69 H/O. Built again in limited numbers, H/O production for this year totaled 904 hardtops and two convertibles, though some sources say an additional six hardtops were built as prototypes and promotional cars.

Olds introduced the W-32 package this year. It combined the 350-horsepower manual-transmission 400-cube V-8 with the M40 automatic transmission. It was billed as a more civilized route to a 350-horsepower 4-4-2. "The W-Machine a mother could learn to love," explained an ad that pictured Dr. Oldsmobile in the company of his mother. The W-32 used the Force-Air scoops, rally hood stripes, and posi-traction rear. This, Dr. Oldsmobile advised, was "a honker with culture. Which means with a refined, unlumpy idle." Only 297 W-32s are thought to have been built: 247 hardtop coupes; 25 post coupes, and 25 convertibles. Production of 4-4-2s fell off in general this year, down to 26,357, of which 4295 were convertibles.

1970

The factory took a cue from the Hurst/Olds and gave all 4-4-2s a 455-cubic-inch V-8 as standard equipment for 1970. The engine was complemented by a facelift that shelved the 4-4-2s blackout grille in favor of a series of bright vertical bars. Also, the taillamps now numbered four instead of two and were moved to within the rear bumper unit.

This was a high-water mark in 4-4-2 specification. The four-barrel 455 was rated at 365 horsepower at 5000 rpm and 500 pounds/feet of torque at 3200. Compression was 10.50:1, dual exhausts were again standard, as was a special handling package with front and rear stabilizer bars and G70×14 glass-belted tires. The W-30 option upped horsepower to 370 via air-induction and other performance goodies, including an aluminum intake manifold and a low-restriction air cleaner. The fiberglass hood with its functional air scoops, plus a rear-deck spoiler, were part of the W-30 package and were also available as free-standing options on other 4-4-2s. Front disc brakes also were available, and the W-32 returned as a detuned, more streetable version of the W-30.

The Hurst camp had proposed something different for the 1970 edition of the H/O. Instead of the previous big-cube, high-roller 4-4-2s, it wanted to create a budget hot rod based on the F-85 coupe body. The car would use the 325-horsepower 350-cubic-inch V-8 that was part of the W-31 option available on the Cutlass S and on the F-85 two-door sedan. Olds didn't accept the idea, so there was no Hurst/Olds in 1970. Olds did, however, apply the concept to the Cutlass and F-85 line as the W-45 option package. Better known as the Rallye 350, these cars were painted Sebring yellow—even the bumpers and wheels were body color—and had orange and black striping, hood scoops, and trunk-lid spoilers. Just 3547 Rallye 350s were

Only minor trim revisions were made to the '69 4-4-2 (top), but for '70 (middle), a robust 365-bhp 455-cid V-8 was made standard. This '70 W-30 has the factory-blueprinted 370-bhp 455, fiberglass hood with functional scoops, and red plastic inner fender liners. W-30 option continued as the top dog for '71 (bottom and opposite), but its 455 dropped to 350 bhp with 8.5:1 compression.

built in this, their only year.

The 4-4-2, meanwhile, saw production fall to just 19,330. That included 14,709 of the $3376 hardtops; 2933 of the $3567 convertibles, and 1688 of the $3312 pillared Sports Coupes.

1971-72

Performance was de-emphasized industry-wide in 1971, the 4-4-2 suffering along with other muscle cars. It was offered only in hardtop and convertible models this year. Unleaded fuel dictated a drop in compression to 8.5:1 and Olds began to rate engines on net horsepower—with all accessories in place—rather than the previous gross horsepower. The standard four-barrel 455 was thus demoted to 340 horsepower and torque was down to 460 pounds/feet. Several "W" options remained, but 4-4-2 buyers seemed to go more for appearance and comfort now. The ultimate Olds performer for 1971 was the 350-gross-horsepower $369 W-30 option, which translated to 300 horsepower net. "It comes factory-blueprinted to save you the trouble and expense," Olds boasted. Output skidded to just over 7500 units, 1304 of them convertibles.

With sales falling rapidly, the 4-4-2 reverted back to a Cutlass option package for 1972. Designated W-29, it cost from $71 to $150 depending upon which of the four hardtops, pillared coupe, or convertible models was ordered. The package consisted of special decals, stripes, and badging, plus the FE-2

suspension with heavy-duty front and rear stabilizer bars, 14×7-inch wheels, louvered hood, and special 4-4-2 grille. Standard engine was now a 160-horsepower 350-cube two-barrel V-8, with a 180-horsepower, four-barrel 350 and 270-horse, four-barrel 455 optional. Fortunately, the 300-horsepower W-30 engine remained on offer with its factory-blueprinted Cold-Air V-8, fiberglass hood with functional scoops, and anti-spin rear end—and a healthy price tag of $599.

Motor Trend tested both the 1971 and '72 4-4-2s, saying, the "drop to 8.5:1 compression ratio was rather like hitting Dr. Oldsmobile with a malpractice suit. But there's still some soul left in Lansing and despite all the furor, a 4-4-2 will still churn up all the smoke and fury the average muscle car driver could need and probably handle." Both test cars were W-30 automatics. The '72 came in a half-second slower in the 0-60-mph sprint, 6.6 seconds versus 6.1. Quarter-mile times were closer, 14.5 and 14.4 seconds, but the '71 was five mph faster with a terminal speed of 97.

A Hurst/Olds was offered again in 1972. Output reached 499 hardtops and 130 convertibles, and as expected, the luxury and executive end of the performance theme was pushed.

Production Cutlass models with the 4-4-2 package rallied a bit to 9845 units for '72, but the true 4-4-2s are remembered as a rather special strain among the thundering herd of muscle cars. "There's always been something special about 4-4-2s," *Motor Trend* said as the car was fading. "They seemed to be the subtle man's GTO...."

1968-72 Oldsmobile 4-4-2

Facts At a Glance

Engine type:	V-8/Oldsmobile	V-8/Oldsmobile
Displacement (cid):	400	455
Horsepower @ rpm:	350 @ 4800 (1968)	365 @ 5000 (1970)
	360 @ 5400 (1968)[1]	370 @ 5200 (1970)
	360 @ 4600 (1969)	340 @ 4600 (1971)
		270 @ 4400 (1972)[2]
		300 @ 4700 (1972)[2]
Torque (lbs/ft) @ rpm:	440 @ 3200 (1968)	500 @ 3200 (1970)
	440 @ 3600 (1969)	500 @ 3600 (1970)
		460 @ 3200 (1971)
		370 @ 3200 (1972)[2]
		410 @ 3200 (1972)[2]
Compression ratio:	10.5:1	10.5:1/8.5:1[1]
Bore (in.):	3.87	4.12
Stroke (in.):	4.25	4.25
Valve lifters:	Hydraulic	Hydraulic
Availability:	1968-69	1970-72

[1]1971-72.
[2]Net ratings.

Engine type:	V-8/Oldsmobile
Displacement (cid):	350
Horsepower @ rpm:	200 @ 4400
Torque (lbs/ft) @ rpm:	300 @ 3200
Compression ratio:	8.5:1
Bore (in.):	4.05
Stroke (in.):	3.38
Valve lifters:	Hydraulic
Availability:	1972

Magazine:	Car Craft	Car Craft
Times:		
0-60 mph (sec):	5.8 (est)	6.3 (est)
0-100 mph (sec):	10.5 (est)	11.5 (est)
¼-mile (sec):	12.97 @ 108.17 mph	13.33 @ 103.56 mph
Top speed (mph):	N/A	N/A
Axle ratio:	3.91:1	3.91:1
Engine (cid/bhp):	455/390[1]	400/360
Model year:	1968 Hurst/Olds	1968 W-30 4-4-2

[1]Hand assembled engine

4-4-2 reverted to a Cutlass option package for '72 (above). It cost $71 to $150 depending on the model and had its own grille and graphics, plus a heavy-duty suspension. The 455 was made an option and the new standard engine was a 350-cid V-8 that made a maximum of 180-bhp net with a four-barrel carb.

1962-65
PLYMOUTH
413/426 WEDGE

MoPar's mighty 400-plus-bhp 413-cid V-8 came to the downsized Plymouths in the spring of '62 as a limited, high-performance option. Most went into bare-bones two-door sedans like this Belvedere.

Street racers were always on the prowl for the Next Hot Thing and in 1962, the ones on the cutting edge were trolling for action in two-door Plymouth sedans. Now, one didn't mess casually with a 421 Super Duty Catalina or even a Ford Galaxie if it had the 405-horsepower 406. But those machines were scarce on the street and rare even at the strip. No, the real top dog was a Chevy Bel Air with a 409-horsepower 409-cubic-inch V-8. It took guts to take on one of these pop-song-prompting 409s. But in 1962 Chrysler did with its new 413-cubic-inch Max Wedge V-8.

Armed with twin 659cfm Carter AFB carburetors mounted in tandem, the 413 made 410 horsepower. Chrysler arrived at the 413 by stroking the B-Block 383, which had been around since 1959, into a taller-deck B-Block known as the "Raised-Block B-Block," or "RB-Block" V-8. It had a bore of 4.19 inches, a stroke of 3.75, solid lifters, dual valve springs to combat valve float over 6000 rpm, magnafluxed rods, wedge-shaped combustion chambers, and short-ram induction manifolds. The Plymouth's engine bay was too narrow to allow the 413's exhaust headers to exit downward. So Chrysler routed the cast-iron headers upward first in a ram's-horn sweep that, along with the tandem carbs, became a trademark of this "maximum wedge" engine.

The 413 Max Wedge came to Dodge and Plymouth full-size cars in the spring of '62 as a limited, high-performance option. Plymouth called it the Super Stock 413; Dodge the RamCharger 413. Most found their way into bare-bones, no-frills two-door sedans ordered primarily for the strip. Already lighter than the full-size Fords, Chevys, Pontiacs—and even its Dodge Dart cousin—a 3100-pound Plymouth Savoy or Belvedere could shed even more weight by being ordered without heater, radio, and sound deadening. Chrysler's push-button TorqueFlite automatic was the hot choice behind the 413; the three-speed manual was actually slightly slower in the quarter, and the company didn't offer a four-speed with the engine.

The Max Wedge 413 was as rare—and as difficult to manage—on the street as any other factory engine built primarily for competition. But even in such exclusive company, it quickly upset the established pecking order. Super Stock/Automatic records fell like flies and while a 413 lost to the dreaded 409 in the NHRA's '62 Super Stock Eliminator world championship, MoPar's new engine did take a Plymouth where no passenger car had gone before. In July 1962, Tom Grove drove his Super Stock Plymouth to an ET of 11.93 seconds at 118.57 mph. His was the first stock passenger automobile to beat 12 seconds in the quarter. It was just the beginning.

For '63, Plymouth's mid-size cars lost some of their eccentric styling and gained a new high-performance engine option. Chrysler enlarged the 413's bore to 4.25 inches to get a 426-cubic-inch Max Wedge V-8 that, in its hottest edition, was dubbed the Stage II. Painted Race Hemi Orange, the Stage II retained the two Carter AFB four-barrel carburetors offset atop a cross-ram intake manifold, as well as the ram's-horn exhaust manifold. It was rated 415 horsepower with 11:1 compression and 425 with 13.5:1 compression. Stage III, a more radical 426 Wedge that appeared midyear, had twin Carter AFBs with larger primary bores, a higher-lift (.520-inch) camshaft, and larger chamber heads. Advertised horsepower/torque ratings of the 426-III were identical to Stage II, though its 425-horsepower version used a 12.5:1 compression ratio. Plymouth offered these Super Stock Max Wedges in any full-size model, and also made available a race-ready lightweight package that could be purchased through any dealer.

The 1964 Plymouth Belvedere was basically a carryover, but a new grille and taillamps were added, while the two-door hardtops got a new roof. Their rear roof pillar narrowed as it went down and created a handsome styling signature. This would be the final appearance for the optional push-button TorqueFlite automatic. It was replaced by a conventional column-shifted automatic in 1965.

Still available was the 426 Max Wedge Stage III. But for those who wished to actually make daily use of a big-block MoPar on the street, the ticket was the new-for-'64 426 Street

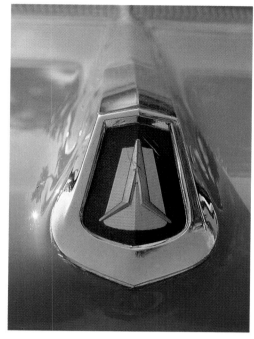

1963-65 Plymouth

Belvedere/Satellite 426 Wedge

Facts At a Glance

Engine type:	V-8/RB-Wedge	V-8/RB-Wedge (Max Wedge)
Displacement (cid):	426	425
Horsepower @ rpm:	365 @ 4800	415/425 @ 5600
Torque (lbs/ft) @ rpm:	470 @ 3200	470/480 @ 4400
Compression ratio:	10.3:1	11.0:1/13.5:1[1]
Bore (in.):	4.25	4.25
Stroke (in.):	3.75	3.75
Valve lifters:	Hydraulic	Mechanical
Availability:	1964 Belvedere,	1965 Belvedere/ Satellite

[1]12.5:1 in 426 Stage III

Magazine:	Motor Trend (Jan. 1964)	Hot Rod (January 1963)
Times:		
0-60 mph (sec):	6.8	N/A
0-100 mph (sec):	N/A	N/A
¼-mile (sec):	15.20 @ 95.5 mph	12.69 @ 111.97 mph
Top speed (mph):	130	N/A
Axle ratio:	3.91:1	
Engine type:	426/365	426/415

With twin Carter AFB carbs, the 413 Super Stock wedge-head mill (both pages) churned out 410 bhp. It supplied the "mean" while base models of Plymouth's full-size cars, on their 116-inch wheelbase and 3100-pound curb weight, took care of the "lean." A Plymouth similar to the '62 Belvederes shown was the first stock passenger car to better 12 seconds in the quarter-mile.

Wedge. Plymouth advertised it as the Commando 426 wedge-head V-8 and billed it as the street version of the 426 Hemi competition engine. It was the sensibile alternative to the Max Wedge Stage III, made so by features like a provision for crossover heat to the manifold, so that it would start in cold weather, and a 10.3:1 compression, so that it could run on something less than aviation fuel. The Street Wedge used a single four-barrel carb on a conventional cast-iron intake manifold. Its exhaust manifold was conventional, too, without the flamboyant ram's-horn sweep that gave the Max Wedge headers such allure. But the Commando was no shrinking violet. It was rated at 365 horsepower and had 470 pounds/feet of torque. High performance valve springs, pistons, plugs, and a hot cam were inside. Hydraulic tappets, dual breaker distributor, nonsilenced air cleaner, dual exhausts, and heavy-duty clutch were part of the package.

This engine was carried over unchanged for 1965, though Beleved ere was repositioned in the Plymouth lineup and an upscale version was added. The basic sheet metal continued but with a new grille, single headlamps, and a "Baby Fury" look. Without changing dimensions, the Belvedere line became a mid-size, as Plymouth put the Fury name on a set of longer full-size models with 119 inch wheelbases. New to the Belevedere roster was the attractive premium-level Satellite. It came standard with front bucket seats, center console, custom wheel covers and some up-level exterior trim to set it apart from the lesser mid-size Plymouths. Inside, the Belvedere and Satellite got a new dashboard with integral instrumentation—a departure from the Jetson look of 1963-64.

The 426 Street Wedge was dropped after '65 and its displacement soon became synonomous with Chrysler's King Kong Hemi. The wedge would return in '66 bored to 440 cubic inches. This was the engine that would carry MoPar into the heart of the muscle years, around which Dodge and Plymouth would build performance cars for a whole new generation of buyers. How many of them, in those fast-changing times, would recall its origins in the barely tamed 413 Max Wedge of 1962?

For '63, Plymouth's full-size cars lost some of their eccentric styling (above) and gained the 426-cid wedge (center) as a new high-performance engine option. The twin-four-barrel mill made 415 or 425 bhp, depending on tune. A less-randy single-quad 365-bhp version of the 426 bowed in '64 as the Street Wedge and made for a better daily driver.

1965-66 PLYMOUTH BARRACUDA 273

Chrysler didn't reach very far when it created its sporty small car in the spring of 1964. The Barracuda was pretty much a Plymouth Valiant from the roofline down, and pure Valiant in power and suspension. It had its own grille, fastback roof, and the rear-end sheetmetal. But these changes weren't enough to emulate the wholesale personality change that Ford accomplished when it rebodied the Falcon as the wildly successful Mustang. The Ford overwhelmed the Barracuda in sales, a snub made worse because the Plymouth actually beat it to the showrooms by a couple of weeks. The scenario was repeated when Chevrolet reskinned the Chevy II as the sleek and successful Camaro in 1967. Barracuda may have been more functional than these pony cars, but it lacked their sexiness and sales appeal.

The first Barracuda actually carried Valiant emblems and was in fact called the Plymouth Valiant Barracuda. It was a five-passenger two door equipped as the top-line Valiant Signet, though it had a fold-down rear seat and a larger cargo area. Built on a 106-inch wheelbase, it came standard with a 225-cubic inch six, but about 90 percent were ordered with the optional 180-horsepower 273-cubic-inch V-8. It cost $2496 and weighed 2905 pounds in base V-8 form. But it was no match for the Mustang, which offered a trio of V-8s, including the 271-horse High Performance 289.

Barracuda beat the Ford Mustang into the sporty-compact market, but Plymouth's aim wasn't as true. Its Valiant-based fastback was more practical than the Ford, but lacked Mustang's flair and range of body styles. The '66 pictured has the sporty Formula S option package, which included upgraded suspension and blue-streak tires.

Chrysler fought back in '65 with the four-barrel Commando 273. A hotter camshaft and Carter carburetion bumped horsepower up to 235. A three-speed manual transmission was standard with the 273; a four-speed or TorqueFlite automatic was optional. Axle ratios varied, but most customers opted for 3.23:1 gears behind their 273s. These Barracudas started at a modest $2571, but the best they could manage were quarter-mile times in the mid- to high-17s. To Plymouth's credit, it recognized that not all performance is measured in straight-line acceleration. Thus, Barracuda's optional Formula "S" sports package. It included the Commando 273; a tachometer; heavy-duty shocks, springs and sway bar; and Goodyear Blue Streak tires on wide-rim 14-inch wheels (replacing the usual 13-inchers). Front disc brakes could be installed by dealers. Circular "Formula S" medallions on the fender identified the package, and many were ordered with the racing stripe that was a regular Barracuda option.

Barracuda production nearly tripled in '65, with 64,596 ready to find customers.

1966

Like Valiant, the Barracuda received a mild facelift for its third year. The sporty bucket seats, a fold-down rear seat, and floor shift continued as standard equipment. The two 273s continued in two- and four-barrel form, with horsepower unchanged. Front disc brakes became a factory Barracuda option for 1966, at $82. Available again was the Formula "S" option that included a 150-mph speedometer, handling package, and other sporty amenities. Production fell to 38,029 for '66. The Barracuda needed more power and a wider choice of body styles if it was to compete with the Mustang and the new GM pony cars due in '67.

1965-66 Plymouth

Barracuda 273

Facts At a Glance

Engine type:	V-8/LA-Block/Wedge	V-8/LA-Block/Wedge
Displacement (cid):	273 (2v)	273 (4v)
Horsepower @ rpm:	180 @ 4200	235 @ 5200
Torque (lbs/ft) @ rpm:	260 @ 1600	280 @ 4000
Compression ratio:	8.8:1	10.5:1
Bore (in.):	3.62	3.62
Stroke (in.):	3.31	3.31
Valve lifters:	Mechanical	Hydraulic
Availability:	1965-66	1965-66

Magazine:	*Car and Driver* (Oct. 1964)	*Car and Driver* (June 1966)
Times:		
0-60 mph (sec):	9.1	9.1
0-100 mph (sec):	26.2	29.6
¼-mile (sec):	17.5 @ 88.5 mph	17.6 @ 81 mph
Top speed (mph):	121	117
Axle ratio:	3.23:1	3.23:1
Engine (cid/bhp):	273/235	273/235

Barracuda for '65 was Plymouth's best-selling car. The hottest versions used the four-barrel Commando 273-cid engine (left), which had a 10.5:1 compression and 235 bhp. The '65 pictured has the Formula S package that included the Commando engine, a tachometer, and heavy-duty suspension.

1966-67
PLYMOUTH
SATELLITE STREET HEMI

Plymouth's restyled 1966 Satellite had clean, muscular lines. The Satellite and its less plush Belvedere sibling began the model year with a 325-horsepower 383 four-barrel as their top performance engine, but when Dodge made the Street Hemi available in its new Charger and Coronet, the corporate-cousin Plymouth intermediates got it, too.

The Hemi option raised the price of the $2695 Satellite two-door hardtop or the $2910 convertible by a steep $907.60. But the engine brought with it a host of performance-enhancing extras and instantly elevated the handsome Plymouth into muscle's upper echelon. *Car and Driver* said the Hemi Satellite was, simply, "the best combination of brute performance and

tractable street manners we've ever driven...even knowledgeable enthusiasts can ride around in the car and never know what a bomb it is."

Its detonator, of course, was the Hemi. Named for its power-enhancing hemispherical-shaped combustion chambers, the engine was first seen in Chrysler vehicles from 1951 to '58. But it never displaced more than 400 cubic inches in those cars. The hemi-head returned in 1964 when Chrysler swapped the wedge-shaped combustion chambers on its 426-cubic-inch V-8 for the domed ones. The engine was bred for the racetrack and with 425 horsepower at 5000 rpm, it captured NASCAR and NHRA checkered flags by the fistful. The Hemi was offered briefly and

Plymouth's handsome '66-'67 mid-size served as the division's first practical application of the mighty Hemi engine. The '67 shown here is a fine example. Its 426 Hemi (below) was tamed for the street, but still put on quite a show with dual Carter quads and 425 bhp. Discreet badging (bottom) and lack of scoops or stripes made the car a sleeper.

1966-67 Plymouth Satellite

Street Hemi

Facts At a Glance

Engine type:	V-8/RB-Block/Hemi
Displacement (cid):	426
Horsepower @ rpm:	425 @ 5000
Torque (lbs/ft) @ rpm:	490 @ 4000
Compression ratio:	10.25:1
Bore (in.):	4.25
Stroke (in.):	3.75
Valve lifters:	Mechanical
Availability:	Belvedere/Satellite

Magazine:	*Car and Driver* (April 1966)	*Car Life* (July 1966)
Times:		
0-60 mph (sec):	5.3	7.1
0-100 mph (sec):	12.8	15.8
¼-mile (sec):	13.8 @ 104 mph	14.5 @ 95 mph
Top speed (mph):	130	130
Axle ratio:	3.54:1	3.23:1

in very limited numbers in some '65 MoPar intermediates, but with a 12.5:1 compression and other competition-quality hop ups, it was too high strung for the street. But that's exactly where the action was—and where reputations had to be upheld.

Bringing the Hemi to the regular production options list in 1966 necessitated some changes in the engine. Cast-iron cylinder heads were substituted for aluminum ones; an aluminum intake manifold of conventional design supplanted a magnesium ram-type manifold; Carter four-barrel carburetors replaced the racing Holley unit; the compression ratio was reduced to 10.25:1; a milder camshaft was installed; cast iron exhaust headers displaced fabricated-steal headers; and cold-weather

Special-order '67 Super Stock Belvedere (white car) had the Street Hemi and a functional hood scoop but no sound insulation. Battery was in the trunk for weight balance. Factory made only 75, but the survivors still win in the drag classes for which they were designed.

starting was made possible by the addition of a choke to the rear primaries and by providing manifold heat.

In the Satellite, Hemi buyers had a choice of four-speed manual or TorqueFlite automatic transmission. A Sure-Grip differential was a mandatory option at extra cost and a cross section of axle ratios was available. Standard tires with the Hemi package were 7.75×14 Goodyear Blue Streaks and a heavy-duty suspension was fitted.

Getting the best out of a Hemi required some skill, but a good run would see 0-60 mph in the low-five-second range with the quarter-mile falling in the mid- to high-13s at more than 100 mph. Stopping one took some talent, as well. Standard with the Hemi engine were police-grade 11-inch drum brakes that gave the car 35 percent more braking area than normal, but testers experienced almost instant rear lock-up and poor directional control in panic stops. The front discs available in larger MoPars weren't offered. And while the Hemi Satellite was quite tractable in normal driving, anything approaching spirited cornering would set the nose-heavy front end to plowing and the body to leaning. Inside, drivers found understated vinyl bucket seats facing a horizontal instrument cluster. About the only ergonomic flaw was that the tachometer—a $48.35 option—was mounted between the seats on the center console, where it was difficult to monitor during full-throttle blasts.

1967

The Satellite received some trim changes for '67, including

a new grille with quad headlamps. Base price for the hardtop was up to $2747, while the $2986 convertible swapped its plastic backlight for a glass one.

All Satellites had V-8 engines, but the Hemi once again topped the options list. Evidently, volume production had its rewards, for the price of the Hemi dropped to $564. Its authority was undiminished, however.

"A quick stab at the throttle pedal—in any old gear—will send the tachometer needle flying around the tach like a teeny little Fiat Abarth, or a Ferrari," wrote *Car and Driver*. "It just doesn't feel like a seven-liter engine—except for the fact that you're suddenly doing 120 and you don't know how you got there."

Even in so potent a form, Satellite still had only discrete "426" badges to identify it as a Hemi. However, this was the year Plymouth finally created a separate performance model of its intermediate, which it called the GTX. That car came standard with the 440-cube Magnum V-8 and had the Hemi as its only engine option. It stole much of the limelight from the Satellite, though with its standard non-functional hood scoops, the GTX wasn't the sleeper a Satellite could be. Plymouth's ultimate Q-ship in this line for '67, however, would have been a special-order Belvedere in what the automaker called Super Stock trim. It came with the Street Hemi and a functional hood scoop, but without sound insulation or sound-deadening material, and with the battery mounted in the trunk for improved weight distribution.

1967-69
PLYMOUTH
BARRACUDA 383/440

Barracuda became a Plymouth series all its own in 1967. It marked the occasion with a two-inch wheelbase stretch, to 108, and with the addition of a two-door hardtop and convertible to go along with its fastback body style. Any resemblance to the Valiant was gone. The styling was more rounded than anything else in the Chrysler line, and the new hardtop was especially continental in flavor. Along with the new body came an engine bay wider by two inches. That was a clue to what Plymouth had in mind for this second-generation Barracuda.

The base '67 Barracudas were equipped with the familiar MoPar slant six engine, while both 273 cubic-inch V-8s remained options. But Plymouth had tracked the performance winds and found them blowing toward more cubic inches. The automaker had apparently intended to offer a fortified version of its 318-cubic-inch V-8 in the '67 Barracuda. But it learned that Mustang would be available with a 390 V-8 for '67, the Chevy Camaro with a 396, and the Pontiac Firebird a 400. Plymouth responded by shoehorning in the 383-cubic-inch B-Wedge V-8. With its single Carter AFB four-barrel and 10.0:1 compression ratio, it was good for 280 horsepower. The 383 was optional only in the top-of-the-line fastback Formula S Barracuda, and brought as standard a four-speed manual transmission; TorqueFlite was optional. The only axle ratio available with the 383 was a 3.23:1.

Like its predecessors, the '67 Barracuda had front torsion-bar and rear leaf-spring suspension, and four-wheel drum brakes. The firm-riding Formula S package included front disc brakes as well as bigger D70×14 tires. What couldn't be fitted, as it turned out, was something the 383 Barracuda

Plymouth widened the Barracuda's engine bay by two inches in a '67 redesign, and made room enough to fit the big 383- and 440-cid engines. The hardtop bowed and in Formula S guise (above) could be ordered with the 383.

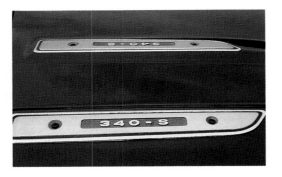

desperately needed: power steering. The 383 engine's exhaust headers occupied the space normally filled by the power steering pump. Trying to park a nose-heavy 383 Barracuda with the standard manual steering was "like trying to dock the Queen Mary," moaned *Car and Driver*.

Customers found enough to like, however, and Barracuda sales increased sharply for '67. Some 94 percent of the 62,534 production total was split about evenly between the fastback and the new hardtop. The new convertible accounted for the balance, with 4228 built.

1968

Except for grille and trim alterations, the 1968 Barracuda was largely a stylistic rehash. But there were important changes under the hood. The 273 V-8s were dropped in favor of the 230-horsepower 318 as the base V-8. The Formula S package was extended to the hardtop and convertible models and now it could be had with MoPar's frisky 275-horsepower 340-cube four-barrel. The Formula S 383, meanwhile, got a boost to 300 horsepower, courtesy of new cylinder heads and a new intake manifold. It did not, however, get a power-steering

option. Both Formula S V-8s were mated with a standard four-speed or an optional automatic. A 3.23:1 rear axle was standard with both this year, but the four-speed also could be fitted with a 3.55:1 or 3:91:1 gear and the automatic with a 3.55:1. Suspension upgrades were tailored to each engine and, combined with wider E70×14 tires, helped improve handling.

Fastest of all were the limited-edition Super Stock Hemi Barracudas, which were built under contract by Hurst Performance. Sold through Plymouth dealers for sanctioned drag racing only, these were 10-second, 130-mph quarter-mile machines. Barracuda sales slipped this year, with only 45,412 coming off the line; ragtop production was down by nearly 40 percent, to 2840.

1969

Plymouth committed itself to Barracuda performance hook, line, and sinker in 1969. It began by using the 'Cuda name officially to denote a new enthusiast package. Sold with the 340 or 383 engines in fastback or hardtop, the 'Cuda tag basically meant an appearance group with Formula S underpinnings. A pair of non-functional hood scoops, two black

MoPar's fine 340-cid four-barrel was new to the Formula S for '68. A good one would turn the quarter in the high 15s. Only 2840 Barracuda convertibles were built that year (opposite). The 'Cuda name was first used formally in '69 and both the fastback and drop top pictured above are stuffed with the 440-cid V-8 that also joined the line that year.

hood stripes, black lower-body paint, and 'Cuda fender decals were its styling cues. The Formula S package could still be ordered on any body style. Cast-aluminum wheels were a new option across the line. The 383 was increased to 330 horsepower and finally was available with power steering.

But the baddest 'Cuda of all came in on a wave that crested mid-year. Feeling pressure again from rival big-block pony cars, Plymouth abandoned all restraint and stuffed MoPar's 375-horsepower 440-cubic-inch four-barrel V-8 into the Barracuda. The results were mixed. On the positive side, Plymouth now had bragging rights to the largest-displacement pony car up to that time. And the 440 sure did get the ETs down, usually into the high 13s at around 104 mph. But there were problems.

The engine bay was once again too crowded to allow a power steering pump. And with 57 percent of the 'Cuda 440's 3400 pounds over the front tires, that was as much a drawback as it had been with the original 383. Neither was there enough room for a booster that was needed to energize the front disc brakes that were standard on other 'Cudas. So the 440 did without those as well, to the detriment of stopping distances. Finally, MoPar engineers feared that a four-speed manual transmission would encourage speed shifts that would destroy the 440 'Cuda's rear-end hardware. So this muscle fish came only with the TorqueFlite. Though it turned a respectable 14.01 at 103.81, *Car Life* magazine said it was disappointed in the 440 'Cuda's drag-strip performance. It was difficult to get the rear tires to bite off the line, and the TorqueFlite—lifted from Plymouth's family sedans—didn't shift with a racer's crispness. The magazine said the 440 'Cuda was at its best on the highway. There its abundant power reserves afforded effortless passing, its steering and braking shortcomings were minimized, and its firm Formula S suspension made it feel secure. *Car Life* recommended that performance enthusiasts fishing for more than acceleration alone cast a line for the 340 'Cuda. "Indeed," it advised, "there are such obvious discrepancies between the superb way the 'Cuda 440 goes, and the way it does other things (like, for example, stop) that in many ways it is a disturbing automobile."

Plymouth wasn't finished with big-block Barracudas, however, not by a long shot. Production of the MoPar compact dipped to 31,987 in this, the last year before a wholesale change would reshape the Barracuda for 1970.

1967-69 Plymouth
Barracuda 383/440
Facts At a Glance

Engine type:	V-8/B-Block/Wedge	V-8/RB-Block/Wedge
Displacement (cid):	383	440
Horsepower @ rpm:	280 @ 4200	375 @ 4600
	300 @ 4400 (1968)	
	330 @ 5000 (1969)	
Torque (lbs/ft) @ rpm:	400 @ 2400	480 @ 3200
	425 @ 3200 (1969)	
Compression ratio:	10.0:1	10.0:1
Bore (in.):	4.25	4.32
Stroke (in.):	3.37	3.75
Valve lifters:	Hydraulic	Hydraulic
Availability:	1967-69	1969

Magazine:	Car and Driver (April 1967)	Car Life (June 1969)
Times:		
0-60 mph (sec):	6.6	5.6
0-100 mph (sec):	18.7	13.8
¼-mile (sec):	15.4 @ 92 mph	14.01 @ 103.81 mph
Top speed (mph):	114 (est)	118
Axle ratio:	3.23:1	3.55:1
Engine (cid/bhp):	383/280	440/375

1967-71 PLYMOUTH GTX 440/HEMI

lymouth had fielded plenty of fast cars prior to 1967, but most were simply big-block versions of regular coupes and sedans. None took the encompassing approach to performance that Pontiac had pioneered three years earlier with its Tempest GTO. When Plymouth finally got around to creating such a vehicle, even its name—GTX—paid homage to that trailblazing Poncho. Be that as it may, the Plymouth GTX turned out to be a fine car in its own right and a corporate cousin to the Dodge Coronet and Charger R/T, which also bowed in '67.

For its supercar, Plymouth turned to the handsome Belvedere/Satellite two-door hardtop and convertible, crisply styled intermediates on a 116-inch wheelbase. The GTX was a Plymouth image car, and so it was flush with upscale appointments, including a top-of-the-line interior with lots of embossed vinyl and brightwork. Plymouth exercised some license in calling the standard front split-bench seats buckets. Body ornamentation was kept to a minimum, save for a pair of small, nonfunctional hood scoops.

The GTX was aimed not at the take-no-prisoners street/strip crowd that could care less about comfort and convenience amenities. Nor was its target the young, budget-minded performance buff. Rather, it was an executive hot rod designed to make gobs of power with a minimum of effort. No question then that Plymouth's choice of the 440-cubic-inch V-8 as the standard engine was a good one. The GTX now had bragging rights as the intermediate with the largest standard motor. But as a lazy, tons-of-torque mill, the 440 was tailored to heavily optioned full-size Chrysler barges. For duty in the GTX, it would have to be fortified.

Plymouth retained the 10.1:1 compression, but revised the camshaft and valve train, freed-up the exhaust manifolding, and added an unsilenced, double-snorkel air cleaner. Plymouth dubbed the result the Super Commando 440 and rated it at 375 horsepower at 4600 rpm. This compared with the regular 440's 350 horsepower at 4400. Both versions of the 440 made 480 pounds/feet of torque, but the Super Commando did it at 3200 rpm, peaking 400 rpm higher than the lesser 440. A double-breaker distributor, a windage tray in the oil pan, even a thicker drive shaft, were among the Super Commando details. In keeping with its sophisticated mission, the GTX came standard with the TorqueFlite automatic, but Plymouth raised its upshift speeds to match the higher-rpm engine. A four-speed manual was optional and Plymouth recommended a 3.23:1 rear axle with either transmission, though it offered a variety of gears.

Underneath, the Belvedere suspension was upgraded with heavy-duty torsion bars and ball joints, and six rear leaf springs instead of five. Its shocks were firmer and its 7.75×14 nylon red-stripe tires were wider. The brakes were upgraded drums, but optional front discs were the sporting driver's choice, as was the extra-cost power steering.

For all its power, the Super Commando 440 with its Carter AFB four-barrel had good street manners, with a gentle lope from its rather radical hydraulic-lifter camshaft. Testers were impressed, seeing low 15s at close to 100 mph in the quarter. And, surprise, at $3178, it was considered somewhat of a bargain.

For those with a little more cash and a bigger appetite for both thrills and wrench time, the GTX could be ordered

With the GTX tag, Plymouth finally bestowed a special name on its mid-size muscle Satellite. MoPar's brawny 440-cid four-barrel was standard in this executive-class hot rod. Hood scoops on the '67 GTX (red car, both pages) were decorative. Plymouth intermediates were restyled for '68, but retained the Hemi-engine option (blue car). Hood now could be equipped with functional cold-air vents.

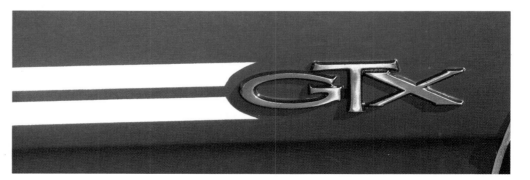

The '70 GTX pictured above is just one of 72 built that year with the optional Hemi engine. King Kong gained hydraulic lifters for easier maintenance and brought with it the functional Air Grabber hood scoop, which deployed at the driver's command. Plymouth intermediates got swoopy new sheetmetal for '71 (opposite). Handling and ergonomics improved and big-blocks returned, but this was the GTX's last season.

with the death-defying 425-horsepower 426 Street Hemi. This was the only GTX engine option. King Kong cost an additional $546 and used the standard GTX transmissions and its other upgrades. The Hemi sliced the car's quarter-mile ET into the 13s, but in cut-and-thrust action on the street, the standard Super Commando 440 could stay with a Hemi up to 100 mph or so. The beauty was that both the 440 and the Hemi GTX "were perfectly happy to motor sedately through town," said *Car and Driver*. Plymouth finally had its image muscle car, though few buyers seemed to notice. Production totaled just 2500 in '67, though a respectable 720 were Hemi-equipped.

1968-69

Chrysler restyled its intermediate line for 1968, with rounded panels and softer lines. The GTX returned with the same powertrain choices, though the standard tires were now F70×14s. Inside, true bucket seats and a console became standard. Performance was the byword in Detroit, and GTX sales were up dramatically, with 18,940 built, including 1026 convertibles and 450 Hemis. But Plymouth's sophisticated supercar was overshadowed by a new entry at the other end of the division's muscle spectrum, the Road Runner. Both the GTX and the 'Runner were built off the Belvedere/Satellite, but buyers could order the lighter, less-expensive Road Runner with all the GTX engines and performance goodies. The new kid outsold the GTX three to one in '68.

A new grille and taillamps were external revisions for '69, while Plymouth massaged some mechanicals. A new "Air Grabber" option allowed either the 440 or the Hemi to gulp cool air through inlets atop the ridges on the hood. A control beneath the dash could shut off the flow. Axle-ratio choices were expanded and 3.54:1 and 4.10:1 gears could be ordered. Hurst linkage was added to the manual transmission and a viscous-drive fan was now standard. The Road Runner continued to steal the limelight and could be ordered with a 440 variation the GTX didn't offer: a triple-two-barrel-carb setup that went by the catchy Six Pack name. The GTX hardtop cost $3416 and had a curb weight of 3465 pounds; the convertible listed for $3635 and weighed 3590. The Hemi was a $700.90 option.

1970

Plymouth performance reached its pinnacle in 1970 and you had only to look at its comprehensive new Rapid Transit System campaign to see why. Here was a range of hot wheels for every budget, from the sleeper Valiant Duster 340, through the all-new 'Cudas and the reskinned Road Runner and GTX, to the full-size Sport Fury GT. The GTX was once again a full-dress Satellite with the 440 V-8 as standard equipment. It rode the previous 116-inch wheelbase, but had new sheetmetal. Its lines were more flowing, the fender creases were ironed out, a fake air intake appeared behind the door, and the grille and tail were new. The GTX convertible was dropped for '70.

Under the hood, the 440 four-barrel endured a drop in compression to 9.7:1, but its horsepower and torque were unaltered. The Hemi's ratings also were unchanged, though its mechanical lifters were replaced by hydraulic lifters. This allowed it to meet emissions standards more easily and enabled the Hemi to go longer between tuneups. Joining the $711 Hemi on the GTX option list was the 440 Six Pack. With its trio of Holley two-barrels and 10.5:1 compression, it was rated at 390 horsepower at 4700 rpm and 490 pounds/feet of torque at 3200. It added just $119 to the GTX's $3535 base price.

If the guy in the next lane wasn't intimidated by the "440+6" decal on the bulge of the new hood, the GTX driver could flip a switch and pop the Air Grabber hood scoop, the sides of which were decorated with a menacing shark-like aggressor reminiscent of those painted on the air intakes of World War II fighter planes. Designed to funnel cold air directly to the air cleaner, the Air Grabber was a $66 option with either 440 engine and came standard with the Hemi.

The TorqueFlite continued standard and the optional four-speed got a pistol-grip shifter for its Hurst linkage. New F60×15 tires were an optional upgrade over the standard F70×14s. In keeping with its comprehensive Rapid Transit System approach, the '70 GTX could be ordered with any of four axle groups.

1967-71 Plymouth GTX

Facts At a Glance

Engine type:	V-8/RB-Block/Wedge	V-8/RB-Block/Hemi
Displacement (cid):	440	426
Horsepower @ rpm:	375 @ 4600[1]	425 @ 5000
	390 @ 4700[2]	
Torque (lbs/ft) @ rpm:	480 @ 3200	490 @ 4000
	490 @ 3200[2]	
Compression ratio:	10.1:1/10.5:1[2]	10.25:1
	9.7:1[3]	
Bore (in.):	4.32	4.25
Stroke (in.):	3.75	3.75
Valve lifters:	Hydraulic	Mechanical
Availability:	1967-69	1967-70

[1]370 @ 4600 in 1971
[2]Six Pack (1970-71)
[3]1970-71

Magazine:	*Car and Driver* (Nov. 1966)	*Car and Driver* (Nov. 1966)
Times:		
0-60 mph (sec):	6.0	4.8
0-100 mph (sec):	15.1	12.5
¼-mile (sec):	14.4 @ 98 mph	13.5 @ 105 mph
Top speed (mph):	118-plus	130

Axle ratio:	3.23:1	3.23:1
Engine (cid/bhp):	440/375	426/425 Hemi

Magazine:	*Car Life* (Feb. 1968)	*Car Life* (Feb. 1968)
Times:		
0-60 mph (sec):	6.3	6.8
0-100 mph (sec):	15.3	17.4
¼-mile (sec):	14.0 @ 96.5 mph[1]	14.6 @ 95.6 mph[2]
Top speed (mph):	144	121
Axle ratio:	3.23:1	3.23:1
Engine (cid/bhp):	426/425 Hemi	440/375
Model:	1968 convertible	1968 hardtop

[1]13.44 @ 104.89 mph with 4.56:1 axle and slicks
[2]13.97 @ 99.77 mph with 4.30:1 axle and slicks

Magazine:	*Car and Driver* (Nov. 1970)
Times:	
0-60 mph (sec):	6.5
0-100 mph (sec):	16.2
¼-mile (sec):	14.9 @ 95.4 mph
Top speed (mph):	130
Axle ratio:	3.23:1
Engine (cid/bhp):	440/370
Model:	1971

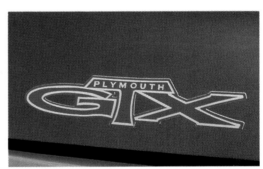

1971

Plymouth intermediates got curvaceous new "fuselage" styling on an inch-shorter wheelbase for '71. With the new body came a three-inch increase in rear track (to 62 inches), which benefited handling, plus a reconfigured interior with a more comfortable driving position and superior ergonomics. But Detroit was being pressured to tone down performance and while MoPar was the slowest to scale back, it too did some detuning. The Road Runner's standard 383 V-8, for instance, lost a whopping 30 horsepower. GTX engines, however, held out virtually unscathed. The standard 440 four-barrel lost only five horsepower, while the optional Six Pack and Hemi were unchanged. Weight was up by about 170 pounds, however, and quarter-mile times began to creep up, by nearly a full second in some tests.

The '71 GTX had the stiffest suspension rates of any Plymouth intermediate and while handling was adequate, most testers concluded that it wasn't good enough to justify the rock-hard ride. Still, the GTX was one of the few muscle cars that had no apologies to make when comparisons were made to its recent ancestors. "All in all," said *Car and Driver*, "we would have to say that the Plymouth GTX is a step forward on a front where all others are retreating. In certain areas, styling and driver comfort, for example, it is vastly improved over the previous model and only in performance, primarily because of increased weight, has it lost ground." The GTX was discontinued after 1971, and while Road Runner lived on, it was a muscle car in memory only. The GTX, at least, died with its big-cube boots on.

Pontiac defined the muscle car with its 1964 GTO, a mid-size Tempest stuffed full of 389 V-8 and all the sporty features then so popular with think-young buyers: bucket seats, floorshift, fancy trim, "performance" styling touches, and a chassis tuned for serious driving. Dodge and Plymouth had similarly fast packages, but it took them several years to imitate the GTO's integrated approach. But by '68 the problem with muscle cars—Pontiac's and Plymouth's included—was that they cost too much for the younger enthusiasts who most wanted them. All it took were a few options to work the price up beyond $5000.

In the spring of 1967 it occurred to Plymouth planners that there might be a sizable market for a bargain-priced factory hot rod. It would have few frills, which would cut costs and allow more money to be spent where it counted—on the hardware. Depending on your source, this notion originated with either Plymouth's sales department or Brock Yates, an outspoken editor with *Car and Driver* magazine.

In any case, Plymouth held back until 1968, partly to take advantage of the smoother new styling scheduled for that year's B-body Belvedere and the companion Dodge Coronet/

Charger. The car would be slotted below the GTX and its target would be what Plymouth marketers had identified as the "Drive-In Set:" twentysomething street cruisers who wanted the maximum bang and beauty for the minimum number of bucks. Division planners aimed to give them a $3000 car capable of 100 mph in the quarter-mile. *Car and Driver* later blasted Plymouth for disregarding Yates' original suggestion that the car be devoid of hood scoops or other gimmicks. But even if it did have a little more gingerbread than Yates had proposed, and even if its base price of $2986 and quarter-mile speed of 98 mph just missed Plymouth's ideal, the kids didn't seem to mind. The Road Runner was a hit from Day One.

The package was predictable enough. Starting with the lightest Belvedere body, the base two-door pillared coupe, Plymouth added a modified version of Chrysler's veteran 383 V-8, with heads, manifolds, camshaft, valve springs and crankcase windage tray taken form the 440 big block. With minor help from an unsilenced air cleaner, the result was 335 horsepower at 5200 rpm and a healthy 425 pounds/feet of torque at 3400. The only engine option was the Hemi. A

Plymouth's small-buck big-bang '68 Road Runner took muscle to the masses with its 335-bhp 383-cid four-barrel V-8 and $2986 base price. The car's "beep-beep" horn imitated its namesake cartoon character. Rival automakers, meanwhile, mimicked the Road Runner with budget high-performance models of their own.

heavy-duty four-on-the-floor manual was the standard transmission, but a beefed-up column-shifted edition of Chrysler's three-speed TorqueFlite automatic was available at extra cost. Suspension was heavy-duty, too, with larger-than-stock front torsion bars and high-rate rear leaf springs. Rounding out chassis upgrades were 11-inch-diameter heavy-duty drum brakes and F70×14 polyglas tires with thinline stripes in red or white. Hemis rolled on F70×15 rubber.

Plymouth's retail price target dictated limiting other standard equipment to the bare essentials, though this was actually a plus for enthusiasts. As *Motor Trend* observed: "The Road Runner is the simplest, most brazenly pure, non-compromising supercar in history, and…its simplicity is a welcome virtue." Still, Plymouth managed to budget for a bulged "performance" hood with incongruous side-facing dummy air intakes that were made functional as a mid-year option (via an underdash pull-knob).

Given its no-frills concept, the Road Runner's options list was surprisingly long. Items split about evenly between show and go. In the latter category were power brakes ($43.75), front-disc brakes ($72.95, which came with 10-inch rear drums), power steering ($94.15), and "Sure-Grip" limited-slip differential ($42.35). Standard axle ratio was 3.23:1, but an $87.50 High-Performance Axle Package grouped a tighter 3.55:1 gearset with Sure-Grip, heavy-duty radiator and fan shroud. The Hemi came with a super-duty Sure-Grip Dana 60 axle turning a 3.54:1 cog, though this was a "mandatory" $138.90 option on top of a formidable $714.30 for the engine itself.

The Road Runner was the right car at the right time, and its combination of low price, high performance, and good-natured fun took the market by storm. Against a first-year sale forecast of only 2500, Plymouth happily moved no fewer than 44,599 Runners. About a third of those represented a companion hardtop coupe that arrived during the year at $3304. Just 1019 '68s were Hemi equipped.

1969

Curiously, Plymouth seemed to back away from the original Road Runner concept for 1969, adding a $3313 convertible model and more luxury options like a center console, front buckets with four-way driver's-seat adjustment, and power windows. But performance was hardly forgotten. No fewer than five new extra-cost axle packages arrived with ratios ranging to 4.10:1. And while the Hemi option and standard hi-po 383 were unchanged, there was a third engine option for the coupe and hardtop: a hot new 440 with three two-barrel Holley carbs on a special aluminum intake manifold, good for 390 horsepower and a massive 490 pounds/feet of torque.

Dubbed "440 Six Pack" and badged as "440+6," it came with a special lift-off fiberglass hood finished in flat-black and furnished with four NASCAR-type tiedown pins, plus a functional, forward-facing "Air Grabber" scoop. The hood was also available with other engines for just $55.30. Additionally, the Six-Pack included a Hurst shifter for the standard heavy-duty four-speed anual, which was good because road testers had generally panned the original Inland linkage. A high-capacity cooling system, 4.10 axle with Sure-Grip, and wider G70-15 Goodyear Red Streaks on 15×6-inch wheels accompanied the Six Pack. With all this, the tri-carb 440 furnished Hemi-style acceleration yet at only about half the money—$462.80 versus $813.45.

All '69 Road Runners received new grille and taillight styling, plus larger cartoon birds outside and a new one on the steering wheel hub. The car was hotter than ever and Road

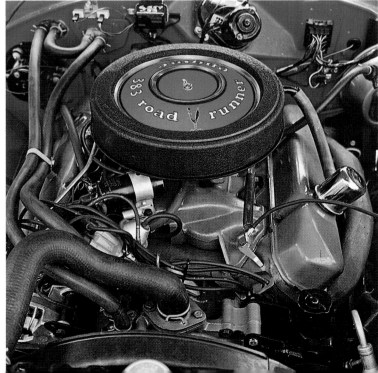

Road Runner reached its peak annual production of 84,420 in '69, but just 2128 were the new drop top model (above). The 440 Six Pack was also added that year. MoPar's 426 Hemi had been an option from the start and continued in the restyled '70 model (opposite), but now with the campy Air Grabber hood scoop. A 383 Road Runner could turn 15-second ETs; the Hemi and 440 Six Pack would run in the mid-13s.

Runner sales almost doubled, to nearly 84,500: 48,549 were hardtops; 33,743 were pillared coupes; and 2128 were convertibles. Hemis went into 788 Road Runners, including 10 ragtops.

1970

The good times rolled on for 1970, the year Plymouth grouped its meanest cars under the "Rapid Transit System" banner. The Washington safety lobby and fast-rising insurance rates were starting to crimp muscle-car sales, but you couldn't tell from looking at the Road Runner. Styling was again freshened with handsome loop-motif front and rear ends, creaseless sides, and a dummy rear-fender scoop. Drivetrains stayed basically the same save two significant changes: the Hemi went from solid to hydraulic lifters in the interest of greater durability and cleaner emissions, and the standard four-on-the-floor manual moved to the options list, replaced by a heavy-duty three-speed.

Naturally, there was a new gimmick for 1970: a planed-off Air Grabber hood in which the scoop now popped up at the driver's command (via an underdash solenoid switch tripping a vacuum-operated trap door). Raising the scoop revealed a toothy-shark cartoon on each side—just the thing for psyching out the opposition at stoplights.

Even more intimidating was a new fourth Road Runner model for 1970. Aptly called Superbird, this was a wild, aerodynamic hardtop with a towering rear wing and extended hidden-headlamp nose cone. It's covered elsewhere in this book. Road Runner sales in '70 barely exceeded the '68 figure, but the car's reputation had been made. Probably no other car of the muscle era except the original GTO was as much a phenomenon as the 1968-70 Road Runner. It was fun, it was fast, it was imitated, and it had something to offer both the hard-core racer and the timid stroker. No one was disappointed, except maybe Brock Yates.

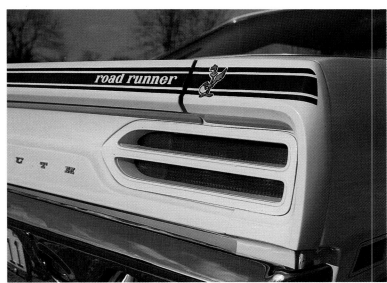

1968-70 Plymouth Road Runner

Facts At a Glance

Engine type:	V-8/B-Block/Wedge	V-8/RB-Block/Wedge
Displacement (cid):	383	440 (3x2v)
Horsepower @ rpm:	335 @ 5200	390 @ 4700
Torque (lbs/ft) @ rpm:	425 @ 3400	490 @ 3200
Compression ratio:	10.0:1	10.5:1
Bore (in.):	4.25	4.34
Stroke (in.):	3.38	3.75
Valve lifters:	Hydraulic	Hydraulic
Availability:	(1968-70)	(1969-70)

Engine type:	V-8/RB-Block/Hemi
Displacement (cid):	426 (2x4v)
Horsepower @ rpm:	425 @ 5000
Torque (lbs/ft) @ rpm:	490 @ 4000
Compression ratio:	10.2:1
Bore (in.):	4.25
Stroke (in.):	3.75
Valve lifters:	Mechanical
Availability:	(1968-70)

1971-73 PLYMOUTH ROAD RUNNER

A radical change hit the Road Runner for 1971—a new slippery-smooth two-door hardtop body with long nose and short rear deck. The convertible and pillared coupe were gone, but the 115-inch wheelbase was retained and the car's rear track grew by three inches, which benefited handling. Referred to by some as the "intermediate ponycar," the '71 Road Runner was otherwise a high-performance repeat for the budget buyer. Base priced at just $3120 this year, the Road Runner remained an excellent muscle value. Still, the writing was on the wall, and the marketing emphasis shifted somewhat from go to show. New options only involved things like color-keyed "elastomeric" front bumper, a semi-functional rear spoiler, trendy backlight louvers and "contour" bucket seats.

As in 1968-70, the 383 four-barrel V-8 was standard, but horsepower dropped by 35, to 300, and torque was down by 25 pounds/feet, to 410, as a result of tougher emissions standards and a compression drop from 9.50:1 to 8.50:1. The 440 Six Pack was down by five horsepower, to 385, as its compression slipped a tad, from 10.5:1 to 10.3:1. At 425 horsepower, the Hemi's specifications were unchanged. A glimpse into the Road Runner's future could be had by ordering the optional 340-cubic-inch four barrel, which was rated at 275 horsepower.

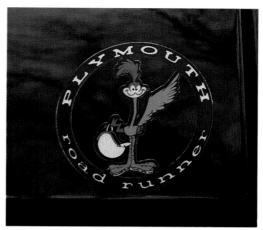

Transmission choices stayed the same and the Air Grabber hood was still available. Included was a heavy-duty suspension, performance hood with bold "383," "440" or "Hemi" graphics, low-restriction dual exhaust system, and the "beep-beep" horn. A reconfigured interior was highlighted by a more comfortable driving position and superior ergonomics.

Motor Trend sampled a couple of '71s: a 383 that went out the door for $4324 with options; and a 440, which cost $4638 with options, the costliest being the $262 Six Pack engine. Both were equipped with vinyl buckets ($106); the power steering group ($200), TorqueFlite automatic ($262); Air Grabber hood ($69), and Goodyear G60×15 Polyglas tires in place of the standard 70-series rubber ($94). Overall, *Motor Trend* liked the 383 better. With its single four-barrel, it was more responsive to the throttle, especially in fluctuating traffic conditions, and it got slightly better fuel economy: 11.1 mpg average versus 10.8. Both cars had what the magazine called "superior" handling, though the slightly softer suspension on the 383 made it more comfortable with no discernable loss in roadholding. Surprisingly, the 383 was quicker. With a 3.91:1 rear axle ratio, the 383 turned a 14.84/94.5 mph quarter; the 440 with a 4.10:1 gear turned 15.02/96 mph. *Motor Trend* said the Six Pack wasn't running as it should, but concluded that the cheaper 383 was the overall better car—and more insurable, to boot.

Despite new skin and the lingering appeal of powerful V-8s, Road Runner sales took a backslide to 14,218 units, with just 55 of them Hemis.

1972

Things got even worse for '72, when the Runner attracted but 7628 buyers. The Hemi was dropped, having become almost unsalable in the fast-shrinking muscle market. Maybe that was for the best, for it saved the legendary powerplant from the embarrassment of being rated under the net horsepower figures Detroit turned to for '72. Unlike the previous gross horsepower ratings, this system calculated the power of the engine as it was installed in the vehicle, with all accessories connected and in operation. That lowered published horsepower ratings considerably.

Even the new ratings system, however, wasn't enough to save the Road Runner's original MoPar 383. It departed, too, replaced as standard power by a Chrysler 340 small-block with a Carter Thermo-Quad plastic-bodied four-barrel carburetor and 10.2:1 compression giving 240 net horsepower. If the 340 didn't fit the bill, big-cube performance was still available in the form of a 400-cubic-inch B-Block, which Chrysler created by punching the 383's bores to 4.34 inches. It was rated at 255 horsepower and also had Thermo-Quad carburetion. You could still get the Air Grabber hood but not the 440 Six Pack engine, the 440 being trimmed to just a single four-barrel with a 8.2:1 compression and 280 horses.

Segmented tape stripes spilling over the front fenders from the side-facing hood scoops were a novel option, but the trend was clear: The Runner was running out of steam. At least the horn still went "Beep-Beep."

1973

Plymouth's bird soldiered on, in name if not spirit, at a time when other hot cars were being dropped with little fanfare. That, plus a still-reasonable $3115 base price, helps explain why sales recovered to 19,056 for 1973. Still, those looking for sleek muscle in a climate hostile to high-performance had to accept the Road

Runner's chunky frontal restyle prompted by that year's newly mandated five-mph "crash" bumpers.

More painful was a further demotion in standard power to a 318 V-8. It had dual exhausts, but ran on a two-barrel carb and netted just 170 horsepower. Most 'Runner buyers opted for the extra-cost 240-horsepower 340 four barrel. Again topped by Thermo-Quad carburetion, the 340 was a high-revving small-block with good street manners. Both the 400, at 260 horsepower, and the 440, with 280, continued as four-barrel options.

And that, as far as enthusiasts were concerned, was pretty much the end of the line. The '74 Road Runner was a carryover, though the 340 was supplanted by a 360-cube four barrel. Though the Runner returned for 1975 as part of Plymouth's restyled, renamed "small Fury" mid-size line, it was a muscle car whose muscles had atrophied to, at most, a four-barrel 400 that left it no quicker than some four-cylinder imports. The name was then applied to a package option for two-door versions of the new-for-'76 Volare compact. Built around 360 power, it was sprightly enough, attention-getting, and arguably the most nimble Road Runner yet, but it was hardly the rip-snorting Beep-Beep of yore.

Road Runner's decline was evident by '72, when the 340-cid V-8 became standard (this page). These cars handled better than their predecessors, but were weaker in the quarter-mile. Four-barrel 440 V-8 continued through '73 (opposite, top) and '74 (opposite, bottom), the last year for this body style.

1971-73 Plymouth Road Runner

Facts At a Glance

Engine type:	V-8/LA-Block/Wedge	V-8/B-Block/Wedge
Displacement (cid):	340	383
Horsepower @ rpm:	240 @ 4800 (72-73)	335 @ 5200 (68-70)
		300 @ 4800 (1971)
Torque (lbs/ft)		
@ rpm:	290 @ 3600 (72-73)	425 @ 3400 (68-70)
		410 @ 3400 (1971)
Compression ratio:	8.5:1	9.5:1 (1971)
Bore (in.):	4.04	4.25
Stroke (in.):	3.31	3.38
Valve lifters:	Hydraulic	Hydraulic
Availability:	1972-73	1970-71

Engine type:	V-8/B-Block/Wedge	V-8/RB-Block/Wedge
Displacement (cid):	400	440 (3x2v)
Horsepower @ rpm:	255 @ 4800 (1972)	390 @ 4700
	260 @ 4800 (1973)	
Torque (lbs/ft)		
@ rpm:	340 @ 3200 (1972)	490 @ 3200
	335 @ 3600 (1973)	
Compression ratio:	8.2:1	10.3:1
Bore (in.):	4.34	4.32
Stroke (in.):	3.38	3.75
Valve lifters:	Hydraulic	Hydraulic
Availability:	1972-73	1971

Engine type:	V-8/RB-Block/Wedge
Displacement (cid):	440 (4v)

Horsepower @ rpm:	280 @ 4800
Torque (lbs/ft)	
@ rpm:	375 @ 3200[1]
Compression ratio:	8.2:1
Bore (in.):	4.32
Stroke (in.):	3.75
Valve lifters:	Hydraulic
Availability:	1972-73

[1]380 @ 3200 1973

Engine type:	V-8/RB-Block/Hemi	V-8/LA-Block/Wedge
Displacement (cid):	426	318
Horsepower @ rpm:	425 @ 5000	170 @ 4000
Torque (lbs/ft)		
@ rpm:	490 @ 4000	270 @ 2000
Compression ratio:	10.2:1	8.6:1
Bore (in.):	4.25	3.91
Stroke (in.):	3.75	3.31
Valve lifters:	Hydraulic	Hydraulic
Availability:	1971	1973

Magazine:	*Motor Trend*	*Motor Trend*
	(Feb. 1971)	*(Feb. 1971)*
Times:		
0-60 mph (sec):	6.7	6.7
0-100 mph (sec):	N/A	N/A
¼-mile (sec):	14.84 @ 94.5	15.02 @ 96.0 mph
Top speed (mph):	N/A	N/A
Axle ratio:	3.91:1	4.10:1
Engine (cid/bhp):	383/300	440/385
Model year:	1971	1971

1970 PLYMOUTH AAR 'CUDA

Rivaling the drag strip as racing's premier showcase for pony power from 1964-70 was the Sports Car Club of America's popular Trans-American Sedan road racing series. Happily for performance enthusiasts, the SCCA required Detroit to build street versions of the cars it raced. Hence, the Boss 302 Mustang and Z-28 Camaro. Chrysler had competed in Trans Am-type events with various Darts and Valiants, but when it finally got legitimate pony cars in 1970, it leaped in with both feet. From Dodge came the Challenger T/A and from Plymouth, the AAR 'Cuda.

Bowing in March 1970, the AAR 'Cuda was named for Dan Gurney's All-American Racers, which would campaign the car in the Trans Am series. Plymouth farmed out actual construction of the coupes to a Michigan aftermarket firm, Creative Industries. The rules required that a minimum of 2500

Striped and spoilered AAR 'Cuda was the street version of Plymouth's Trans Am racer. The competition car used a 305-cid four-barrel, but its road counterpart (both pages) had a 340 with three two-barrel Holleys (below). This car has the optional Elastomeric body-colored front bumper.

production examples be built and the best evidence is that Plymouth produced 2724 AAR 'Cudas. With a base price of $3966, the AAR 'Cuda was about $800 more expensive than a regular 'Cuda coupe.

Those production versions may have looked much like their competition counterparts, but of course there were some important differences. The Trans Am race cars were limited to a maximum displacement of 305 cubic inches and a single four-barrel carburetor. MoPar de-stroked its potent 340-cube four-barrel V-8 to qualify. On the street, however, there was no such limit. So Chrysler went a little wild. It retained the 340-cubic-inch displacement, but added a trio of Holley two-barrel carburetors and placed them atop an Edlebrock aluminum intake manifold. The carbs were borrowed from MoPar's 440 Six Pack, with calibration and jetting changed to suit the smaller engine. Other changes from the run-of-the-mill 340s included heavier main webbing, a stronger new casting for the cylinder heads, and Hemi-grade valve springs. The 340 six barrel was exclusive to the AAR 'Cuda and Challenger T/A and appeared for 1970 only. It was conservatively rated at 290 horsepower at 5000 rpm and 340 pounds/feet of torque at 3200. A choice of four-speed or TorqueFlite was offered with a 3.55:1 gear standard and a 3.91:1 rear-axle ratio optional.

Since the Trans Am series emphasized handling as well as power, the AAR 'Cuda got a suspension that made it arguably the best cornering Plymouth of the era. The rear springs were recambered, a change that helped raise the tail 1¾ inches over regular 'Cuda specification. The lift permitted clearance for exhausts pipes that exited in front of the rear wheelwell. Curiously, the exhaust actually was routed to the standard muffler beneath the trunk, then fed forward to the chrome-tipped side outlets. A little deceptive, perhaps, but it sure looked cool. Plymouth also used the elevated tail to fit G60×15 rear tires; E60×15s were used in front. Both sets were Goodyear Polyglas GTs on Plymouth's Road Wheels. In tandem with stiffer rear shocks and sway bars fore and aft, this tire arrangement helped the AAR 'Cuda keep its tail planted under power in the turns. Brakes were discs in front and 11-inch drums in back. The car came with normal-ratio manual steering,

Quick and nimble AAR 'Cuda was offered for '70 only. Its body was raked to clear the oversized rear tires and the side-exit exhaust. Black fiberglass hood with functional scoop and duck-tail spoiler were standard.

1970 Plymouth AAR 'Cuda

Facts At a Glance

Engine type:	V-8/LA-Block/Wedge
Displacement (cid):	340 (3x2v)
Horsepower @ rpm:	290 @ 5000
Torque (lbs/ft) @ rpm:	340 @ 3200
Compression ratio:	10.5:1
Bore (in.):	4.04
Stroke (in.):	3.31
Valve lifters:	Hydraulic
Availability:	1970 AAR 'Cuda

Magazine:	Car Life (July 1970)	Car and Driver (July 1970)
Times:		
0-60 mph (sec):	N/A	5.8
0-100 mph (sec):	N/A	14.4
¼-mile (sec):	14.50 @ 98.68 mph	14.3 @ 99.5 mph
Top speed (mph):	N/A	128 (est)
Axle ratio:	3.55:1	3.55:1

but could be ordered with a special fast-ratio power alternative.

The AAR 'Cuda could be ordered in any 'Cuda color, but no other 'Cuda had its rake or its blacked-out grille with anodized aluminum trim. It also had an exclusive matte-black fiberglass hood held down by NASCAR-style pins and sporting a sexy molded cowl-induction scoop that fed the Holleys. A strobe tape stripe traced the upper body line and ended with the word "Cuda" and an AAR shield beneath a black, duck-tail spoiler. The cabin was standard 'Cuda issue, though a surprising variety of options was available considering that the AAR was strictly a performance car. Customers could order the body-colored Elastomeric front bumper, a vinyl top, power windows, and bench/bucket seats. Rear-window louvers also proved popular.

With ETs in the mid 14s at 98 mph or so, the AAR 'Cuda was a tick slower than the class leader, the Camaro Z-28, which weighed less than the Plymouth's 3500-3600 pounds and packed a larger engine, a 350-cube V-8 rated at 360 horsepower. The rumble fish outhandled the Z-28, however, and only the Boss 302 Mustang had better overall balance in the turns. Alas, the AAR 'Cudas raced by Gurney and Swede Savage lacked the development time to make much dent in the Trans Am points tally, and Ford won the series in '70. All the factories except AMC pulled out of Trans Am the following year, and Plymouth killed both the racing and street version of its AAR 'Cuda.

1970 PLYMOUTH ROAD RUNNER SUPERBIRD

To Plymouth in 1969, the only thing more painful than relinquishing its superspeedway dominance to Ford was losing Richard Petty to the blue-oval boys. Plymouth gave up an 11-year association with NASCAR's most successful driver and its biggest star when it refused to let him race for sister division—and racing rival—Dodge. Petty wanted to run Dodge's new aerodynamic Charger Daytona. Plymouth said no. So he bailed out of the crate-shaped Belvedere and skipped to Ford. Petty drove the wind-cheating Torino Talladega to 10 NASCAR wins in '69, helping Ford snare the manufacturer's championship. Plymouth saw the light. It went out and built its own winged wonder, refined it some over Dodge's version, and christened it the Superbird.

There it was in a Plymouth ad in early 1970, pictured in a garage, with the familar number 43 on the door and the familiar face of smiling King Richard behind it. "The obvious reason Richard Petty came back," read the tag line, triumphantly. With Pete Hamilton behind the wheel, the new Superbird went right out and won the 1970 Daytona 500. Those were the days.

Plymouth had created its winner in the mold of the Charger Daytona. Basically, it planted a wind-piercing nose cone on the front of its intermediate coupe and a 25-inch-tall air foil on the tail. This created enough downforce to keep the car ground-bound during 200-mph blasts around the superspeedway. Ford had similarly modified its Torinos and Mercury Cyclones, but they weren't as radical in appearance as the MoPar efforts.

NASCAR, meanwhile, was troubled by these outlandish deviations from stock-looking cars. Rather than outright banning them, however, the sanctioning body upped the number that the manufacturer had to build for sale to the public before a design could qualify for racing.

For the 1969 Charger Daytona, the requirement had been 500; Dodge built 503. For 1970, the requirement was hiked to 1000. No problem, said Plymouth. It claimed it had orders for 2000 Superbirds, though, like the Charger Daytona and Ford's Talladega, the car experienced a sudden burst of unpopularity upon reaching the dealerships. It took a while, but Plymouth eventually sold 1971 of these birds of a decidedly different feather.

What the customer got was basically a Road Runner modified by Creative Industries, an aftermarket contractor that had built the Charger Daytona and its less-radical antecedent, the 1969 Charger 500. As with the Charger, the Road Runner's front was extended by about 18 inches via a drooping sheetmetal snout. Plymouth used a slightly different grille opening than did Dodge, but both featured a small lower air dam and also employed fiberglass housings for pop-up headlamps. Plymouth had to use the front fenders from a '70 Dodge Coronet because the Belvedere's wouldn't mate well with the nose. Atop the fenders were a pair rear-facing scoops. On the race car these allowed the lowered fenders to clear the tires, but they were merely ornamental on the street Superbird. The rear roofline followed the one pioneered by the

Plymouth hatched the limited-edition Road Runner Superbird to meet NASCAR homologation requirements. It was produced only for '70. All race versions were Hemis, but the street cars were based on 440 or Hemi Road Runners. Both versions used basically the same elongated aero snout and soaring rear wing. Dodge Coronet fenders helped mate the nose to the body. All street models had a black vinyl top to hide scars inflicted during creation of the flush rear window. Fender scoops were decorative on the street version.

Charger 500 and used a flush-fitted backlight in place of the stock tunneled rear window. All street Superbirds came with a black vinyl roof to cover up the fabricator's patchwork. Straddling the trunk was an aluminum horizontal stabilizer supported some 25 inches over the rear fenders. Perhaps even more than the nose, this was the distinguishing trait of the Daytona and Superbird, though the Plymouth's vertical supports were slightly wider at the bottom.

The Superbird came standard with MoPar's 375-horsepower, 440-cubic-inch Super Commando four-barrel V-8. Some 716 were built with the optional 390-horse 440 Six Pack, and another 135 got the extra-cost 425-horsepower 426 Hemi. Transmission choices were the four-speed manual or TorqueFlite automatic. Power steering and power front disc brakes were standard, as was bench seating in black or white vinyl; buckets were optional. The suspension was heavy duty and extra-cost G60×15 tires could be substituted for the standard F70×14s. Color choices included Vitamin C Orange, Lime Light , Blue Fire Metallic, Alpine White, Lemon Twist, Corporation Blue, or TorRed. "Plymouth" was spelled out in large letters on the rear fenders—just like on the racing cars—and a Road Runner cartoon likeness encircled by the words "Road Runner Superbird" appeared in decal form on the air foil uprights and on the left headlamp closure.

Though it was an obvious head-turner, the Superbird drove no differently than a similarly equipped '70 Road Runner. It was most tractable with the 440 four-barrel and with any of the engines, balancing throttle and brake off the line to limit wheelspin would result in quarter-miles from the mid 13s to low 14s at more than 100 mph. The ride was extremely stiff, but roadholding was good, given the 3900-pound car's front weight bias. As with other MoPars of this vintage, the steering wheel was mounted too high for a comfortable driving position. No testers complained about poor rear vision, but in light of the unprotected nose, there were admonitions against tailgating or parking carelessly. Some criticized the car's horn. The Superbird used the Road Runner's standard-issue "beep-beep" unit. "It's cute, but absolutely lacks the authority the car deserves, authority absolutely necessary on the highway," said *Road Test* magazine.

As it turned out, these magnificently extreme MoPars were more conversation pieces than cutting-edge muscle cars. Their aerodynamic aids didn't work until 80 to 100 mph and they were heavier and more expensive than comparable standard models. On the race track, their record-shattering speeds scared NASCAR into legislating them out of existence. Dodge built the Charger Daytona for only one year, 1969, and Plymouth shelved the Superbird after 1970. Chrysler fielded sleeker new mid-size bodies for '71, and the winged cars languished on dealers' lots, curiosities waiting to turn collectible.

1970 Plymouth Superbird

Facts At a Glance

Engine type:	V-8/RB-Block/Wedge	V-8/RB-Block/Hemi
Displacement (cid):	440	426
Horsepower @ rpm:	375 @ 4600	425 @ 5000
	390 @ 4700[1]	
Torque (lbs/ft) @ rpm:	480 @ 3200	490 @ 4000
	490 @ 3200[1]	
Compression ratio:	9.7:1/10.5:1[1]	10.2:1
Bore (in.):	4.32	4.25
Stroke (in.):	3.75	3.75
Valve lifters:	Hydraulic	Mechanical

[1]Optional 440 Six Pack engine

Magazine:	Car and Driver (1970)	Road Test (April 1970)
Times:		
0-60 mph (sec):	4.8	N/A
0-100 mph (sec):	12.5	N/A
¼-mile (sec):	13.5 @ 105 mph	14.26 @ 103.7 mph
Top speed (mph):	139	N/A
Axle ratio:	3.23:1	N/A
Engine (cid/bhp):	426/425 Hemi	440/375

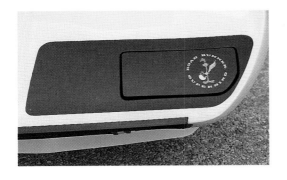

Tail spoiler kept NASCAR Superbirds on the track at 190 mph; didn't do much but draw stares at highway speeds (top). Fiberglass hidden-headlamp pods were set into the steel nose (left). Superbird used the Road Runner's "beep-beep" horn; it's the purple component in the upper-left photo. Superbird was most successful as a NASCAR racer, but a few showed up on the drag strip. MoPar mavens Sox and Martin ran one (above).

1970-71
PLYMOUTH
'CUDA 440/HEMI

Not only was Plymouth's redesigned '70 Barracuda beautiful, it was downright beastly when fitted with the 426 Hemi (both pages). Hemi 'Cudas could turn sub-14-second quarter-miles, but were too nose heavy to handle well. Car in the bottom-right photo has aftermarket wheels and tires.

By 1970, the pony car field had been saturated with strong entries from Ford, Chevrolet, Pontiac, and even AMC. This was the year Chrysler finally jumped in with an entry that had the long-hood/short-rear deck essential to the genre. A 110-inch-wheelbase version went to Dodge, where it wore a new name, the Challenger. Another version, on the same platform but with a two-inch-shorter-wheelbase, went to Plymouth. There it got the Barracuda tag that had been worn by the division's Valiant-derived sporty cars since 1964.

By this time it was difficult to do anything really new in the pony arena, but Chrysler's E-bodies set themselves apart with a rainbow of engine selections—seven V-8s and a six-cylinder. When it came to appearances, Dodge wanted the Challenger to look tough and brawny, but the result was a small car that rather self-consciously wore big-car styling cues. At Plymouth, the stylists went for a leaner, less pretentious look. The Barracuda coupes and convertibles had an economy of line that's fresh even today. The available wide rubber, Elastomeric body-colored bumpers, and hood scoops complemented the fluid shape. And a palette of extra-cost colors—Lime Light, TorRed, In Violet, and Lemon Twist—were traffic stoppers.

The Barracuda came as a base model and as the upscale Gran Coupe, but enthusiasts were drawn to the 'Cuda derivation. Standard on the 'Cuda was MoPar's fine 335-horsepower four-barrel 383. Optional was the scampy 275-horsepower 340 four barrel. A trio of big-block stormers rounded out the options list: the 440, which made 375 horsepower with a single four barrel or 390 in triple two-barrel Six Pack guise; and finally, the all-conquering dual-quad 425-horsepower 426 Hemi.

Standard with the 340 and 383 was a three-speed floor-shift manual. A high-upshift TorqueFlite was optional but standard on the 440 and 426. Its Slap Stik T-handle allowed quick manual upshifts of the automatic. A New Process A-833 four-speed manual was optional across the board and was available with Hurst Pistol-Grip linkage. Depending on the powertrain, axle ratios of 3.23:1, 3.55:1, 3.91:1, and 4.10:1 were offered. Sure-Grip was a mandatory option in Chrysler and Dana axles.

This was the year Plymouth grouped its hot cars under

the Rapid Transit System umbrella and the 'Cuda was a textbook study in this all-encompassing approach to performance. For example, heavy-duty suspensions were not only 'Cuda standards, but were tailored according to the engine fitted. The 340s and 383s had handling-oriented spring rates and front and rear stabilizer bars. Suspensions on the 440s and Hemis, meanwhile, were set up to withstand heavy-metal acceleration; they had no aft stabilizer bar, but their rear springs consisted of five full leaves plus two half-leaves on the left and six full leaves on the right. 'Cuda brakes were larger than those on regular Barracudas, though front discs were optional. Standard on 383 and 440 models were F70×14 white-letter tires; the 'Cuda 340 wore E60×15 skins; while the Hemi smoked F60×15s on seven-inch rims. Externally, 'Cudas were identified by their dual non-functioning hood scoops and the pair of driving lights mounted beneath the front bumper. An option

exclusive to the 'Cuda and the companion Challenger R/T was the functional shaker scoop, which mounted to the air cleaner through a hole in the hood and quivered with the vibration of the engine. It was standard with the Hemi.

Each 'Cuda had its own personality. The 340 was by far the best balanced, while the 383 offered the most flexible power delivery. Either one would turn the quarter in the mid 14s at around 96-98 mph. Drag racers were drawn to the 440, especially the Six Pack. This big block was fortified with a forged-steel crankshaft, heavy-duty connecting rods and steel-reinforced, cast-aluminum pistons. Its radical-profile camshaft mated with hydraulic lifters. At full bore, its trio of Holleys sucked 1300 cubic feet of air per minute. With ETs in the mid- to low-14s at 100 mph, it could stay with the Hemi on the street, though around town, its vacuum-actuated front and rear carbs could open with little warning, making for some

interesting drives to the supermarket.

Hot rodders quickly shortened the name of the ultimate Plymouth pony to Hemicuda. This was one bad sea horse. It could click off quarter-miles in the 13s at 102-108 mph on street tires. Specify the TorqueFlite, buckle the seat belt, and hang on. Leave the driving to Mr. Hemi and its forged-steel crankshaft, heavy-duty connecting rods (with floating pins to support its massive high-dome pistons), and mechanical high-lift camshaft. Twin Carter AFB four-barrels metered the mixture, while a Chrysler dual-point distributor aided ignition.

The 'Cuda coupe started at $3164 and weighed 3395 pounds; the convertible cost $3433 and tipped the scales at 3480. The Hemi added $871 and the Six Pack $250. Public reception of the Challenger was a little more enthusiastic than it was for the Barracuda, with Dodge building 83,000 of its ponies in the first year, to 55,472 Barracudas. However, performance drivers took to the Challenger R/T and 'Cuda in virtually equal numbers. Plymouth built 19,515 'Cudas for '70; just 635 of them were convertibles, and only 666 were Hemis.

1971

Twin-set headlamps and a multi-pocketed grille for 1971 destroyed the spare beauty of the '70 Barracuda's face, while its sexy profile was defiled by a quartet of gill-like fake air extractors on the front fenders. Segmented taillamps, meanwhile, busied its rump unnecessarily and the 'Cuda's previous hockey-stick rear-fender graphics gave way to a less tasteful tape option that covered virtually the back one-third of the body.

Muscle power had peaked in 1970; economic and environmental forces began to take their toll in earnest beginning in '71. The 'Cuda, of course, wasn't immune. The 440 four-barrel, never a popular choice anyway, was dropped. Compression on the standard 383 four-barrel slipped from 9.5:1 to 8.5:1 and horsepower declined with it, down to 300. The 440 Six Pack lost five horsepower, but the 340 and Hemi were unchanged. Sales took a dive, with just 6228 'Cuda hardtops and only 374 convertibles built. Hemi production fell to 115. The 'Cuda hung on until 1974, by which time a four-barrel 360-cube V-8 had replaced the four-barrel 340 as the hottest engine. Hard driving and rust problems doomed most 'Cudas to an early grave. But for one shining moment at the dawn of the decade, no predator prowled the street with more style or bite.

Plymouth built just 14 Hemi 'Cuda convertibles for '70; value of one today can be more $200,000, depending on its condition. Dual-quad Hemi mill came standard with the shaker scoop (opposite, left), which mounted to the air cleaner and quivered with the engine. 'Cuda's beauty was compromised for '71 by fake fender vents and segmented grille (above), but the performance remained appealing.

1970 Plymouth 'Cuda 440/Hemi

Facts At a Glance

Engine type:	V-8/RB-Block/Wedge	V-8/RB-Block/Hemi
Displacement (cid):	440 (4v)	426 (2x4v)
Horsepower @ rpm:	375 @ 4600 390 @ 4700[1]	425 @ 5000
Torque (lbs/ft) @ rpm:	480 @ 3200 490 @ 3200[1]	490 @ 4000
Compression ratio:	9.7:1/10.5:1[1]	10.2:1
Bore (in.):	4.32	4.25
Stroke (in.):	3.75	3.75
Valve lifters:	Hydraulic	Mechanical
Availability:	1970-71[2]	1970-71

[1] Six Pack
[2] In 1971, 440 Six Pack horsepower was 385 at 4600 on a compression of 10.3:1.

Magazine:	Motor Trend (May 1970)	Motor Trend (Sept. 1969)
Times:		
0-60 mph (sec):	5.9	6.9
0-100 mph (sec):	14.4	N/A
¼-mile (sec):	14.04 @ 100 mph	13.70 @ 101.2 mph[1]
Top speed (mph):	109	N/A
Axle ratio:	3.55:1	4.10:1
Engine (cid/bhp):	440/390	426/425 Hemi

[1] *Car Craft* recorded a quarter-mile time of 13.10 @ 107 mph with a four-speed and 3.54:1 Sure-Grip.

Just as it had with the Road Runner in 1968, Plymouth scored a budget-muscle bull's-eye in 1970 with the Duster 340. Using the strategy that created the original Barracuda in 1964, the division once again tapped the Valiant platform for its new offering. The Duster used the Valiant sedan's 108-inch wheelbase, most of its mechanicals, its front-end sheetmetal, and its windshield. But Plymouth gave its new compact a light, strong, fastback body that was inexpensive to produce. It could be ordered as an economy-oriented six-cylinder car or made moderately lively with the 318-cubic-inch two-barrel V-8. But the hottest ticket was the 340 four-barrel. It furnished 275 horsepower, quarter-mile times in the high 14s, and a $2547 base price that made it the least expensive car in Plymouth's Rapid Transit System.

Plymouth's Rapid Transit System brochure said the division had planned the Duster 340 as "a sleeper that would blow the doors off hulking, pretentious behemoths twice its size." With a base curb weight of 3110 pounds, the trim Duster wasted none of the 340 pounds/feet of torque furnished by its

high-revving V-8. MoPar's 340 was one of Detroit's most efficient and respected small blocks. Plymouth fitted a Carter AVS carb and gave the engine big-league credentials with a 10.5:1 compression ratio and camshaft timing only slightly less radical than that used on the mighty 440 Six Pack.

A heavy-duty three-speed manual transmission was standard; optional was a heavy-duty four-speed or high-upshift TorqueFlite. The Duster 340 came with a 3.23:1 rear axle, but 3.55:1 and 3.91:1 gears and Sure-Grip limited-slip were available. The three-speed turned out to be the quickest, with ETs in the mid-13s at 107 mph recorded on street tires and the 3.91:1 gear. A good four-speed would run in the 13.9s at 100, while the automatic made for a 15-second machine.

Since it was a member of the Rapid Transit System, the Duster 340 was treated to an array of performance enhancers, including dual exhausts, a heavy-duty suspension, front stabilizer bar, and six rear leaf springs on either side. Standard tires were E70×14s on 5.5-inch rally wheels. This little Plymouth had the distinction of being the only car in the Rapid Transit

1970 Plymouth Duster 340

Facts At a Glance

Engine type:	V-8/LA-Block/Wedge
Displacement (cid):	340
Horsepower @ rpm:	275 @ 5000
Torque (lbs/ft) @ rpm:	340 @ 3200
Compression ratio:	10.5:1[1]
Bore (in.):	4.04
Stroke (in.):	3.31
Valve lifters:	Hydraulic
Availability:	1970-71

[1]10.3:1 (1971)

Magazine:	*Car Life* (March 1970)
Times:	
0-60 mph (sec):	6.2
0-100 mph (sec):	17.5
¼-mile (sec):	14.72 @ 94.24 mph
Top speed (mph):	120
Axle ratio:	3.23:1
Model year:	1970

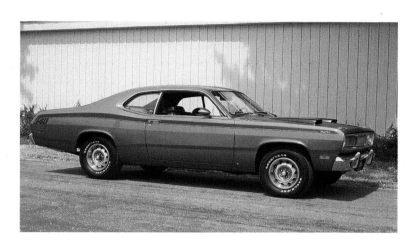

System to come standard with front disc brakes.

Inside, the three pod instrument panel from the previous-generation Barracuda had been borrowed while bucket seats and a center console with floor shift could be ordered in place of the front bench. A pistol-grip for the four-speed, an 8000-rpm tach, and power steering were attractive extra-cost items.

Testers found that the Duster 340's light weight and stiff suspension could make for a punishing ride. And they found the car's composure in hard cornering was undermined by front-end plow. The power steering, quicker at 3.5 turns lock-to-lock than the manual at 5.3 turns, was recommended as an aid to handling. But overall, the Duster 340 was taken quite seriously as a high-performance car, especially by certain pretentious behemoths. Plymouth had a hit on its hands, building 218,000 Dusters that first year, with a respectable 24,817 of them Duster 340s.

Duster 340 lost none of its performance but relinquished a little of its sleeper quality for '71. The grille was flashier with vertical bars, the taillamps were changed, and the side stripe now culminated in "340" script on the rear fender. Its secret identity could be blown completely by ordering an optional flat-black hood treatment that contained a huge "340" in white script with the word "Wedge" stenciled in orange within.

Beneath that hood, Plymouth had switched to a Carter Thermo-Quad four barrel and the 340 V-8's compression slipped to 10.3:1, but its rating of 275 gross horsepower was unchanged. Incidentally, Plymouth also listed a net horsepower figure of 235 this year, evidence that the muscle age was on the shoals. Further indication was a new Duster Twister model with one of two six cylinder engines or the 318 two barrel.

Duster 340 soldiered on through compression-ratio decreases in '72 and '73, but still was an excellent performance value with at least 240 net horsepower. It became the Duster 360 in '74 when displacement was bumped and horsepower rose to 245 net. But weight was up, too, and quarter-miles in the 16-17-second range were the norm. This last performance Duster was phased out in 1976.

1963-66
PONTIAC
421

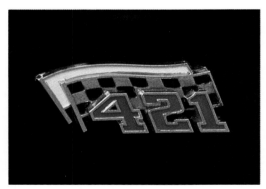

Pontiac's redesigned full-size line for '63 set style trends and packed some of the world's most fierce engines. The most ferocious were Catalinas with 421-cid V-8s. Big new threat on the street was the 370-bhp Tri-Power 421 (above). It could turn mid-14-second ETs. Aimed primarily for strip use was the Super Duty 421 (opposite, top). With dual quads it made 405 bhp with a 12.0:1 compression or 410 bhp with 13.0:1. Sub-14-second ETs were within its grasp. Early muscle gets no better than this.

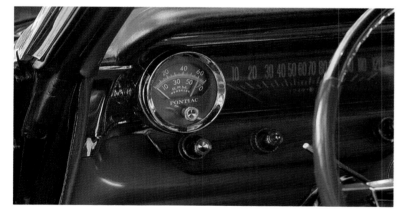

Pontiac's 421-cubic-inch Super Duty V-8 was introduced in 1961 and promptly put a Poncho in the winner's circle of the Daytona 500. It was equally potent on the drag strip, and factory-built aluminum-front-end Catalinas consistently ran low 12s at more than 116 mph. Occasionally, a '61 or '62 Super Duty Catalina would show up on the street. With its dual-quad, 405-horsepower, 11.0:1-compression 421, it was feared by anything with wheels.

Then in 1963, with little warning, Pontiac withdrew from organized racing. Luckily, the 421 carried on without missing a beat. Pontiac made the widely respected big block available in all of its full-sized cars for the first time in '63, a move that coincided with a breakthrough redesign of its full-size line. "Here's What The Other '63s Wished They Looked Like," declared a Pontiac ad and it was no idle boast. The new Bonneville and Star Chief ran on 123-inch wheelbases, while the Catalina and Grand Prix had a 120-inch wheelbase. Their styling was crisp, dynamic, and pacesetting. Their stacked headlamps would quickly be copied by Ford and Plymouth. Their split grille would become a Pontiac trademark. And their clean lines lent credibility to Pontiac's sports-luxury image.

The standard engine on these wide-track '63 Pontiacs was a 215-horsepower two-barrel 389-cubic-inch V-8 that could be boosted to 313 horsepower with an optional triple two-barrel-carburetor setup. The 421 was available at extra cost and came in two versions for the street.

With a four-barrel carburetor it had 353 horsepower at 5000 rpm and 455 pounds/feet of torque at 3400. This version cost between $291 and $343, depending on the model and transmission.

But it was the new-for-'63 triple-deuce version that had a real impact on the street scene. Known as the Trophy 421 HO, it cost $404 to $445 extra and was rated at 370 horsepower at 5200 rpm and 460 pounds/feet of torque at 3800. Its three Rochester two-barrels were borrowed from the Tri-Power 389 and used progressive throttle linkage. It had a four-bolt block and forged crank, medium-port 389 cylinder heads, and a hydraulic camshaft. Both of the street 421s had 10.75:1 compression ratios and each was available with a three- or four-speed manual transmission or Pontiac's Super Hydra-Matic automatic. Pontiac recommended a 3.42:1 rear-axle ratio as a good acceleration/cruising compromise with the 421, though dealer-installed ratios up 4.44:1 were available.

In a two-door Catalina—the lightest and least expensive big Pontiac—a Tri-Power 421 four-speed could turn mid-14-second quarter miles right out of the box. Even the 4000-pound Grand Prix was capable of running in the low 15s at around 92 mph with this motor.

Reserved primarily for drag-strip use was the Super Duty 421, which came in three different levels of tune for '63. Each had less torque, but more horsepower and higher rev capabilities than the regular 421s. Pontiac's Special Equipment catalog warned that these engines were "designed only for all-out performance enthusiasts," with versions tailored for "maximum acceleration" or "sustained high-speed."

The artillery began with the single four-barrel Super Duty rated at 390 horsepower at 5800 rpm and 425 pounds/feet of torque at 3600. Its compression was 12.0:1. Next up was a dual-quad version making 405 horsepower at 5600 rpm and 425 pounds/feet of torque at 4400. It too had a 12.0:1 compression. The highest-horse Super Duty ever offered was the 13.0:1-compression version of the dual-quad 421. It was rated at 410 horsepower at 5600 rpm and 435 pounds/feet of torque at 4400 rpm. *Motor Trend* ran one of the four-speed, dual-quad Super Duty Catalinas to a 0-60 mph run of 5.4 seconds and a quarter-mile of 13.9 seconds at 107 mph—on street tires. Only 88 of these engines came out of the factory for '63. Most went into Catalinas, though 11 were installed in the compact Tempest body.

1964

Only minor changes were made to the full-sized Pontiacs for 1964, with the sharp-edged body gaining slight contours front and rear. Enthusiasts were greeted by the first complete performance option offered on a big Pontiac. Known as the 2+2, it was available only on the Catalina convertible and Catalina two-door Sport Coupe hardtop. It cost $291 and included bucket seats and a console with either a four-on-the-floor or Hydra-Matic. The standard engine was the 389 rated at 283 horsepower with the manual or 267 with the automatic.

Testers generally found that the 421 four-barrel was the more adept around-town cruiser because the Tri-Power tended to delay throttle response. Part of the problem was that automatic-transmission Tri-Powers used a vacuum linkage; response was much quicker with the mechanical linkage used on the stick-shift cars. The four-barrel also could stay with the Tri-Power up to about 70 mph. The big Ponchos were ponderous handlers with the standard suspension, though the 2+2 with beefed-up underpinnings was probably the best full-size roadholder of its day.

Pontiac's restyled full-size cars had helped it increase sales to record levels in '63, and '64 was even better.

1965

Pontiac had fully redesigned its compacts for 1964 and now it was the big cars' turn. The wheelbase was stretched an inch, to 124 on the Bonneville and Star Chief, and to 121 on the Catalina and Grand Prix. Aggressive new sheetmetal made them look even larger.

Mechanically, the new three-speed Turbo-Hydra-Matic was installed when the optional automatic transmission was ordered and its shifts were notably smoother than the four-speed Hydra-Matic's. The 389 remained standard, but the 421 was again the optional performance choice. Horsepower was 338 with a four-barrel carb. A 356-horsepower Tri-Power was added. Top of the heap was the 421 HO. It was rated at 376 horsepower and 461 pounds/feet of torque.

The 2+2 option came into its own this year and made a Catalina convertible or hardtop into one of the best-performing full-size cars ever to come out of Detroit. Vertical louvers on the front fenders and "2+2" badging were identifying marks. The 338-horsepower 421 was now a 2+2 standard, with the Tri-Power 421s optional. The package included bucket seats and heavy duty springs, shocks and stabilizer bar. A heavy-duty three-speed manual with short-throw Hurst shifter was standard; a four-speed manual and the Turbo-Hydra-Matic were options, as was a sports steering wheel coupled to a 17.5:1 power steering ratio. Extra-stiff springs, center console, tachometer, Safe-T-Track limited-slip differential, transistorized ignition, and aluminum wheels completed the package.

In logging its fastest-ever 0-60-mph test cars, *Car and Driver* in July 1980 recalled running a '65 Pontiac 2+2 with a blueprinted engine and other go-fast enhancements bestowed by Royal Pontiac, a Royal Oak, Michigan, dealer specializing in high-performance Ponchos. It turned what the magazine termed "a rather preposterous, 3.9-second zero-to-sixty time...."

Pontiac built 11,521 Catalina 2+2s in '65, and a surprisingly high 5316 had manual transmission.

1966

Pontiac celebrated its 40th birthday in 1966 and marked the occasion by building its 11-millionth car. Styling changes to the big cars were subtle. The 2+2 became its own model, still based on the Catalina. The Catalina and the Grand Prix lost three inches of overall length, though their 121-inch wheelbase was unchanged.

While most Pontiacs were equipped with the two- and four-barrel 389s, the 421 still was available in 338-horse four-barrel guise or in 356- and 376-horse Tri-Power form.

Elevation of the 2+2 to model status symbolized Pontiac's commitment to the full-size muscle car market.

At $3492, the Grand Prix was the most expensive Pontiac hardtop, and sales, along with those of the other big Ponchos, declined for '66. Just 6383 2+2s were built; the convertible cost $3602, the coupe, $3298. Tempest and LeMans production was up, however, and Pontiac, like the other automakers, would begin to concentrate its street-performance efforts on the smaller cars from here on. But for a time, the full-size Pontiacs reigned at the pinnacle of the early muscle world.

1963-66 Pontiac 421

Facts At a Glance

Engine type:	V-8/Pontiac
Displacement (cid):	421
Horsepower @ rpm:	353 @ 5000 (1963)
	370 @ 5200 (1963-64)[1]
	350 @ 4600 (1964)
	338 @ 4600 (1965-66)
	356 @ 4800 (1965-66)[1]
	376 @ 5000 (1965-66)[1]
Torque (lbs/ft) @ rpm:	455 @ 3400 (1963)
	460 @ 3800 (1963-64)[1]
	454 @ 3200 (1964)
	459 @ 2800 (1965-66)
	459 @ 3200 (1965-66)[1]
	461 @ 3600 (1965-66)[1]
Compression ratio:	10.5:1/10.75:1
Bore (in.):	4.09
Stroke (in.):	4.00
Valve lifters:	Hydraulic
Availability:	1962-66

[1]Tri-Power

Magazine:	Motor Trend (April 1965)	Car Life (1965)
Times:		
0-60 mph (sec):	8.1	7.2
0-100 mph (sec):	NA	17.5
¼-mile (sec):	16.40 @ 88 mph	15.5 @ 95 mph
Top speed (mph):	115 (est)	NA
Axle ratio:	3.42:1	NA
Engine type:	421 (4v)	421 (3x2v)
Model year:	1965	1965

Another restyle of the big Ponchos for '65 kept them at the cutting edge of '60s design. Catalina with 2+2 option (opposite) had 421 power and a beefy suspension. It was one of the world's best performing full-size cars. Car and Driver claimed a 0-60-mph time of 3.9 seconds with a blueprinted '65 2+2. For '66, the 2+2 became its own model (this page). Interior was inviting with buckets, console, gauges. Bodyside vents were a decorative signature.

225

1964-65 PONTIAC GTO

Pontiac's 1964 Tempest GTO lit the fuse on the muscle-car era. It was the first modern mid-size car with a big-block high-performance engine. And it was the first factory hot rod with an identity all its own. Even the name was magic. GTO stood for *Gran Turismo Omologato*, a tag Pontiac appropriated from no less than the Ferrari 250 GTO. Translated from the Italian, it meant a grand touring production car that had been homologated, or officially sanctioned, to race.

The GTO was conceived either by Pontiac ad man Jim Wagners or by engineers John DeLorean and Bill Collins, depending on your source. The idea was to stuff the 389-cubic-inch V-8 from the full-size Pontiac into the all-new intermediate Tempest that arrived for the '64 model year. The scheme was complicated by a couple of factors. In January, 1963 General Motors pulled Pontiac out of racing, a move that could have had a chilling effect on street performance. The other factor was a corporate ban on putting any engine larger than 330 cubic inches into an intermediate body.

Development of the '64 GTO was a deep secret. Engineering prototypes appeared as though they were equipped with the Tempest's 326 four-barrel V-8 when, in reality, they held 389s and even the 421-cubic-inch Pontiac V-8. DeLorean and his people elected to make the GTO a LeMans option, which wouldn't require approval from the GM hierarchy. By that subterfuge, they got their potent package to market. Offered on all three LeMans body styles, the option was priced at just $296. With it, the two-door pillared Sports Coupe cost $2852, the two-door hardtop listed for $2963, and the convertible started at $3081.

The GTO package started by beefing up the 389 with such goodies as 421 High Output heads, a high-lift camshaft (for hydraulic lifters), Carter AFB four-barrel carburetor and, to perk up appearances, chromed valve covers. In base four-barrel

form, the GTO's 389 made 325 horsepower at 4800 rpm. Optional Tri-Power carburetion added 23 horsepower.

Beyond the standard Hurst-shifted three-speed, there were two Muncie four-speeds (close or wide ratio). A three-speed automatic transmission based on the Turbo Hydra-Matic was also available, specially programmed for the GTO's level of performance. A ten-bolt GM differential offered a number of different ratios, ranging from 3.08:1 to 3.90:1. Pontiac's Safe-T-Track limited-slip differential was an option. An extra-heavy-duty suspension included a thicker (¹⁵/₁₆-inch) front sway bar, heavy-duty Delco shocks, and stiffer spring rates front and rear. Special red-line Tiger Paw high-performance 7.50×14 tires were fitted. Finned drum brakes were standard, but savvy street racers opted for the $75 "roadability group" which consisted of sintered metallic brake linings, a heavy-duty radiator, and Safe-T-Track. Since the standard steering ratio was a woefully slow 25.5:1, another smart move was to order the quick ratio steering, which came in ratios of 20:1 with no assist or 17:1 with power assist. However, with a nose-heavy 56/44 distribution of its 3400 pounds, handling needed all the help it could get, so dropping an additional $3.82 for even heavier duty shocks and springs was advised.

Car and Driver had the audacity to compare Pontiac's GTO to Ferrari's in a 1964 "road test" showdown. Though it never actually ran the two cars head to head, the magazine concluded that the 348-horsepower Pontiac would leave the 280-horsepower Ferrari eating dust in a straight line. It also suggested that a NASCAR suspension setup would give the Yankee an edge over the Italian on a road course. *Car and Driver* recorded an unholy 4.6-second 0-60 mph time and a positively devilish 13.1-second quarter-mile at 115 mph with its Tri-Power GTO. These times were nearly a full second quicker than other magazines were getting, and the top speed was faster by about 10 mph.

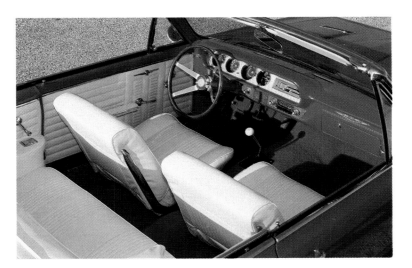

Car and Driver noted that its GTO had been prepared by the performance wizards at Royal Pontiac, a Royal Oak, Michigan, dealer specializing in high-performance Ponchos. Among the modifications were richer-running carbs, advanced timing, blocked-off heat risers, and other work that brought the compression ratio close to 11.0:1.

Some skeptics have since argued that unbeknownst to Car and Driver, the GTO it tested wasn't even a 389, but that Pontiac had slipped in a Tri-Power 421. Regardless, so excited were automotive enthusiasts about this new Pontiac that mentioning it as a legitimate challenger to a Ferrari seemed perfectly reasonable. By the end of the 1964 model year, 32,450 GTOs had been assembled, 8245 of them equipped with Tri-Power.

1965

Though still clearly a GTO, a reskin gave it crisper contours and the stacked headlamps of the bigger Pontiacs. The scoop on the new hood still wasn't functional, but a revised induction system along with an improved camshaft profile upped the 389 four-barrel to 335 horsepower and boosted the Tri-Power to 360.

The standard three-speed, Hurst-shifted box could be replaced by a variety of optional transmissions including a heavy-duty three-speed, close or wide ratio Hurst-shifted Muncie four-speeds, and a two-speed automatic. Axle ratios came in six flavors, from 3.08:1 to 4.33:1. Aluminum front brake drums and stylish Rally I wheels were new options. The cabin changed little, and power windows, air conditioning, and rear window defogger were joined on the options list by such items as a rally cluster with full instrumentation and an AM/FM radio.

Early in '65 Pontiac introduced "Ram Air," a dealer-installed package that included a metal shroud with three openings to fit over the trio of Tri-Power carbs.

Power and style made the 1965 GTO the standard for muscle cars and production more than doubled, to 75,352. The Goat would soon grow into its own model, and into larger, heavier bodies. And while other supercars would surpass it in horsepower and speed, it's likely that few of them would have seen the light of day if not for this original.

Reskin for '65 gave GTO a whiff of big-Poncho style and included "hidden" taillamps. Horsepower increased to 335 on the four-barrel and 360 for the tri carb. About 200 '65s were fitted with optional ram air, which included revisions to make the hood scoop functional.

1964-65 Pontiac GTO

Facts At a Glance

Engine type:	V-8/Pontiac	V-8/Pontiac
Displacement (cid):	389 (4v)	389 (3x2v)
Horsepower @ rpm:	325 @ 4800[1]	348 @ 4900[1]
	335 @ 5000	360 @ 5200
Torque (lbs/ft) @ rpm:	428 @ 3200[1]	428 @ 3600[1]
	431 @ 3200	424 @ 3600
Compression ratio:	10.75:1	10.75:1
Bore (in.):	4.06	4.06
Stroke (in.):	3.75	3.75
Valve lifters:	Hydraulic	Hydraulic
Availability:	1964-65 GTO	1964-65 GTO

[1]1964

Magazine:	Road & Track (March 1964)	Road & Track (March 1964)
Times:		
0-60 mph (sec):	6.9	5.7
0-100 mph (sec):	18.3	13.2
¼-mile (sec):	15.0 @ 91.5	14.1 @ 104.2
Top speed (mph):	122	NA
Axle ratio:	3.23:1	3.23:1
Engine type:	1964 389 (4v)	1964 389 (3x2v)

Magazine:	Car Life (May 1965)
Times:	
0-60 mph (sec):	5.8
0-100 mph (sec):	14.5
¼-mile (sec):	14.5 @ 100 mph
Top speed (mph):	114
Axle ratio:	4.11:1
Engine type:	1965 389 (3x2v)

1966-67 PONTIAC GTO

The success of the 1964-65 GTO prompted rival automakers to field a host of imitators. From Chevrolet came the Chevelle SS 396 and from Dodge and Plymouth came intermediates with Street Hemis. Buick built the Skylark Gran Sport, Oldsmobile the 4-4-2, and Ford the 427 Fairlane.

But Pontiac wasn't resting on its laurels. The GTO still was based on the Tempest, but it got promoted to its own series in 1966. The move coincided with a new Tempest/LeMans/GTO body. Retained were the stacked headlamps and the 115-inch wheelbase, but the car got a slightly wider stance with more voluptuous Coke-bottle contours. The backlight was recessed from the swept-back rear roof pillars and the stern sported fluted taillamps. New options included a reclining passenger seat, headrests, and red plastic inner fender liners.

The four-barrel 389 again made 335 horsepower and the Tri-Power 389 still was rated at 360. But at mid-year, General Motors ordered a ban on all multi-carb performance packages, so this would be the last year for the factory triple two-barrel setup. Transmission and axle-ratio choices were unchanged.

While faulting the GTO's heavy front end, *Car Life* noted that it "has an engine that loves to work and willingly turns well past the red-line—seemingly without harm."

With the new styling helping it along, GTO fever reached its peak in '66 and model-year production hit an all-time high of 96,946.

The '66 GTO (both pages) holds the record for the highest one-year production of any muscle car in history — 96,946. Fanning its popularity was a gorgeous new body. Details included fluted taillamps (opposite, bottom left), recessed backlight (opposite, top left), and turn-signal/parking lights in a plastic grille (bottom right). Hood scoop functioned only with Ram Air package. GTO became its own series for '66, but this was the final season for the celebrated Tri-Carb setup (bottom). Note rare red inner fender liners on the blue hardtop.

For '67, GTO taillamps lost their brows and were more visible (left). A 400-cid V-8 (below) replaced the 389 as standard. It had 335 bhp in base form and 360 bhp when Ram Air was ordered. A wire-mesh grille was new and the rocker-panel molding was raised to highlight the lower beltline.

1967

The mildly-revised GTO had a new chrome-mesh grille, taillamps with improved visibility, and minor interior refinements. But the big news was under the hood, where the 389's bore was increased, pushing displacement up to 400 cubic inches.

With a Quadrajet four-barrel carburetor, the base 400 engine had 335 horsepower at 5000 rpm. The optional 400 High Output added a long-duration cam and improved exhaust manifolds. In this trim it made 360 horsepower at 5100 rpm. Order the Ram-Air V-8 and Pontiac responded with a functional hood scoop and another 360-horsepower rating, but this time at 5400 rpm. The Ram-Air V-8 came with a 4.33:1 rear axle ratio. All these engines had a compression ratio of 10.75:1 and such beefy components as heavy-duty Moraine 400 main and rod bearings; flat-top pistons with valve indents; high-performance valve lifters and springs; high-output cam and springs; dual exhausts with low-restriction mufflers; and a declutching seven-blade 18-inch fan.

Though rarely ordered, Pontiac also offered the 400 with a two-barrel carb as an economy GTO. The engine could be had at no extra cost and only with Turbo Hydra-Matic. It was rated at 225 horsepower.

Both four-barrel 400s were available with standard three-speed stick, optional Muncie four-speed, or Turbo Hydra-Matic. The axle-gearing list grew even longer for '67, with eight available ratios ranging from 2.78:1 to 4.33:1. A Safe-T-Track limited-slip differential was optional. *Motor Trend* testers took a liking to the GTO's three-speed Turbo Hydra-Matic, especially with the optional Hurst Dual Gate shift quadrant, naming it a "formidable foe" for the four-speed, even though 0-60 mph times were a trifle slower.

An optional hood-mounted tachometer appeared during the model year. Other options included an eight-track stereo tape player, power front disc brakes, Rally II wheels, and Wonder Touch power steering.

At $2871, the pillared Sports Coupe was the least expensive 1967 GTO and with a weight of 3425 pounds, it was the lightest. The hardtop cost $2935 and shipped at 3430 pounds; the convertible listed for $3165 and tipped the scales at 3515 pounds. With competition from a host of other muscle intermediates, GTO sales were down in '67. Production totaled 81,722, including 9517 convertibles, and 39,128 manual-transmisson models.

1966-67 Pontiac GTO

Facts At a Glance

Engine type:	V-8/Pontiac	V-8/Pontiac
Displacement (cid):	389	400
Horsepower @ rpm:	335 @ 5000	335 @ 5000
	360 @ 5200[1]	360 @ 5100[2]
		360 @ 5400[3]
Torque (lbs/ft) @ rpm:	431 @ 3200	441 @ 3400
	424 @ 3600[1]	438 @ 3600[2]
		438 @ 3800[3]
Compression ratio:	10.75:1	10.75:1
Bore (in.):	4.06	4.12
Stroke (in.):	3.75	3.75
Valve lifters:	Hydraulic	Hydraulic
Availability:	1966	1967

[1]Tri-Power [2]High Output [3]Ram Air High Output

Magazine:	Car and Driver (March 1966)	Car Life (May 1966)
Times:		
0-60 mph (sec):	6.5	6.8
0-100 mph (sec):	12.5	19.2
¼-mile (sec):	14.05 @ 105 mph	15.4 @ 92 mph
Top speed (mph):	120	125
Axle ratio:	3.55:1	3.08:1
Engine type:	389 (3x2v)	389 (4v)
Model year:	1966	1966

1967-70 PONTIAC FIREBIRD

Pontiac hustled into the pony car act on February 23, 1967, with introduction of the Firebird. Built on the Chevrolet Camaro platform and sharing the Chevy's 108-inch wheelbase, the Firebird was offered in convertible and two-door hardtop body styles. Its name was drawn from an Indian symbol and had been used on a series of experimental General Motors gas turbine cars in the 1950s.

Pontiac gave it the division's trademark split grille, added quad headlamps, fluted taillamps, and some fake side vents, but, in profile especially, its kinship to the Camaro was unmistakable. Firebird had trailed Camaro into the pony car market by about six months and Pontiac, perhaps hoping to make up for lost time with the appearance of a wider model line, advertised each Firebird engine option as a separate model.

The base Firebird hardtop listed for $2666 and came with a single-barrel overhead-cam 165-horsepower six-cylinder. Add $116.16 to a base convertible or hardtop and you got the Sprint, which used a four-barrel version of the OHC six to make 215 horsepower. Next was the Firebird 326. It had a 250-horsepower 326-cubic-inch two-barrel V-8. Buyers looking for reliability plus a taste of performance opted for the Firebird HO, which used the 326 four-barrel High Output V-8. It cranked up 285 horsepower with dual exhausts and a 10.5:1 compression.

"Anything our light heavyweight can't handle," said a

Pontiac advertisement beneath a photo of the Firebird HO, "our heavyweight can." Pictured below was the heavyweight: the Firebird 400. This was the Firebird that would carry Pontiac's high-performance pony car banner.

Its heart was the 400-cubic-inch V-8 that Pontiac had introduced earlier that year in its full-size cars and in the GTO. Pontiac took the successful 389-cubic-inch V-8 with its 4.06-inch bores and opened them up to 4.12 inches, but left the stroke unchanged. The result was nearly the 389 Tri-Power's horsepower from a single four-barrel carburetor. Two versions were offered. The base 400 produced 325 horsepower at 4800 rpm. This package raised the asking price of the coupe to $2777 and to $3177 for the convertible. For another $616 the buyer got the Ram Air 400. Pontiac opened the Firebird's hood scoops for this one. It too was rated at 325 horsepower, but at a higher-revving 5200 rpm.

Behind the 400 engine, Pontiac offered a mix of transmissions and axle ratios. Most opted for the Muncie close-ratio four-speed, or GM's Turbo Hydra-Matic. A three-speed, manually shifted transmission was standard. Standard features with either Firebird 400 included chrome engine dress-up, dual exhausts, heavy-duty battery, Power Flex fan, sport suspension and F70×14 tires. Eleven-inch front disc brakes were optional, but didn't prove as popular as the

Pontiac got its pony car for '67 with the Firebird, an upscale cousin to the Chevy Camaro. The hottest version was the Firebird 400; the models pictured are '68s. The 400-cid V-8 (below, center) made 330 bhp for '68. Hood scoops were nonfunctional unless Ram Air option was ordered. Hood-mounted tachometer was optional (opposite). Multi-leaf rear springs for '68 helped cure '67 400's rear-wheel hop on take off and, coupled with optional heavy-duty suspension, improved handling.

mag-style Rally II wheels, which were an $84.26 extra.

Inside, all Firebirds came with bucket seats standard. The instrument panel with its two deeply recessed circular dials was borrowed from the Camaro; a tachometer in a pod on the hood was optional. Despite the late start in its opening season, 82,560 Firebirds were built by Pontiac as 1967 models.

1968

Firebird was altered only minimally for 1968, the most obvious change being deletion of wing windows as a cost-cutting measure. Under the hood, Pontiac replaced the 326 as the base Firebird V-8 with a bored-out version displacing 350 cubic inches. Horsepower was 265 in the two-barrel version and 320 with the $181 four-barrel High Output option. Changes to the 400 came under the heading of refinements. Compression increased to 10.75:1, and horsepower was up by five for both the base 400 and Ram Air version. The rear suspension got multiple-leaf springs in place of single-leaf springs and staggered shocks were added to combat the wheel hop that plagued the '67 400s under hard acceleration.

Sports Car Graphic tested a '68 Ram Air, which listed for $3484, but shot to $4295 with the addition of such options as custom trim, power steering with 17.5:1 ratio, power (drum) brakes, Rally II wheels, heavy duty suspension and differential,

235

Firebird got its first facelift for '69 (top), but was all-new the next year (above). The '70's fenders seemed pulled taut over the wheels, the curved A-pillars and single side glass bespoke a European influence. It was sexy, original, and would prove a modern classic. Handling was outstanding. The Formula 400 (above and opposite) had a fiberglass hood; its aggressive scoops were opened with the Ram Air option.

Muncie four-speed close ration gearbox, tinted glass, custom seat belts, auxiliary gauges, tachometer, tilt steering wheel and AM-FM radio.

"Motoring gently down the city streets, the occasional hiss from the quadrajet carburetor and the throaty chug from the dual exhausts gave the impression of enormous power," wrote the editors, "but the docile clutch and butter-smooth Hurst shifter on the close-ratio Muncie four-speed gearbox made the car more hospitable with boulevard traffic."

The Firebird 400 was a more luxurious alternative to the Camaro SS or Mustang GT, a grand touring coupe or drop top to the Chevy and Ford pony cars. With a full year of production, Pontiac built 90,152 Firebird coupes and 16,960 convertibles.

Firebird got its first facelift for 1969, with revisions similar to those given the Camaro. A boxier, split grille appeared with headlamps set into square body-colored Endura bezels. The roofline also was altered.

Pontiac's 350 and 400 engines remained popular choices for Firebird buyers, with an array of transmission and axle combos. The potent Ram Air IV mill got a boost to 345 horsepower at 5400 rpm and was an $832 option.

Despite its styling update, the 1969 Firebird suffered a sales slump. Combined with a delayed introduction of the '70 models, the downturn prompted Pontiac to carry over some remaining '69s for sale as 1970 models. Production for '69 totaled 75,362 Firebird coupes, 11,649 convertibles, and 697 Trans Ams.

1970

Pontiac's launch of the second-generation Firebird was in some ways a repeat introduction of the original car back in 1967. And as in '67, the car was late, debuting on February 26, 1970.

Though still a kissing cousin to the Camaro, the new F-body Firebird departed dramatically from the mini-Pontiac it had been. Built on the same wheelbase but now offered only as a two-door coupe, Firebird was slipperier and wider than its predecessor with a gaping split grille and single headlamps.

Four models were offered. At $2875, the base Firebird had a 155-horsepower six-cylinder 250-cubic-inch Chevrolet engine. The $3241 Esprit used the 350 two-barrel V-8, rated at 255 horsepower. Next came the Formula 400 and its 400-cube four-barrel rated at 330 horsepower at 4800 rpm on a 10.25:1 compression. Standard was a heavy-duty Hurst-shifted three-speed manual, front and rear stabilizer bars, high-rate springs, windup rear axle controls, F70×14 tires, manual front disc and rear drum brakes, hidden windshield wipers, and dual sport mirrors. It also included a fiberglass hood with two molded-in scoops that were non-functional, but very aggressive-looking. It listed for $3370 and tipped the scales at 3470 pounds without options. For another $168.51, Pontiac opened the scoops and added the Ram Air option to the 400. It was good for 345 horsepower at 5000 rpm on a 10.5:1 compression. This engine also was used by the Trans Am. With these powerplants came a manual three-speed or the optional four-speed or Turbo Hydra-Matic transmission. Axle ratios on the 400 started at 3.31:1 and included 3.55:1 and 3.73:1 gears, as well as a 4.10:1 ratio, which was usually installed at the dealer. With the automatic and standard gear, the base 400 ran the quarter in around 15 seconds at 93 mph or so. The Ram Air with a lower gear would turn mid-14s at 100. These cars handled better than any previous Firebirds and represented a high-water mark in early-'70s roadability. The floor pan had been lowered and the transmission tunnel raised for improved suspension movement and a better center of gravity.

Sales, however, were disappointing. The pony car field was more crowded than ever and Firebird production for 1970 was 48,739 (including 3196 Trans Ams). Firebird continued to struggle through the early 1970s, nearly was phased out in 1972, but then staged a comeback, primarily on the strength of the popular Trans Am.

1967-70 Pontiac Firebird

Facts At a Glance

Engine type:	V-8/Pontiac	V-8/Pontiac
Displacement (cid):	326	350
Horsepower @ rpm:	250 @ 4600	265 @ 4600
	285 @ 5000[1]	320 @ 5100[1]
Torque (lbs/ft) @ rpm:	333 @ 2800	355 @ 2800
	359 @ 3200[1]	380 @ 3200[1]
Compression ratio:	9.2:1/10.5:1[1]	9.2:1/10.5:1[1]
Bore (in.):	3.72	3.88
Stroke (in.):	3.75	3.75
Valve lifters:	Hydraulic	Hydraulic
Availability:	1967	1968-69

[1]High Output

Engine type:	V-8/Pontiac	V-8/Pontiac
Displacement (cid):	350	400
Horsepower @ rpm:	255 @ 4600	325 @ 4800 (1967)
		325 @ 5200 (1967)[2]
		330 @ 4800 (1968)
		335 @ 5300 (1968)[2]
		335 @ 5000 (68-69)[1]
		330 @ 4800 (1969-70)
		345 @ 5400 (1969)[2]
		265 @ 4600 (1970)[3]
		345 @ 5400 (1970)[2]
Torque (lbs/ft) @ rpm:	355 @ 2800	410 @ 3400 (1967)
		410 @ 3600 (1967)[2]
		430 @ 3300 (1968)
		430 @ 3600 (1968)[2]
		430 @ 3400 (68-69)[1]
		430 @ 3300 (1969)
		430 @ 3700 (1969)[2]
		397 @ 2400 (1970)[3]
		430 @ 3000 (1970)
		430 @ 3400 (1970)[2]
Compression ratio:	8.8:1	10.75:1/10.5:1[4]
Bore (in.):	3.88	4.12
Stroke (in.):	3.75	3.75
Valve lifters:	Hydraulic	Hydraulic
Availability:	1970	1967-70

[1]High Output. [2]Ram Air. [3]Low-compression (8.2:1). [4]Reduced in 1970.

Magazine:	Car and Driver (March 1967)	Car and Driver (June 1970)
Times:		
0-60 mph (sec):	5.8	6.4
0-100 mph (sec):	14.4	15.0
¼-mile (sec):	14.4 @ 100 mph	14.7 @ 98.9 mph
Top speed (mph):	114 (est)	N/A
Axle ratio:	3.90:1	3.07:1
Engine type:	400 Ram Air	400 (4v)
Model year:	1967 Firebird 400	1970 Formula 400

1968-72
PONTIAC
GTO

GM's intermediates were fully redesigned for 1968, but none had the impact that new GTO did. Enthusiasts breathed a sigh of relief when they saw that Pontiac didn't slip and somehow declaw the original muscle car. Its shape was beautiful, its powertrains beastly. Plus, its string of innovations continued. Not only had the GTO been the first real muscle car, it had helped introduce mass-produced cars to such items as ram-air induction and a hood-mounted tachometer. And now, for '68, it was the first car with an energy-absorbing bumper. Molded and color-keyed to form the car's clean new nose, the Endura bumper symbolized Pontiac's performance-car design leadership.

"Others have caught on. But they haven't caught up," boasted the new GTO ad with only a hint of hyperbole. Indeed, the '68 Goat was a masterpiece of proportion, a collection of compound curves that was both organic and brawny. It differed radically from its predecessor, with high-swept quarter panels, a short rear deck, elongated front end, and convex beltline. Two body styles were available, hardtop coupe and convertible. The wheelbase had shrunk by three inches, to 112, and the body by six inches, but some observers said the car looked even smaller—high praise for the stylists. This leadership was carried over to the cabin, where standard Strato bucket seats (a bench was optional) faced a tri-pod gauge cluster that *Hot Rod* magazine declared "the best instrument panel in super-car-land."

Though most GTOs ending up listing for $4000-$4500 once options were added, in base form, it still was an affordable performance car. Its $3103 base sticker price bought a 350-horsepower, 400-cubic-inch Pontiac V-8 (up 15 horsepower from 1967). Optional again at no additional cost was a two-barrel, low-compression version of the 400 V-8 with a modest 265 horsepower and automatic transmission only. Also optional, the 400 High Output four-barrel V-8 yielded 360 horsepower at 5100 rpm. The Ram Air option was rated at 360 horsepower at

Fully redesigned GTO for '68 (opposite) was a masterpiece of proportion. Hidden headlamps were optional, but all Goats had an impact-absorbing Endura bumper. Side marker light was shaped like the Pontiac crest (opposite, bottom). A new Endura nose with exposed quad lights and bodyside creases marked the '70 GTO (below). A 455-cid V-8 was optional in place of the 400 that had been standard since '67.

5400 rpm. In March 1968, it was superseded by the Ram Air II, a new engine also rated at 360 horsepower at 5400 rpm, but with new cylinder heads, forged pistons and lighter-weight valves, among other improvements.

A three-speed manual with Hurst shifter was standard with the base engine; optional were a Muncie M21 close-ratio four-speed or M40 Turbo Hydra-Matic. Ram Air V-8s were available only with the four-speed or the automatic, only with a 4.33:1 rear axle, and could not be ordered with air conditioning.

With a curb weight of 3506 pounds on the base hardtop, GTO was about 100 pounds heftier than the '67 version. But the shorter wheelbase, another year of suspension tuning, and standard G77×14 tires improved its handling enough to rival that of the best GM intermediate, the Olds 4-4-2. Front disc brakes were optional. Few GTOs had the standard unconcealed headlamps so most people are surprised to learn that the hidden headlamps were optional as well. Critics still complained that the Goat's steering transmitted too much road shock and too little feel. Some also said the GTO's doors and front fenders had a tinny sound not found on the Buick GS 400. And while the GTO's mufflers were tuned to an image-enhancing resonance, some drivers found their sound too intrusive.

Still, these were minor beefs compared to the car's overall appeal and sales improved. Pontiac built 87,684 '68 GTOs, including 9980 convertibles.

1969

Only minor cosmetic changes were made to the 1969 GTO inside and out, but bigger things were brewing under the hood. The base 350-horsepower 400 and the "economy" 265-horse version remained. The 400 HO engine was dropped and replaced by the 366-horsepower Ram Air 400. The Ram Air induction system was made available only as a factory-installed option. This engine came to be known as the Ram Air III and used revised "D" port heads, free-breathing cast iron exhaust headers, a Power Flex fan for reduced drag, and Rochester Quadra-Jet carburetor. But the big news was the arrival of the new 400 Ram Air IV engine. This option was conservatively advertised at 370 horsepower. It built upon the Ram Air III with a special aluminum intake manifold, a radical camshaft, and free-breathing exhaust manifolds. A serious performance engine, the Ram Air IV was available only with 3.90:1 or 4.33:1 gears. Safe-T-Track and a heavy-duty cooling system were mandatory; air conditioning was forbidden.

For 1969, the GTO had a revised grille with an eggcrate pattern. The split Endura bumper remained a trademark. Ram Air hood graphics were a warning to any upstarts looking for action. Despite refinements and more usable horsepower, GTO sales began to slide. Production slipped to 72,287.

1970

The second-generation GTO got its first significant sheetmetal alterations and there was a portentous change in the engine bay.

Standard was the 350-horsepower 400-cube V-8, with a choice of three-speed, four-speed, or Turbo Hydra-Matic. Axle choices were fewer this year, ranging from 3.07:1 to 4.33:1. As in 1969, two powerful 400s remained—the Ram Air III and

IV—with 366 and 370 horsepower, respectively, though compression was down a tad, to 10.5:1. The low-compression 400 was dropped, though curb weight was up another 100-200 pounds and power accessories were proliferating. This caused another powerplant to join the line.

General Motors had lifted the corporate ban on engines displacing more than 400 cubic inches for intermediate sized automobiles, so Pontiac took the 455 cubic-incher out of the Bonneville and offered it as a new GTO option. With a 10.25:1 compression ratio and a single four-barrel, the 455 was rated at 360 horsepower at 4300 rpm and packed a whopping 500 pounds/feet of torque at 2700. This engine also was available with the Ram Air treatment. In that form, it had a 10.5:1 compression and was rated at 370 horsepower at 5500 rpm, but torque was down to 445 pounds/feet at 3900. A Ram Air 400—with its higher rpm ability—would outrun either 455 in the quarter-mile. The 455 , however, was a more flexible and less temperamental street engine.

While GTO's body got a new look, the interior remained a 1969 carryover, though the seat and door-panel patterns were altered and the thick-rimmed steering wheel from the Firebird Trans Am was made available as an option. Production fell to 40,149, of which 3783 were convertibles.

1971

Pontiac revised the GTO's sheet metal again for 1971. The split Endura grille was lowered and the new hood had scoops close to its leading edge. The scoops were functional with all engines.

Compression ratios and horsepower ratings dropped for 1971 as a result of governmental pressure and tougher emission standards. The standard 400 four-barrel was rated at 300 horsepower with 8.2:1 compression, making it a high

performance V-8 that could safely operate on lower octane fuels. Gone were the Ram Air III and IV engines. Taking their place was a 335-horse 455 High Output V-8 with an aluminum intake manifold, 8.4:1 compression, and available Ram Air. Available only with Hydra-matic was a 325-horsepower version of the 455.

A three-speed manual transmission remained standard for both the 400 and 455 engines, though GM's Muncie four-speed and M40 Turbo Hydra-Matic were mainstream choices for 1971 GTO buyers. Axle ratios ranged from 3.08:1 to 4.33:1.

1972

After five years as its own car line, the GTO, again, became a LeMans option. Both a hardtop coupe and two-door sedan were available; no 1972 GTO convertibles are known to have been produced. The '71 body was carried over with only minor trim changes because GM's new "A" body had been delayed one year due to a United Auto Workers strike. Two spoiler packages were available, although just one was produced in significant numbers: the single-plane, pedestal-style decklid spoiler.

Engine and driveline packaging remained much as it was in 1971, though horsepower was now rated as a net figure to represent the engine's output installed in the car and with all accessories connected. The 400 was rated at 250 horsepower, as was the automatic-transmission-only 455. The High Output 455 rated 300 horsepower. Improved emissions and angry insurance companies made their presence known in axle ratios that started at 3.08:1 and topped at 3.55:1.

GTO production skidded to just 5807. Pontiac had turned its performance emphasis to the Firebird Trans Am and the proud GTO tag would be shuffled to the A-body LeMans in '73 to finally wither and die on the Ventura options list in '74.

1968-72 Pontiac GTO

Facts At a Glance

Engine type:	V-8/Pontiac	V-8/Pontiac
Displacement (cid):	400	455
Horsepower @ rpm:	265 @ 4600 (68-69)	360 @ 4300 (1970)
	350 @ 5000 (68-70)	370 @ 4600 (1970)
	360 @ 5100 (1968)	325 @ 4400 (1971)
	300 @ 4800 (1971)	335 @ 3600 (1971)
	250 @ 4400 (1972)	250 @ 3600 (1972)
		300 @ 4000 (1972)
Torque (lbs/ft) @ rpm:	397 @ 2400 (68-69)	500 @ 3000 (1970)
	445 @ 3000 (68-70)	455 @ 3200 (1971)
	445 @ 3600 (1968)	480 @ 3600 (1971)
	400 @ 3600 (1971)	375 @ 2400 (1972)
	325 @ 3200 (1972)	415 @ 2400 (1972)
Compression ratio:	10.75:1/10.25:1[1]	10.5:1/10.0:1[2]
Bore (in.):	4.12	4.15
Stroke (in.):	3.75	4.21
Valve lifters:	Hydraulic	Hydraulic
Availability:	1968-72	1970-72

[1]Dropped to 8.2:1 in 1971-72. 265-horsepower engine had 8.6:1 compression.
[2]8.4:1 in 1972.

Engine type:	V-8/Pontiac	V-8/Pontiac
Displacement (cid):	400 (Ram Air II)	400 (Ram Air III)
Horsepower @ rpm:	360 @ 5400	366 @ 5100
		370 @ 5500[3]
Torque (lbs/ft) @ rpm:	445 @ 3800	445 @ 3600
		445 @ 3900[3]
Compression ratio:	10.75:1	10.75:1/10.5:1
Bore (in.):	4.12	4.12
Stroke (in.):	3.75	3.75
Valve lifters:	Hydraulic	Hydraulic
Availability:	1968	1969-70

[3]Ram Air IV

Magazine:	Motor Trend (Feb. 1968)	Car and Driver (Jan. 1970)
Times:		
0-60 mph (sec):	6.5	6.6
0-100 mph (sec):	N/A	16.0
¼-mile (sec):	14.45 @ 98.2 mph	15.0 @ 96.5 mph
Top speed (mph):	N/A	120 (est)
Axle ratio:	4.33:1	3.31:1
Engine type:	400 Ram-Air	455 High Output
Model year:	1968	1970

Restyle for '71 (above) included functional hood scoops with all engines. Strongest motor was the 335-bhp Ram Air 455 HO (above, left). Air cleaner extensions mated to underhood fresh-air baffles. GTO again became a LeMans option for '72 (opposite). Air extractor vents on front fenders are functional. Honeycomb wheels were an option introduced in '71. Pontiac built 503,000 '64-'72 GTOs.

1969-70
PONTIAC FIREBIRD
TRANS AM

Launched with little fanfare in 1969, it took the Firebird Trans Am only three years to push the GTO off Pontiac's performance throne. Within eight years it was second only to the Grand Prix as the best-selling Poncho. Most significant of all, however, was that it alone among affordable cars kept the high-performance flame burning during the fuel crises and recessions of the 1970s and early '80s.

Trans Am began life in March 1969 as a cosmetic option group for the Firebird 400. Pontiac had introduced the GTO Judge package earlier that year, and thought it might be nice to do something along those lines with the Firebird. But the Judge was far better promoted; there wasn't even a Trans Am customer brochure, just a single-sheet insert in the dealer sales album. The package's name was taken from the Sports Car Club of America's popular Trans American sedan racing series, then the premier competition bracket for pony cars.

The 1969 Trans Am was unveiled in both convertible and hardtop body styles. Officially called the Trans Am Performance and Appearance Package, this limited-production option cost $725 over the base price of a Firebird. Pontiac said its most striking feature was "a floating 60-inch air foil spanning the rear deck," but didn't mention whether it actually was a

functional aerodynamic aid. It also had a special hood with full length, functional hood scoops and functional air outlets behind the front wheel opening. The car's Polar White paint was offset by two blue full-length racing stripes and a tail panel painted to match. Trans Am emblems were incorporated into the side window glass.

Under the hood, the 400-cubic-inch Ram Air III with its 335 horsepower was standard and the 345-horsepower Ram Air IV was an option. A three-speed manual running a 3.55:1 rear end and Safe-T-Track limited-slip axle came with the car. Extra-cost transmissions included a four-speed manual and the Turbo Hydra-Matic with either a column-mounted lever or a floor shift; the later mandated the purchase of a center console. Also optional were 3.36:1, 3.90:1, and 4.33:1 rear-axle ratios.

Special high-effort variable ratio power steering and high-effort power brakes with front discs were fitted, and Pontiac said "these specially designed systems have a higher degree of road feel than ordinary power steering and brakes." Heavy duty springs and shocks and a heavy-duty one-inch stabilizer bar with high-rate bushings were used, as were F70×14 Fiberglass belted tires on seven-inch wheels. Inside, bucket seats and a

Pontiac's most successful performance car bowed during the '69 model year as a cosmetic option group for the Firebird 400. The original Trans Am (both pages) was the only one offered as a convertible. Spoilers were largely for decoration, though the hood's functional scoops fed the standard Ram Air V-8. Steering, suspension, and brakes were upgraded, but the cabin was virtually standard Firebird 400.

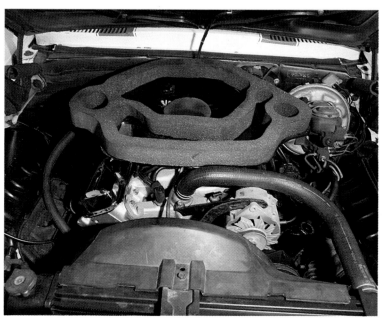

1969-70 Pontiac Trans Am

Facts At a Glance

Engine type:	V-8/Pontiac	V-8/Pontiac
Displacement (cid):	400	400
Horsepower @ rpm:	335 @ 5000	345 @ 5000
	345 @ 5400[1]	370 @ 5500[1]
Torque (lbs/ft)		
@ rpm:	430 @ 3600	430 @ 3400
	430 @ 3700[1]	445 @ 3900[1]
Compression ratio:	10.75:1	10.5:1
Bore (in.):	4.12	4.12
Stroke (in.):	3.75	3.75
Valve lifters:	Hydraulic	Hydraulic
Availability:	1969	1970

[1]Ram Air IV

Magazine:	*Hot Rod* (1969)	*Car and Driver* (June 1970)
Times:		
0-60 mph (sec):	5.6 (est)	5.7
0-100 mph (sec):	14.0	13.4
¼-mile (sec):	14.10 @ 100.78 mph	14.1 @ 103.2 mph
Top speed (mph):	115 (est)	115 (est)
Axle ratio:	3.90:1	3.73:1
Engine (cid/bhp):	400/345	400/345
Model year:	1969	1970

Magazine:	*Sports Car Graphic* (April 1969)
Times:	
0-60 mph (sec):	6.5
0-100 mph (sec):	14.2
¼-mile (sec):	14.3 @ 101.7 mph
Top speed (mph):	108
Axle ratio:	3.55:1
Engine (cid/bhp):	400/335
Model year:	1969

new 14-inch diameter sports steering wheel were standard. Optional were a rally gauge cluster with a tachometer, though buyers also could order a hood-mounted tach.

Sports Car Graphic criticized the absence of a front air-dam, saying nose lift was discernible even on the freeway. It also found that putting 57 percent of the Trans Am's 3815 pounds on its front tires compromised rear traction enough to prematurely lock the rear brakes and to prevent the car from turning anything better than what it called a "not-so-low e.t. of 14.3...." But despite these handicaps, a mountain road proved the Trans Am a more-than-capable road car. "We were safely passing chains of cars, eight, nine, ten at a whack like a cable car a mile up in the sky—and not having to brake for the corner, but carving the turns at high speed..." wrote *Sports Car Graphic*.

Just 697 Trans Ams were produced during the late-starting model year, making it the rarest of the T/A Pontiacs. Of that number, only 55 had the more potent Ram Air IV engine and just eight were convertibles.

1970

The Trans Am came into its own in 1970 with introduction of the all-new second-generation Camaro and Firebird. Built on the same 108-inch wheelbase, GM's new pony cars were slipperier, more European in nature. Available only in a two-door hardtop, they were a mid-year introduction in February of 1970 and labeled '70½ models.

Standard in the $4305 Trans Am was the Ram Air 400 engine rated at 345 horsepower at 5000 rpm; the Ram Air IV was optional and returned 370 horsepower at 5500 rpm. Pontiac made a floor-mounted Hurst-shifted four-speed manual standard; Turbo-Hydra-Matic was optional. Standard gearing was 3.55:1, though the four-speed was available with a 3.73:1 gear. Much attention was paid to the car's road manners. The

padded Formula steering wheel worked variable-ratio Saginaw power steering in a quick 12.1:1 ratio. Stiffer springs and heavy-duty front and rear sway bars teamed with Goodyear Polyglas F60×15 tires on Kelsey-Hayes Rally II wheels. Power front disc brakes also were standard.

Visually, Pontiac went all-out with a road-racer look for the street. The Trans Am shared the Firebird's fastback roof and impact-absorbing snout, but it was its own model now and was treated to some unique features. Pontiac said the front air dam and fender air extractors created 50 pounds of downforce on the nose at expressway speeds. The same amount of downforce was applied to the tail by a big deck lid lip and the small spoilers in front of the rear wheels. On the hood was a rear-facing shaker scoop, which was connected to the air cleaner through a hole in the hood and vibrated with the engine. Pontiac said it drew in cooler ambient air for improved performance by taking advantage of the high air pressure that develops close to the windshield. Inside, the Trans Am was the sporting driver's delight, with bucket seats, floor shifter, thick-rimmed steering wheel, and an engine-turned aluminum instrument panel insert. The standard tachometer had its redline in the straight-up position for easy checking. The '70 Trans Am was a hit with the critics. *Car and Driver* called it "a hard muscled, lightning-flexed commando of a car, the likes of which doesn't exist anywhere in the world, even for twice the price."

At 3782 pounds, *Sports Car Graphic's* 345-horsepower test car was slightly lighter than the '69 it had run, but 57 percent of the weight was still over the front wheels. Nonetheless, said the magazine, "Overall handling feel—for a production car—was as near to a front engine race car as we have ever driven."

Production for 1970, however, remained sluggish. Only 3196 Trans Ams were built. Rarest was the Ram Air IV, with only 29 four-speed and 59 automatic versions produced.

1969-71 PONTIAC GTO JUDGE

It was no secret that the 1968-69 GTO had been criticized in some quarters as a high-priced, over-optioned muscle car usually sold only with lots of luxury features that few performance buffs wanted. Intermediate-sized rivals like the Plymouth Road Runner and Chevrolet Chevelle SS could be had as leaner vehicles designed to do one thing only—go fast. Pontiac conceived a special GTO for '69 in an effort to regain some of those serious enthusiasts who had been lost to the Goat's upscale image and price. It was called the Judge.

Rowan and Martin's Laugh-In was at that time snaring top TV ratings with its wacky reflections of the irreverent 1960s. "Here come de judge!" was a catch phrase in one of its skits and quickly became part of the American lexicon. In straight society, the term "judge" denoted power and respect, which of course is a great image for a muscle car. But in *Laugh-In's* world, "Here come de judge!" was a giddy poke at authority, and Pontiac seemed to be saying that here was a car with all the GTO's power, but in a package that didn't take itself quite so seriously—much like the Road Runner and its "beep-beep" horn. As envisioned, the Judge was to have been offered for one year only, maybe as a pillared coupe in a single color, with rubber floor mats and the GTO's hottest performance equipment standard. The Judge that was unveiled in December 1968 wasn't quite what the product planners had proposed.

The Judge actually was a GTO option package priced $332.07 over the cost of a base Goat. But for that money, the buyer got a host of performance features that would have cost much more than $332 if purchased individually. At $3161 for the hardtop and about $3700 for the convertible, the Judge probably had more performance hardware than available most anyplace else for the price.

Standard was the 366-horsepower Ram Air III engine with functional hood scoops, which could be closed in rainy weather by a knob under the dashboard. The base three-speed manual transmission with Hurst shifter was fitted, but each Judge had a heavy-duty suspension and rode G70×14 Wide Tread fiberglass belted tires. To save a few dollars, the standard Rally II wheels came without trim rings. The interior was standard GTO, but the exterior was individualized by a rear-deck spoiler, blacked out grille, "The Judge" decals, and a bodyside tape stripe. All the regular GTO power and convenience options were available, including the 370-horsepower 400 Ram-Air IV mill, four-speed manual and automatic transmissions, and hidden headlamps.

Car Life saw nothing very special about the Judge, other than its eye-catching graphics. Its test Judge retailed for $4439 and included the Ram Air IV engine ($390), four-speed trans ($195), front-disc brakes ($64), power steering ($100), and hood-mounted tachometer ($63). It ran the quarter in 14.45 at 97.8 mph with 3.55:1 gears. The magazine had this to say about the powerplant: "The Ram Air IV is a very peaky engine. The idle is a rough, rolling bark, music to the driver's ears and a warning to people in the next lane." The car was difficult to drive around town and difficult to launch, its handling was ill-suited to the road course, and its rear brakes locked prematurely. "The Judge is at its best on the highway," *Car Life* concluded, "where the engine runs fast enough to be happy and the suspension needn't do things it doesn't like to do."

By the end of the 1969 model year, 6833 Judges were assembled, including 108 convertibles.

1970

Pontiac gave the GTO some new sheetmetal for 1970, which the Judge got, too. Also, it offered the Judge in hardtop and convertible at $337 over the base Goat. The package included a redesigned air foil and new multi-hued stripes placed like eyebrows over the bodyside creases. Orbit Orange was offered as an exclusive Judge color, but all other GTO hues were

The Judge grouped GTO's hottest performance options into one package. The name was '60s-trendy and enabled Pontiac to advertise that "The Judge can be bought." Opposite is a '69. The first 2000 Judges were painted Carousel Red; any GTO color was available after February '69. The '70 Judge (below) got the GTO's new sheetmetal, plus revised graphics and a new rear spoiler.

available. No longer did the Judge come standard with the heavy-duty suspension, but it again was delivered with the Ram Air III engine that was optional in the standard GTO. Optional on the Judge was the Ram Air IV. Pontiac made a 360-horsepower 455-cubic-inch V-8 available on GTOs from the start of the '70 model year, but the engine wasn't offered as an option on the Judge until the last quarter of the model year. Transmissions were shared with the standard Goat.

Production of the Judge for 1970 mirrored the standard GTO—down considerably at 3797 units. Just 168 were convertibles.

GTOs got a revised fascia for 1971 and so did the Judge, but the special edition was otherwise a 1970 carryover. The principal difference was beneath the hood, where the 335-horse 455 High Output V-8 was the only available engine.

Soured by insurance rates, deteriorating fuel quality, and general public attitude toward the factory "hot rod," buyers had little appetite for the garish muscle option. The Judge was discontinued in mid-year after just 357 hardtops and 17 convertibles had been built. This was twilight muscle at its most extroverted, though, and shows that Pontiac was willing to make even the original supercar car a follower in the chase for sales.

1969-71 Pontiac GTO Judge

Facts At a Glance

Engine type:	V-8/Pontiac	V-8/Pontiac
Displacement (cid):	400 (Ram Air III)	455
Horsepower @ rpm:	366 @ 5100	360 @ 4600 (1970)
	370 @ 4600[1]	335 @ 4800 (1971)
Torque (lbs/ft) @ rpm:	445 @ 3600	500 @ 3100 (1970)
	445 @ 3900[1]	480 @ 3600 (1971)
Compression ratio:	10.75:1	10.25:1 (1970)
		8.4:1 (1971)
Bore (in.):	4.12	4.15
Stroke (in.):	3.75	4.21
Valve lifters:	Hydraulic	Hydraulic
Availability:	1969-70	1970-71

[1]Ram Air IV

Magazine:	Muscle Car Review (1968)	Car Life (March 1969)
Times:		
0-60 mph (sec):	5.7	6.2
0-100 mph (sec):	12.5	15.3
¼-mile (sec):	13.20 @ 104 mph	14.45 @ 97.8 mph
Top speed (mph):	N/A	124
Axle ratio:	3.90:1	3.55:1
Engine type:	400 Ram Air IV	400 Ram Air IV
Model year:	1969	1969

The 366-bhp Ram Air III engine was standard on the '70 Judge (opposite), though later in the year the car was available with the tamer but torquier 360-bhp 455. A slightly detuned 455 was the only engine offered with the '71 (above and left). The Judge was discontinued in mid-'71 with just 357 hardtops and 17 convertibles built.

1971-73
PONTIAC FIREBIRD
TRANS AM

As the 1971 model year opened, the Trans Am was poised to eclipse the GTO as Pontiac's premier performance offering—and to send the rest of the pony field scurrying. Its weapon was the biggest V-8 ever offered in the class, the 455 cubic-inch four-barrel High Output (HO) V-8. This was the only engine offered with the Trans Am for '71 and could also be found beneath the hood of the Firebird Formula 455.

With 335 horsepower, the 455 HO had less advertised muscle than the Trans Am's previous engines: the 345-horsepower Ram Air 400 and the 370-horse Ram Air IV. Both those 400-cube mills had a 10.5:1 compression ratio and made their peak horsepower at 5000 rpm or more. But tighter emissions standards and the dwindling availability of high-octane fuels had caused Pontiac to turn to the 455. It had a compression ratio of 8.5:1, which was compatible with a wider-range of gasolines. It couldn't wind as high as the 400s, peaking at 4800 rpm, but it was less temperamental than the Ram Air IV and with 480 pounds/feet of torque at 3600 rpm, it packed a real wallop around town.

With just half a year's production under its belt, Pontiac decided not to tamper with the appearance of the '71 Firebird and thus the Trans Am differed little from its 1970 predecessor. Carried over were the Endura nose, the spoilers, air dams, and air-extractor vents on the front fenders. The shaker scoop returned, connected again through the hood to a Rochester Quadra-Jet four-barrel carburetor atop a cast aluminum high-rise intake manifold. The backward-facing scoop was designed to suck in high-pressure air that collected at the windshield base. It had a hinged door that opened under hard throttle. A low-restriction dual exhaust system with chrome tips further aided the 455's breathing. Pontiac used round-port Ram Air IV-style cylinder heads with this engine for better breathing

through the mid- and high-rpm range. Formerly standard, the chrome-happy Engine Dress Kit was now a dealer option. A three-speed manual was standard; a four-speed and the Turbo-Hydra-Matic were back as options. Trans Am's Safe-T-Track differential carried a standard axle ratio of 3.42:1; the manuals could be had with an optional 3.73:1, but not with that gearing and air conditioning, and if air was ordered with the automatic, Pontiac fitted a 3.08:1 gear.

The underpinnings consisted of heavy-duty shocks and springs, a 1¼-inch front stabilizer bar and a ⅞-inch rear bar, power brakes with discs in front, and raised-white-letter F60×15 bias-belted tires on Rally II wheels. Ultra-quick Saginaw variable-ratio power steering was fitted. High-back bucket seats, console, engine-turned aluminum cluster insert, Formula steering wheel, and sculptured door panels made up Trans Am's interior package.

At $4590, the 3578-pound Trans Am coupe was no cut-rate Pegasus and demand was paltry; only 2116 were built.

1972

A strike at the Lordstown, Ohio, plant that produced Camaros and Firebirds reduced output of GM's pony cars in 1972, and what labor strife didn't accomplish, the market did. Sales in the segment were dropping rapidly and Pontiac made few changes in the '72 Firebird and even fewer in the Trans Am.

The biggest news was that Pontiac's 455 HO V-8 had a revised power rating as a result of Detroit's new method of calculating horsepower. Beginning with the 1972 model year, horsepower was rated as a net figure, that is, with all engine accessories in place and operating. That snipped the 455's rating to 300 horsepower at 4000 rpm with maximum torque—415

Trans Am returned visually unchanged for '71 (both pages), but in place of the previous 400-cid V-8 was the 455-cid High Output mill. Horsepower was down, but the 455 was more tractable in daily use than the hot Ram Air 400s. This was the largest engine ever offered in a pony car and was fitted with the functional rear-facing shaker hood scoop.

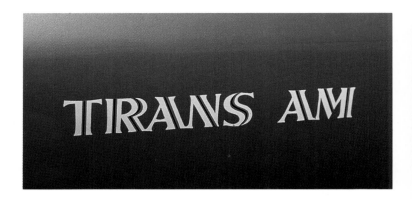

Trans Am sales plummeted for '72 and Pontiac considered killing the Firebird. A rebound in '73 saved that car as well as Chevy's Camaro and marked the start of Trans Am's second golden age. By the time the '72 pictured here was built, Trans Am had eclipsed the GTO as Pontiac's premier performer. The '73 model was visually identical and also came standard with the 455-cid V-8.

pounds/feet—coming at 3200 rpm.

Trans Am came standard with a four-speed manual transmission this year, a Hurst-shifted Muncie unit. A 3.42:1 rear-axle ratio was the only one offered unless you ordered the Turbo Hydra-Matic and air conditioning, which brought a 3.08:1 ratio. Safe-T-Track was again a standard feature.

Pontiac actually reduced Firebird prices for '72; the Trans Am was down $340, to $4256. Nonetheless, production plummeted to just 1286, 458 of which were equipped with the four speed.

1973

The Firebird made a comeback in 1973, with production up 55 percent to 46,313. Fueling the jump was renewed interest in the performance editions. Sales of the Formula nearly doubled to 10,166 while Trans Am production nearly quadrupled, to 4802.

Even though big-cube performance had faded at Ford, Chrysler and Chevrolet, Pontiac continued to push development of large, high-output engines for the Formula Firebird and Trans Am and two 455 V-8s were available for the '73 Trans Am. The vast majority of '73 Trans Ams were delivered with the standard 250-net-horsepower version with 8.0:1 compression. Called the 455 HO, it sported two-bolt main bearing caps, hydraulic lifters, and Quadra-Jet carburetion. Functional Cold Air ram-induction was no longer available due to stricter emission standards. But the real performance ticket was the 455 cubic-inch Super Duty (SD) V-8.

The 455 SD V-8 was introduced early in 1973 and was rated at 310 net horsepower at 4000 rpm. It originally used the radical camshaft from the 400 Ram-Air IV, but a cam revision in March

to reduce emissions dropped the horsepower to 290. It was nonetheless a powerplant that recalled the heyday of factory performance development. The 455 SD heads were blessed with large, round ports based on the 400 Ram Air IV and were said by some engineers to move more air than Chrysler's Hemi heads. Its large wedge chambers resisted knock and ping as a result of a larger squash area and their ability to dissipate heat. The SD engine's bottom end was a masterpiece of bulletproof technology, equipped with a nodular iron crankshaft with nitrated bearing surfaces, and was good for revs as high as 7000 rpm.

Again standard on the Trans Am was a four-speed manual transmission; it used a 3.43:1 rear-axle ratio with either the standard 455 or the SD. Turbo Hydra-Matic also was available with either engine and could be mated to a 3.08:1 gear in place of the 3.43:1.

Trans Am was back, and its appeal would continue to grow throughout the '70s and into the late 1980s. Its classic 108-inch-wheelbase '70½ body would undergo some changes to nose and tail, but would remain substantially the same until 1982. The 455 would survive until 1976 and Trans Am would be available with 400-cubic-inch power until 1979. Never again, however, would it approach the big-block majesty of the 1967-73 muscle years.

1971-73 Pontiac Firebird

Trans Am

Facts At a Glance

Engine type:	V-8/Pontiac	V-8/Pontiac (Super Duty)
Displacement (cid):	455	455
Horsepower @ rpm:	335 @ 4800 (1971) 300 @ 4000 (1972) 250 @ 4000 (1973)	310 @ 4000 290 @ 4000 (3-73)
Torque (lbs/ft) @ rpm:	480 @ 3600 (1971) 415 @ 3200 (1972) 370 @ 2800 (1973)	390 @ 3600 395 @ 3200 (3-73)
Compression ratio:	8.5:1 (1971-72) 8.0:1 (1973)	8.4:1
Bore (in.):	4.15	4.15
Stroke (in.):	4.21	4.21
Valve lifters:	Hydraulic	Hydraulic
Availability:	1971-73 Trans Am	1973-74 Trans Am

Magazine:	*Car and Driver (1972)*
Times:	
0-60 mph (sec):	5.4
0-100 mph (sec):	12.7
¼-mile (sec):	13.90 @ 104.6 mph
Top speed (mph):	132
Axle ratio:	3.42:1
Engine type:	455
Model year:	1972

INDEX